PL 550
5-12-11

ARC 2412

DEPARTMENT OF THE ENVIRONMENT
BUILDING RESEARCH ESTABLISHMENT

Principles of
Modern Building

Volume II

Floors and Roofs

LONDON
HER MAJESTY'S STATIONERY OFFICE
1961

First published 1961
Fifth impression 1973

This publication was originally issued by the Department
of Scientific and Industrial Research which is now dissolved and this *reprint* is issued by the Department of the
Environment - Building Research Establishment

SBN   11 670297 4

Printed in England for Her Majesty's Stationery Office
by A Wheaton & Co, Exeter

PREFACE

THE present volume follows the same general plan as Volume 1, which dealt in Part I with the principles of the functional performance of a building as a whole and in Part II with their application to walls. This book carries on the application to floors and roofs. After a short general section on matters common to both these elements of a structure, it deals separately with suspended floors, solid floors, and floor finishes. In the case of roofs, there are many functional principles that are common to both flat and pitched roofs. These are discussed before proceeding to their more detailed application, in separate sections, to flat and pitched roofs. This form of treatment will, it is hoped, have the advantage of fixing principles in the reader's mind, and that is the first purpose of "Principles", even though it leads in places to a semblance of repetition, and some division of related subject-matter which is alleviated by back-reference.

As with Volume 1, this book is supplementary to, and not a substitute for, a text-book on building construction. The application of principles to practice is illustrated but not all details of construction.

The preparation of this volume is the work of numerous officers of the Station, and it is published as the collective work of its staff.

F. M. LEA,

Director of Building Research

Building Research Station,
Garston,
Watford, Herts.
July, 1961

iii

CONTENTS

Chapter 1

INTRODUCTION

FUNCTION

FLOORS and roofs form the horizontal elements of building structures, the former being essentially platforms for the work or leisure of the occupants, and the latter, together with external walls, providing the necessary protection from the weather.

Apart from the obvious requirements that floors and roofs must be sufficiently strong to carry safely the loads to which they are likely to be subjected, and that roofs must keep out the rain and snow, there are many features that must be kept in mind if the owner and the occupant are to be satisfied with the building.

Although the structural design may be such that the floors will not collapse (and the structural engineer will always introduce a margin of safety to ensure this), the flexibility of a floor may be enough to cause deflections that are a nuisance. The deflections themselves may be too small to see, but large enough to cause cracking of a plaster ceiling or local crushing or cracking of a weak partition wall. Such blemishes should be avoided as far as possible but can hardly ever be completely eliminated. Apart from the flexibility of the floor under applied loading, similar defects can sometimes result from differential shrinkage or thermal effects.

In buildings of more than one storey, the floors are in general dividing elements between the people and activities at the various levels. These dividing elements must act as barriers to the passage of sound, so that the people on one level are not unduly disturbed by the noise created on another level. They must also prevent or delay the passage of fire vertically through the building, just as party walls must act as barriers to the spread of fire horizontally. The necessary standards of sound insulation or of fire resistance will depend very much on the individual circumstances. For example, sound insulation through a floor in a domestic building is usually considered of less importance if the rooms immediately above and below the floor are in the same dwelling, as in a house or maisonette, since a family is more ready to put up with noise of its own creation than with that of a neighbour. The degree of fire resistance necessary will depend on the amount of combustible material likely to be present in the building, on any special precautions, such as the installation of sprinklers, taken to control an outbreak, and on the provision for escape of occupants.

Ground floors and roofs have to afford some degree of thermal insulation; that is, they must act as adequate barriers to the passage of heat into or out of the building. In recent years thermal insulation has received considerable attention, having regard both to the comfort of the occupants and the need to conserve fuel for heating buildings.

Finally, the floors or roofs must be durable to give trouble-free service with a minimum of maintenance for a long time. A floor should have a surface that will stand up to the treatment that it is likely to get, whether it be the continual scrape of children's shoes in a school, the frequent passage of heavily-laden trucks in a factory, or even exposure to a corrosive environment. Roofs require special consideration to ensure adequate durability in relation to the exposure to sun and rain, and to an atmosphere sometimes heavily polluted with chemicals.

STRENGTH AND STABILITY

Floors and roofs are structures that are supported at their ends (or edges) so that they can carry loads above a void. There are three primary structural systems that can be adopted for spanning across space: the hanging chain, the arch, and the beam. The characteristic feature of the hanging chain is that all its parts are in tension; of the arch, that they are all in compression. In the beam the top fibres are in compression and the bottom fibres in tension, their combined effect being a resistance to bending.

Provided that the necessary elevated support is available, the hanging chain or cable is the lightest form of supporting structure for any particular span to be covered and load to be carried. For bridges of very long span, for instance, the suspension bridge is the only practical type. However, this system of construction is inherently flexible under changes of load, and large deflections would be objectionable in a permanent building. For a temporary building (e.g. for exhibitions) its use can combine lightness with aesthetic interest. For other temporary coverings its lightness and consequent portability are a great advantage, as in the tent; there is no way of roofing over a large space so economical in weight as the circus 'big top'.

In a true arch, the whole of the structural material is in compression, and this makes the arch ideal for covering a wide space with material that is strong to resist compression even if laid with a weak jointing material, such as stone or brick masonry laid with lime mortar. Sufficient room must be spared for the rise of the arch, and substantial abutments are needed to take not only the weight of the arch and whatever load it carries, but also its horizontal thrust. It should be noted that the lower the ratio of rise to span, the greater is the thrust. If this ratio is to be very low, the best means of dealing with the thrust may be to use a tie rod to connect the two abutments.

For the material of the arch to remain wholly in direct compression, an arch would have to have a special shape for each particular arrangement of loads. Since loading is usually very variable, the chosen form of arch will not be ideal for all loading conditions, and it will be subject to some bending as well as compression, acting as a combination of the primary arch and the beam.

The basic structural unit of most floors is the beam (or the slab, which, for the present, may be regarded merely as a wide beam), and considerable attention has been given during the last fifty years to the development of the most efficient sections for beams of various materials. With timber, the simple solid rectangular section has long been popular and economical, but greater structural efficiency is possible, for important engineering construction, by the use of built-up sections. With steel, there is no difficulty in rolling a section of I-shape, and there are great advantages in doing so, since the resistance of the beam is increased by arranging most of the material in two flanges, as far apart as possible, with merely a connecting web between that is just thick enough to ensure that the two flanges work properly together (that is, the web must be able to transmit shearing forces). With cast iron, as used for girders in buildings and bridges in the 19th century, the strength in tension is much less than in compression; the girders were therefore made with small top flanges and wide bottom flanges, so that the total forces that could be withstood by the two flanges were roughly the same.

Concrete is strong in compression but very weak in tension, and hence reinforced concrete was developed as an extremely valuable composite material in which most of the compressive forces developed in a beam or slab are resisted by the concrete and most of the tensile forces developed are resisted by the steel reinforcement.

In a rectangular reinforced-concrete beam, well over half of the concrete is usually in the tensile zone. Since, for design purposes, it is usual to assume that it has no tensile strength, this concrete is of little structural value; it merely adds to the dead weight that must be supported by the rest of the beam. (The concrete in the tensile zone is sometimes sufficient to resist shearing forces, and it also increases the stiffness of the beam; however, these effects are relatively unimportant.) Accordingly, a more efficient section for reinforced concrete is the T-section, in which most of the concrete is in the compression flange, the main reinforcement is near the bottom of the web, and secondary reinforcement is provided to link together these two elements and to resist shearing forces.

With normal reinforced concrete, as spans are increased, the weight of material in the beam or slab itself becomes increasingly disproportionate to the loads to be carried, and so a limit is set to the length of span that can economically be used. An additional disadvantage with long spans is presented by the concrete surrounding the steel on the tension side of the beam, which adds nothing to the strength of the beam and which would crack excessively if the steel were allowed to take really high stresses. Because of such cracking, it is not practicable to take full advantage of the great load-carrying capacity of high-tensile steel. If, however, the steel is either pre-tensioned by stretching it in the forms before the concrete is cast (in pre-cast concrete construction), or is threaded through ducts formed in the concrete and subsequently post-tensioned, it is possible to put the whole of the concrete in compression and hence also to take advantage of the high stresses permissible with high-tensile steel wire. With this modern system of prestressed concrete, the self-weight of a beam can be much less than that of a normal reinforced concrete beam, and the limiting economic span is much increased.

Modern aluminium alloys developed for structural purposes have strengths similar to that of mild steel, and the structural shapes in general follow the same basic pattern. The modulus of elasticity of aluminium alloys is, however, much lower than that of steel, so that the problem of keeping deflections within reasonable limits becomes of special importance with beams of this material. It is also necessary to consider the possibility of local instability of parts of the section such as outstanding flanges, but fortunately there is no difficulty in producing a wide variety of sectional shapes with, for example, stiffened edges to the flanges. Since aluminium is very much lighter than steel, an increasing use of aluminium is to be expected for large-span structures, although the present high basic cost of the material sometimes rules out its use.

For maximum structural efficiency, a beam is given the form of a truss. The truss is a beam in which the compressive, tensile and shearing forces, which distribute themselves throughout the body of a solid beam, are localized by building up the beam as an open linkwork. The top boom is generally in compression, the bottom boom in tension; and the farther these booms are apart, the greater the load they can carry for the same cross-section. The two booms are connected by members which resist the shearing forces, and the position and method of connection is chosen so that all elements of the truss are subjected as far as possible to direct tension or compression, with bending effects reduced to the minimum.

For the same load to be carried per unit area of floor or roof, the force to be resisted by either boom of a girder or truss of given depth is proportional to the spacing between girders and to the square of the span. Long spans and wide spacings are therefore expensive in material. The modern tendency in industrial buildings is towards clear spans and few columns, to give freedom in layout of machinery and routing. It is, however, essential to remember that spans longer than are really required are a luxury leading to unnecessary expense.

Floors and roofs commonly extend over several bays of their supporting structure, and an important economy can be effected by designing them as continuous structures. Figure 1.1 compares the bending of non-continuous

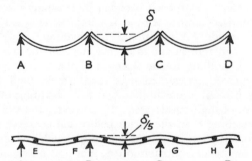

FIG. 1.1

Effect of continuity in beams over points of support

and continuous beams or slabs of the same section carrying the same uniformly distributed loads. The deflections are equally exaggerated in the two diagrams; the deflection at mid-span of the continuous beam is only one-fifth of that in the simply-supported beam. It will be observed that the direction of the bending in the continuous beam changes at about one-fifth of the span from each side of the support; at these 'points of contraflexure', such as E, F, G and H, the stresses in the fibres change sign (from tension to compression, or vice versa) so that, in continuous floor and roof slabs, it is over the supports that tension develops at the top of the slab and cracks may be formed in applied coverings and finishes.

In all the examples so far cited, the structural systems for spanning space are one-way systems; that is, in each system the internal forces and moments act in a series of parallel planes in the direction of the span. Such systems are not so economical in material as two-dimensional or three-dimensional systems whereby the loading can be supported by forces spreading through the structure in all directions. These more efficient systems may be called spatial structural systems, and include domes and barrel-vault floors and two-way slabs supported on columns to form a three-dimensional system.

The shell roof is one type of space structure that has been developed considerably in recent years. It carries load mainly through internal forces in the plane of the shell surface, usually without important bending moments. For an internal bay of a series of adjacent cylindrical shells of long span, it is possible to consider the shell as a beam spanning between the gable ends, the upper part of the shell acting in direct compression and the lower edges where the adjacent shells meet acting in tension, with the help of the reinforcement in the edge beam. But in general, this simple conception needs considerable modification to deal with single shell roofs or end bays of multiple roofs, particularly when the span is relatively short (in relation to the radius of curvature of the shell). With the shell roof, there is scope for a wide variety of roof shapes, the behaviour of some of which are not readily amenable to structural analysis; in these circumstances loading tests on scale models are necessary to establish the safety of a design.

DIMENSIONAL STABILITY

Dimensional changes in floors or roofs can occur as a result of elastic or inelastic deformations caused by the self-weight of the member and by imposed loading, and as a result of temperature changes and of changes in moisture content.

Floors in buildings normally reach equilibrium between their moisture content and the surrounding air conditions within a few months of construction; and the temperature fluctuations are usually small. Dimensional changes arising from the effects of loading, dead and imposed, are observed as deflections of the floor, sometimes accompanied by cracking. The elastic deflections due to the self-weight of the floor do not usually matter, since they are too small to be unsightly, but subsequent inelastic deformations of the floor after the finishes have been completed may lead to progressive cracking in these finishes. The deflections due to applied loading must also be seriously considered from this point of view. Very great flexibility of a floor or excessive vibration may also feel uncomfortable to people walking on it. With some types of floor, such as the traditional timber floor, the scantlings are chosen, on the basis of experience, so that the floor is within suitable limits of flexibility rather than so that the timber is within permissible limits of stress.

Roofs are usually not subjected to high imposed loading, but they are liable to large temperature variations. With extensive areas of roofing, heating by solar radiation and consequent expansion leads to the development of forces on other parts of the structure, which commonly result in unsightly cracking of internal and external walls. Bowing of the roof slab, as a whole or in panels, may be caused by a temperature gradient through the roof, and may in time cause cracking of walls and partitions in the top storey of the building. Examples are given in Volume 1, pp. 25-7.

These troubles have been found to be particularly serious with flat concrete roofs, and the design of such roofs in relation to thermal effects is one of the chief problems in attempting to ensure the dimensional stability of buildings. It is considered in detail in Chapter 7.

Although designers are mainly concerned with *downward* deflections of floors and roofs, upward deflections can sometimes be troublesome. This condition can arise with floors and roofs consisting of a series of precast prestressed concrete beams laid side by side. The beams are commonly prestressed in such a way that they bow upwards, so that their initial deflections, and the corresponding stresses in the concrete, are of opposite sign to those caused by the subsequent additional dead load and imposed loading. For flooring, this arrangement works admirably, although it is necessary to control the manufacture very carefully (particularly the positioning of the prestressing wires) so that all units of a floor have the same initial camber, to avoid difficulties in bringing the finished surfaces above and below the floor to a continuous level surface. For roofing, however, where the imposed load is usually small, the upward camber may increase steadily as a result of creep of the concrete under the internal prestressing forces.

SOUND INSULATION

The broad principles of sound insulation have already been discussed in Volume 1, in relation to walls. Mass is the main factor determining the sound insulation, provided there is no 'leakage' of sound, for instance via air paths, and a first estimate of the airborne sound insulation of a floor can be obtained from Fig. 2.6 (p. 36). The main additional problem presented by floors concerns the effect of impact transmission; this is of little importance with walls but of great importance with floors. Airborne and impact sound insulation differ in principle and in method, so that floors, which require both, present a more complicated problem than do walls.

Roofs, like external walls, are exposed to outdoor noise, though usually they are less exposed to the noise of traffic and more to that of aircraft.

FIRE PROTECTION

In Volume 1 the fundamental principles of fire protection are discussed, and one element of the building, the wall, is dealt with in detail. The underlying principle of all structural precautions to reduce spread of smoke, hot gases and fire is simply that of confining the fire within any room, group of rooms or compartments, and thus restricting the size of the fire that can develop. In this respect the floor, and in certain circumstances the roof, can play an important part.

A staircase may provide an opening for fire to spread from one floor to the next; and in some circumstances it may act as a flue into which hot air and fire are drawn. The placing and enclosure of staircases and landings, in relation to corridors and rooms opening on to them, must therefore be considered carefully, taking into account both spread of fire and means of escape for the occupants.

DURABILITY AND MAINTENANCE

This section is concerned with structural materials; the finishes for floors and roofs are discussed in later chapters. The principal materials used are concrete (plain and reinforced), timber, and metal (usually steel but occasionally aluminium). The structural parts of floors and roofs are protected from the weather; thus the causes of deterioration are, for the most part, different from those affecting external walls, though their effects may be just as serious. In the first place, it cannot be assumed that no moisture is present; it may get into the structure by rising from the ground, by leakage, or by condensation. Moreover, in spaces within a building, the air may be stagnant, and this, in one respect at least, may be worse than exposure to the weather: the dry-rot fungus, *Merulius lachrymans*, will attack timber in stagnant, damp conditions within a building but has rarely been found to flourish in timber exposed to the elements. Rapid deterioration can occur also where there is an aggressive atmosphere due to manufacturing processes such as paper-making or metal plating.

As a general principle, it is better to use a material that is itself durable rather than to rely on a protective coating. The protection offered by a coating is limited to that of its poorest or thinnest part; once a breakdown has occurred there, deterioration will spread rapidly to other, better-protected areas. Moreoever, any structural movement leading to cracking can cause a breakdown of the protective coating and render it useless.

Concrete

Concrete is affected only very slowly by water and air. Its sensitivity to attack by sulphates, by acids and by animal and vegetable oils was discussed at some length in Volume i (pp. 90–94). The rate of attack depends largely on the extent to which the concrete has been consolidated. With a dense concrete, free from voids, chemical attack only proceeds gradually from the surface; with a porous concrete, whether it be poorly consolidated or made with a porous aggregate, attack can occur throughout the mass and cause rapid breakdown. This is particularly true with sulphate attack, as the associated expansion causes disruption. With acid attack the main effect is a gradual solution of the cement, releasing particles of aggregate. At first sight, it might be assumed that an aggregate that would itself be attacked by the acid, for instance limestone, would produce a concrete having very poor chemical resistance. In practice, the reverse is found to be true; the attack on the aggregate neutralizes some of the acid, and the gradual solution of the aggregate enables the surface to erode more uniformly and confers on the concrete a greater resistance to attack. Where exposure to acid is serious, special constructional measures are required.

The comments in Volume i were based on the behaviour of concrete of average quality. Where assurance can be given that the concrete will be free from voids or other local defects, a rather more corrosive environment can be tolerated. If even high-quality Portland cement concrete cannot be relied upon to give good service, the use of other cements must be considered. Sulphate-resisting cement is similar in most respects to Portland cement but can tolerate much higher strengths of sulphate solution without suffering expansion. It is not, however, immune from attack. For very severe conditions, either high-alumina cement or supersulphate cement will be required. The alternative is to protect the concrete by covering it with an impervious coating. Materials commonly used for this coating are tar or bitumen, chlorinated-rubber paint, epoxy resin paint or, where a thicker coating is needed, gunned asphalt. Epoxy-resin paint is claimed to have better adhesion than have the other materials to concrete that is damp. Floors in some factories handling chemicals need more elaborate systems of protection.

These comments apply equally to reinforced concrete, though here the quality of the concrete itself is usually more carefully controlled, giving a rather higher resistance to destructive agencies. There is, however, an additional hazard in that the steel reinforcement may corrode.

The alkaline environment afforded by concrete provides some protection for the steel, and reliance is usually placed upon this to prevent corrosion. If the concrete is dense, is present in sufficient thickness, and is free from local defects, little oxygen and carbon dioxide can reach the steel, and corrosion is inhibited. For slabs and beams not exposed to the weather a minimum cover of 1 in. of concrete is needed, but for external work and also internal work exposed to corrosive conditions at least $1\frac{1}{2}$-in. cover is necessary. Extra care is needed where solutions of mineral salts, particularly chlorides, are present. In such cases, even a $1\frac{1}{2}$-in. cover of dense concrete may not be sufficient and other measures, such as the incorporation of an impervious membrane or protective coating, will be needed. Small amounts of chlorides (e.g. up to 2 per cent calcium chloride by weight of the cement), incorporated at the time of mixing to increase the speed of hardening or as an anti-freeze additive, are usually permissible. As the cement sets, the chloride enters into chemical reaction with some of its constituents and is then no longer harmful. Chloride that is free after the cement has set and hardened will accelerate corrosion of the steel; it may come into concrete from outside, for instance in brackish water, or it may be present within the concrete from the use of excess additions or in porous aggregate contaminated with sea salt.

With reinforced concrete made with *lightweight aggregates*, the risk of corrosion of the steel may be somewhat greater than with dense, gravel aggregate concrete. Lightweight concrete is more porous and so offers less resistance to the migration of moisture and of oxygen and carbon dioxide, both as gases and in solution. Moreover, there is a greater propensity to cracking as a result of drying shrinkage. Nevertheless, exposure tests indicate that the protection afforded to embedded reinforcement by the surrounding concrete is affected much more by the quality of the concrete and properties such as compaction, workability, cement content, concrete cover, and the grading of the aggregates, than by the type of aggregate used.

Reinforcement to be embedded in lightweight concrete can be protected against corrosive influences by simple measures. The surface of the steel bars might be covered with a cement slurry before casting the concrete. Galvanized steel can be employed, but the zinc coating is slowly attacked by the alkalis present in cement. Where reinforced lightweight concrete is exposed to the weather, the concrete cover over the reinforcement should not be less than 2 in., and the maximum aggregate size should not exceed $\frac{1}{2}$ in.

More recently *aerated concrete* has been used for precast reinforced concrete members of subsidiary character, such as roof, floor and wall slabs. In aerated concrete the reduction of density is achieved by an infusion of air or gas in a mix containing cement or lime, with sand, pulverized fuel ash, or burnt shale. After casting and initial setting, the material is cut to size and then cured in superheated steam in an autoclave.

Aerated concrete has very little resistance against the penetration of moisture or oxygen, and takes up carbon dioxide from the air readily. Bare bars embedded in structural members exposed to the weather or to humid atmospheric conditions such as are common with some industrial processes or in unventilated roof spaces where condensation occurs, tend to become vulnerable to corrosion. Bars embedded in aerated concrete therefore must be adequately protected by coating them with a bituminous solution or a cement-rubber mix, before embedment.

The effects of corrosion of the steel are two-fold. There is a gradual loss in strength whenever the cross-section of the steel is reduced. Of greater importance, however, is the change in volume that occurs; the corrosion products occupy more space than the original metal, and so severe rusting will cause disruption of the surrounding concrete. Once this has occurred, the protection afforded by the concrete is completely lost and corrosion can proceed at a greater rate. Repairs in such cases are usually made by cutting back the concrete so as to expose the rusty reinforcement, cleaning off most of the rust, and then applying a further protective coating of concrete by means of a spray gun. Since the applied concrete will tend to shrink, it should be given a mechanical key. As much of the reinforcement as possible should be totally embedded in the new material, and at the edges of the repaired patch the existing concrete should be under-cut.

Another common defect is the cracking of concrete. This may result from deflection under load (p. 5), from drying shrinkage and, sometimes, from thermal movement. Drying shrinkage can be minimized by ensuring that the aggregate to be used is clean and that the mixes employed are the leanest that will have adequate strength. Some aggregates of the dolerite and sandstone types suffer, in themselves, an appreciable moisture movement and drying shrinkage, and such aggregates should be avoided, except for concrete that is not likely to dry out.

The thermal movement of ballast concrete is roughly of the same order as that of steel. In places where a big temperature range must be tolerated, use of limestone or broken brick aggregate should be considered; these aggregates give a concrete that suffers little more than half the thermal movement of ballast concrete.

Timber

Timber is attacked only slowly by acids, and hardly at all by solutions of mineral salts or by oils. Its chief vulnerability is to biological attack—by fungi or by insects.

Fungal attack. A number of fungi will attack timber in buildings, but by far the most common and most insidious is the dry-rot fungus *Merulius lachrymans*. To gain a hold it requires timber that is not too dry and not too wet, having perhaps 20–24 per cent of moisture present, in a stagnant atmosphere, so that no rapid changes of moisture content occur. These conditions are favourable for the development of the air-borne spore of this fungus, and a fibrous material, known as mycelium, will grow and permeate the timber and any other porous materials in the vicinity. This mycelium is usually out of sight. Later, fruiting bodies develop on the surface; this is often the first stage at which the presence of dry rot is noticed. The fruiting bodies ripen and liberate millions of spores which float away and may start new growths elsewhere. It is only where stagnant and damp conditions are provided by badly designed or badly constructed buildings that this fungus can thrive. Structural timber is often incorporated in buildings at a moisture content that would make it vulnerable to attack, reliance being placed on drying within the building to save it. The need for drying has to be borne in mind both at the design and construction stages.

Once established, *Merulius lachrymans* can spread to other drier timbers. Its mycelium has been known to travel up to 30 ft in brickwork. It can live for quite a long time—up to 9 months—before it dies from lack of nourishment. Because of these characteristics, immediate action is required as soon as an outbreak of dry rot is found. All infected timber must be removed and the surroundings sterilized. Heat-treatment with a blow-lamp is a common technique employed in the sterilization of brickwork and concrete. There is however, the danger of not attaining and maintaining a sufficiently high temperature to ensure that all the fungus is killed. A temperature of at least 110°F is required for several hours to be sure that no life remains. Another treatment that is widely adopted is the application of a toxic solution. Until recently, sodium fluoride solution was employed for this purpose, but laboratory tests have shown that this chemical is rendered inert by the action of lime and so this fungicide is no longer effective where there is concrete or mortar present. Other toxic substances, such as sodium pentachlorphenate, are now preferred. Preliminary heating of the wall with a blow-lamp encourages penetration of the toxic liquid.

Where there has been an outbreak of dry rot, replacement with ordinary timber should be avoided. Another material, not susceptible to fungal attack, or timber that has been pressure-impregnated with preservative can be used. In most parts of a building it is desirable to have a non-staining, inodorous preservative rather than creosote.

Another common, though far less dangerous fungus is *Coniophora cerebella*, also known as 'cellar fungus'. This attacks timber that is too wet to encourage *Merulius*, and produces the effect commonly known as wet rot. It will attack timber that is sealed on one side by a paint coating, for instance skirting boards in contact with damp walls. It is less dangerous than *Merulius* because it cannot spread to other, drier timbers; it dies if the timber on which it is living dries out.

Details of the common fungi, their identification and treatment, are discussed in Forest Products Research Laboratory Leaflet No. 6, and more fully in that Laboratory's Bulletin No. 1, 'Dry rot in wood'.

Insect attack. Timber is susceptible also to attack by certain insects. For the most part, they confine their attentions to mature timber, but do not require a particular moisture content or the stagnant conditions that encourage fungi. The effect of insect attack is to weaken the timber mechanically. Often the skin of the timber is left intact, apart from a few small exit holes, and the extent of the damage cannot be detected by superficial examination.

Attack starts with the female beetle depositing eggs in a crack or crevice of the wood; these eggs hatch into larvae ('wood-worms'), which eat their way through the timber for a period of months or years and so do most of the damage. In due course they bore to a place near the surface of the wood and there spend some weeks as pupae. When the beetles emerge they gnaw their way through the thin wood covering and fly away.

From this description, the uselessness of treating only exit holes with an insecticide will be appreciated. The holes are present only when the insects have gone. To eradicate wood-worm, all exposed timber surfaces need treatment; injection into exit holes and crevices helps, as it is in places such as these that the mature female deposits its eggs.

Sterilization of infected timbers can sometimes be effected by heat-treatment. The treatment required is rather more drastic than that needed for killing fungus; a temperature of at least 130°F needs to be maintained for several hours. Usually this treatment is not practicable and reliance must be placed on a surface treatment with a toxic solution. Recently, insecticides have been developed that remain effective for a number of years, and it can now be expected that one treatment will ensure total eradication of the pest. Insects that emerge after several years in the grub stage will be killed, and the surface of the timber will remain repellent to other insects that might attempt to lay their eggs in it.

Much of the damage to structural timbers in building is caused by the furniture beetle, *Anobium punctatum*. This beetle will attack most timbers but has a preference for sapwood. The largest of the *Anobium* family, the death-watch beetle, is responsible for the breakdown of structural timber in many of the historic monuments. It has a preference for mature oak that has been softened by fungal attack.

Detailed information concerning the common beetles damaging timber, their recognition and destruction, is given in Forest Products Research Laboratory Leaflets No. 3 'Lyctus powder-post beetles', No. 4 'The death-watch beetle', No. 8 'The common furniture beetle', and No. 14 'The house long-horn beetle', For a fuller account reference should be made to Forest Products Research Bulletin No. 19 'Beetles injurious to timber and furniture'.

Steel

Though unprotected steel rusts rapidly, structural steel with protective coatings remains durable in the average internal environment. Hot-rolled sections of structural mild steel have now been in use for about 50 years in all-steel frames, and for a considerably longer period for single members such as beams and filler joists. By modern standards, the protection given to many of the earlier examples was seldom good but, where buildings containing internal steelwork have been demolished, few examples of serious deterioration have been noted except where there has been prolonged exposure to moisture, for instance through leakage of rain, or where the steelwork has made contact with corrosive substances. In such circumstances there are many cases of severe corrosion.

The prevention of corrosion received only brief mention in Volume 1 (pp. 86–90). Much structural steelwork is encased in dense concrete which serves to protect it not only from fire but also from corrosion. Where the steelwork is exposed, or is encased only in porous materials, additional protection against corrosion is needed and is usually supplied in the form of a paint treatment. The first step is to clean off all mill-scale and rust and to apply a rust-inhibitive primer, such as one based on red lead, zinc chromate or calcium plumbate. The primer is followed by undercoat paint and a gloss finish, to make the whole coating as impervious as possible. In some circumstances, as in corrosive atmospheres, a paint system of this kind may not be adequate; for greater protection the rust-inhibitive primer should be followed, after it has fully hardened, by a substantial coating of bitumen.

The need for thorough cleaning of the metal surface before painting cannot be over-emphasized. All unwanted substances, including moisture, should be removed. One merit of flame-cleaning is that it provides a thoroughly dry surface.

Another treatment for steel or iron that would otherwise be exposed to a risk of corrosion is to coat or 'plate' it with a metal less liable to attack, those most commonly used being zinc, tin, cadmium, chromium, nickel and aluminium.

The mechanism of corrosion is complicated and cannot be discussed here in detail, but the process is in part electrolytic. Two metals, in contact both with one another and with water or some damp material, will act as the poles of a short-circuited electric cell. The positively charged metal (the 'anode') is dissolved, the more rapidly if strong mineral acids or their salts (e.g. sulphates or chlorides) are present. A number of metals are listed below in order of decreasing vulnerability to this kind of attack, the electrolytic action being the stronger the farther apart the two metals concerned stand in the list.

Iron, about half-way down the list, is protected either by a coating that is more vulnerable, such as zinc, or one that is less vulnerable, such as chromium, tin or nickel, so long as the coating is complete and continuous. An anodic covering is generally preferred, zinc being commonly used, as when steel components are 'hot-dip galvanized' by dipping in a bath of molten zinc. Zinc is vulnerable to attack by alkali as well as by acid; galvanized iron or steel parts built into mortar or concrete, particularly in places likely to be damp, should be dipped in, or painted with, bitumen to protect the zinc coating from attack by the alkali. Hot-dip galvanized surfaces that are to be painted must either be weathered for a few months or be etched to ensure satisfactory adhesion.

Corroded (anodic) metals	magnesium
	zinc
	aluminium
	aluminium–magnesium—silicon alloys
	cadmium
	aluminium–copper alloys
	iron and mild steel
	chromium
	tin
	lead
	nickel
	brasses
	bronzes
Protected (cathodic) metals	copper

Hot-rolled steel has a substantial section, and slight corrosion of the surface does not cause much loss in strength; consequently, a properly designed paint coating is considered to give adequate protection in most circumstances. Cold-formed steelwork, on the other hand, has a much lighter section, and little corrosion can be tolerated. For external exposure, or where there is a likelihood of condensation, coating with a non-ferrous metal prior to painting is recommended. In less corrosive environments, a phosphate treatment followed by a rust-inhibitive primer and two further protective coats of paint should be adequate. Details of the protection required in a range of circumstances are given in British Standard P.D. 420 'Recommendations on methods of protection against corrosion for light gauge steel used in building'.

Aluminium

The alloys of aluminium used in building vary widely in their resistance to corrosion. The more corrosion-resistant alloys need no protection where they are exposed to air but should be given a paint treatment based on a chromate primer (*not* a lead primer) where they are in a corrosive atmosphere or where they are in contact with alkaline materials, such as concrete or mortar. Corrosion may also develop where there are crevices in which moisture can be retained; where crevices cannot be avoided, as at the junction of two members bolted together, they should be packed with a protective material such as a barium chromate jointing compound.

Contact with another metal, or even with water that has run over the surface of another metal, can cause rapid corrosion of aluminium. Copper is particularly troublesome in this respect, but zinc is relatively harmless and aluminium members can be joined and fixed in place by galvanized steel bolts without appreciable loss of durability.

THERMAL INSULATION

The standard of thermal insulation in the traditional building of this country has generally been fortuitous or incidental to other functions of the structure, except in such buildings as cold stores, where high standards are desirable to limit capital and operational costs. In post-war years, however, the high costs of fuels and, at one time, shortages of fuel, together with the developments of light materials and cladding techniques using them, have directed attention to the rate at which heat can be lost from buildings by conduction through the enclosing structure. The need for effective heat conservation has now encouraged a rapid development of materials and methods primarily used for insulation, and it has also been recognized in the formulation of legal requirements. In particular, under the Thermal Insulation (Industrial Buildings) Act, 1957, a standard of insulation has been prescribed for the roofs of certain classes of building; for houses, the Model Byelaws stipulate a minimum standard of insulation for the main building elements.

Every improvement in the insulation of walls, floors or roofs, besides restricting the rate of heat flow through these elements, also moderates the influence of outdoor conditions on the internal climate of buildings. Physically the two effects are inseparable, but in practice the first is often given the more attention because it can be related easily to the economics of heating.

The economic case for insulation is judged by considering how much it would cost to maintain a building at a given temperature with different standards of insulation and comparing this with the cost of attaining each standard. The comparison is closest in buildings that need to be heated continuously, for here the capital cost of insulating can be balanced directly against the saving in heating equipment and the recurrent saving of fuel that would otherwise be needed to maintain the required temperature. The cost relationship is rather less direct in intermittently heated buildings, but even so, insulation may often be shown to be profitable. Where the control of overall heat loss is regarded as a potential investment, much depends on the designer's detailed treatment of the structure, since any specific standard of resistance to heat loss can be achieved in different ways and at different capital costs. Compact planning is obviously valuable; beyond this, however, there is the significant effect of the basic shape of a building, which determines the proportional areas of the structural element. The effect of shape can be assessed roughly by expressing the areas of the walls, roof and ground floor as multiples of the gross floor area. Thus the ratios of wall, roof and ground-floor area might be computed as $2 \cdot 6 : 1 \cdot 0 : 1 \cdot 0$ in a two-storey detached house, compared with $0 \cdot 7 : 1 \cdot 0 : 1 \cdot 0$ for a single-storey factory building. Taking account only of surface area and the degree of external exposure, insulation would appear to be of most benefit in the walls of the house and in the roof of the factory, but this would need to be confirmed by an assessment of the basic heat resistance of each of the exposed elements, and of the ease and cost of improving it. Table 1.1 gives some very broad estimates of the relative heat losses through roofs, floors and walls (including windows), and by ventilation, for a few types of building.

The effect of insulation on the indoor climate of buildings is seldom easy to interpret in economic terms though there are specific circumstances where the

TABLE 1.1

Relative heat losses by conduction and by ventilation

Building	Ratio, wall/floor area	Ratio, roof/floor area	Wall $U = 0.3$ Roof $U = 0.4$			Wall $U = 0.3$ Roof $U = 0.1$			Wall $U = 0.2$ Roof $U = 0.2$		
			Conduction	Conduction + ventilation		Conduction	Conduction + ventilation		Conduction	Conduction + ventilation	
				2 a.c./h	3 a.c./h		2 a.c./h	3 a.c./h		2 a.c./h	3 a.c./h
900 sq. ft house (detached) .	1·4 : 1	0·5 : 1	0·92	1·24	1·40	0·77	1·09	1·25	0·68	1·00	1·16
900 sq. ft house (semi-detached) .	1·0 : 1	0·5 : 1	0·80	1·12	1·28	0·65	0·97	1·13	0·60	0·91	1·08
900 sq. ft house (terrace) .	0·6 : 1	0·5 : 1	0·68	1·00	1·16	0·53	0·85	1·01	0·52	0·84	1·00
1500 sq. ft house (detached) .	1 : 1	0·5 : 1	0·80	1·12	1·28	0·65	0·97	1·13	0·60	0·92	1·08
1500 sq. ft bungalow (detached) .	0·6 : 1	1 : 1	0·98	1·30	1·46	0·68	1·00	1·16	0·72	1·04	1·20
				3 a.c./h	6 a.c./h		3 a.c./h	6 a.c./h		3 a.c./h	6 a.c./h
5000 sq. ft factory (single-storey, double height) . .	0·6 : 1	0·7 : 1	1·16	2·12	3·08	0·85	1·81	2·77	0·86	1·82	2·78

Rates of heat loss by conduction and by ventilation
(Btu/hour °F sq. ft gross floor area)

connection is fairly clear. For example, in a building where heating is intermittent, insulating the structure by lightweight linings of low heat capacity can reduce the period needed to warm the building to a comfortable air temperature. Moreover, a general improvement in insulation can be expected at any time to bring the radiant temperature of the occupants' surroundings closer to the region of thermal comfort for a given expenditure of fuel.

Apart from the general use of thermal insulation in roofs and floors to reduce the rate of heat transfer between the inside and the outside of the building, particular use may be made of it in conjunction with embedded heating installations. Such uses include the provision of edge insulation to a solid floor on the ground in which heating units are embedded, and the incorporation of insulation in a roof or intermediate suspended floor construction in which ceiling heating units are provided. The insulation must of course be placed so that the heat output is directed towards those parts of the building for which it is intended.

Intermediate suspended floors rarely need to be insulated, so long as the air temperatures to be maintained are much the same on either side. However, there are occasions when the floor may project beyond the exterior of a part of the building below it; consideration should then be given to insulating the projecting part. An intermediate floor that separates two parts of a building with very different temperature requirements (for example, the floor above a boiler house) may also need to be designed so as to restrict heat transfer.

Chapter 2

SUSPENDED FLOORS

THE main function of a suspended floor is to support the loads placed on it during the life of the building. With some types of building, loadings are easy to predict and unlikely to increase with time. With others, particularly with industrial buildings, change of occupancy or developments in production may require floor strengths greater than those originally adequate, and this possibility needs to be considered at the design stage. Strengthening an existing floor is normally inconvenient, difficult and expensive. On the other hand, design for improbably high loadings will result in excessive cost of the floor construction itself, of the supporting framework or walling, and of the foundations.

Apart from the loadings to be carried, the choice between timber and concrete construction for intermediate floors will be governed mainly by cost and by such requirements as sound insulation and fire protection. Many other factors may need consideration. Thus, a decision on a particular type of concrete floor, for instance a precast or a cast *in situ* floor, may depend on the need for speed of erection, or on the facility with which openings may be formed in the floor after construction. The services, conduits and trunking that are required in a building should be considered before the choice of floor is made, as these may influence the thickness of screed, the provision of holes, the preference for solid or cavity construction, the provision of a suspended ceiling, and in some cases the choice between solid or open-web supporting beams. The floor finishes to be used throughout the building must also be taken into account at an early stage in the design, to ensure that suitable levels for the constructional floor and the supporting beams are provided to allow for possible variations in the thickness of screeds and finishes.

Other special requirements for floors may arise. The function of the floor structure is often complex in modern buildings and frequently demands detailed consideration in the early stages of the building design.

STRENGTH AND STABILITY

Loadings

The standard imposed loadings for which floors must be designed are specified in the building byelaws of the various local authorities, and are usually based on the recommendations in British Standard Code of Practice CP 3, Chapter V, Loadings (1952) as given in Table 2.1.

Imposed loadings are often very variable, both between one building and another in the same loading class and between the various elements of flooring in the same building. The standard loadings specified for design purposes are not necessarily the highest loadings that may occur in practice. They are such that, when they are used in conjunction with the design methods and permissible stresses recommended in other codes of practice, the margin of safety against structural failure is always adequate for the highest actual loads without being unreasonably large for the loads that most commonly occur.

As was shown in Vol. I (p. 8), the average load per square foot of floor area depends on the size of floor considered. The imposed loading, unlike the dead weight of the floor itself, is rarely distributed uniformly over the floor, but consists of a number of isolated loads producing a range of local intensities of pressure on the floor. For a large floor carrying many such isolated loads, the effect of these loads, on the stresses in the flooring material and on the resulting deflection, is often little different from that of the same total load uniformly distributed over the whole floor area. For smaller areas, however, there is a chance that the full effect of a local concentration of load will be sustained without the compensation of appreciable parts of the area being without load. For this reason Table 2.1 includes, besides the basic load requirements in column (3) that will normally be used in design, alternative minimum loads in columns (4) and (5) that become operative for slabs at spans of less than 8 ft, and for beams when the area of floor supported is less than 64 sq. ft. For very small spans or supported areas, the intensities of loading corresponding to these alternative minimum loads are very high, gradually reducing with increase in span or area to the standard values of column (3).

Except where floors are used for storage purposes, the average intensity of loading, in practice, tends to decrease as the floor area increases; and a rational design method should include allowance for this by relating the assumed loading intensity to the area of floor considered. Although such a relationship has not yet been adopted, it is usual to permit a reduction in the assumed imposed loading for the design of supporting beams or girders (but not of the floor slab itself), where a single span of the beam or girder supports not less than 500 sq. ft of floor at one general level. For these conditions, the imposed loading may be reduced by 5 per cent for each 500 sq. ft supported, subject to a maximum reduction of 25 per cent.

The loadings specified in Table 2.1 are stated in the Code to be sufficient to provide for normal effects of impact or of the acceleration of moving loads. However, special consideration must be given, where necessary, to the effects of vibration from machinery and of dynamic stresses arising from the operation of cranes, hoists and the like. Impact resistance is not usually of much importance in buildings but it is possible that, for the lightly loaded floors of small dwelling houses, new unconventional flooring systems may be developed that are of adequate general strength but need checking for satisfactory resistance to impact. For this purpose it has been suggested that three standard impact tests should be made on a prototype of a new type of floor:

  (i) 10-lb weight dropped on to an area 1 in. square of the floor from a height of 4 ft;

  (ii) 100-lb weight dropped on to an area 1 in. square of the floor from a height of 6 in.;

  (iii) 56-lb weight of sand in a standard bag dropped on to the floor from a height of 4 ft.

These standard impacts represent likely blows to which floors in dwellings will at some time be subjected; when a floor is tested with these impacts, it should not suffer serious damage. It is not possible to put forward definite proposals for deciding, from the extent of damage sustained, whether a floor is to be considered satisfactory or otherwise: clearly it would be unsatisfactory if the floor were perforated or if a ceiling below were badly cracked; some indentation of the floor surface may be tolerated, but this should not be deeper than about $\frac{1}{16}$–$\frac{1}{8}$ in.

The assumed distributed loadings are not a sufficient basis for design if any of the actual isolated loads produce local distress of the floor. The likelihood of trouble from this cause is small for solid reinforced concrete floor slabs, since this type of floor is capable of effective lateral distribution of loading, whereby the load is supported by the bending of the slab over a much greater width than that over which the load is directly applied to the floor surface. The effects of concentrated loads are more serious for flooring systems in which the floor slab is built up of a series of separate adjacent beams; however, in practice, even with this type of floor, there is often considerable interaction between the beams so that a heavy local load on one of them would be shared by neighbouring beams.

In general, therefore, no special consideration of the localized effect of the individual loads is required for most types of loading. For garage floors, however, it is necessary to check the strength of the floor to resist the local loads from vehicle wheels. In each design, the floor should be strong enough to withstand the worst combination of actual wheel loads; it is commonly found that, having designed the floor to satisfy the basic loading requirement in column (3) of Table 2.1, the resistance to the actual local loading is adequate.

Floor types

The methods of designing floors in appropriate materials are sufficiently covered in works on building construction and structural engineering, and in the relevant B.S. Codes of Practice; it is not necessary therefore to discuss design in detail here. However, certain general principles should be mentioned.

A floor is usually supported by a rectangular grid of either walls or beams. If the floors are carried by a steel or reinforced concrete framework, the main beams spanning between the columns are often too far apart for the most economic design of the floor slab; in these circumstances, the main beams support secondary beams so that the floor is carried by a grid of smaller dimensions, being thus divided into a series of panels.

It is desirable, and common practice, to arrange that the floor acts as a continuous system over the supporting grid rather than that each panel should behave as an independent structural element.

In general, also, it is advantageous to design the slab to span in two directions so that the load is transmitted to the supporting grid at all four sides of the panels. This is an easy matter when solid reinforced concrete slabs are used, since all that is required is to introduce reinforcing bars in two layers, the upper layer being transverse to and, during construction,

TABLE 2.1

Minimum and alternative minimum imposed loads

In this table, a reference to a floor includes a reference to any part of that floor to be used as a corridor; 'slabs' includes boarding and beams or ribs spaced not further apart than three feet between centres, and 'beams' means all other beams and ribs.

Loading class No.	Types of floors	Minimum imposed loads	Alternative minimum imposed loads*	
			Slabs	Beams
		lb per sq. ft of floor area	lb (uniformly distributed over span) per ft width	lb uniformly distributed over span
(1)	(2)	(3)	(4)	(5)
30	Floors in dwelling houses of not more than two storeys designed for one occupation.	30	240	1920
40	Floors (other than those of Class No. 30) for residential purposes including dwelling houses of more than one occupation, tenements, hospital wards, bedrooms and private sitting rooms in hotels, dormitories.	40	320	2560
50	Office floors above the entrance floor; floors of light workrooms without storage.	50	400	3200
60	Floors of banking halls; office entrance floors and office floors below entrance floor; floors of classrooms in schools.	60	480	3840
80	Shop floors used for the display and sale of merchandise; workrooms generally; places of assembly with fixed seating,† churches and chapels; restaurants; circulation space in machinery halls, power stations, etc. where not occupied by plant or equipment.	80	640	5120

Minimum imposed loads, lb/sq ft of floor area	Type of floor	Concentrated load
100	Floors of warehouses, workshops, factories and other buildings or parts of buildings of similar category for lightweight loads; office floors for storage and filing purposes; places of assembly without fixed seating (public rooms in hotels, dance halls, etc.).	—
150	Floors of warehouses, workshops, factories and other buildings or parts of buildings of similar category for medium-weight loads; floors of garages for vehicles not exceeding 4 tons gross weight.	80
200	Floors of warehouses, workshops, factories and other buildings or parts of buildings of similar category for heavy-weight loads; floors of book stores and stationery stores; roofs and pavement lights over basements projecting under the public footpath.	6400
Garage floors Minimum imposed loads, lb/sq ft of floor area. The worst combination of actual wheel loads Slabs 80 Beams 50 or the worst combination of actual wheel loads, whichever is the greater.	Floors used only for the parking of passenger vehicles and light vans not exceeding 2½ tons gross weight	For garage floors only, 1.5 × maximum wheel load, but not less than 2000 lb considered to be distributed over a floor area 2 ft 6 in. square. —
	Floors used for garages for vehicles not exceeding 2½ tons gross weight	

* Minimum load for slabs becomes operative at spans of less than 8 ft. Minimum load for beams becomes operative on areas less than 64 sq. ft. Beams, ribs and joists spaced at not more than 3 ft centres may be calculated for slab loadings. For alternative loads on cantilever balconies, the span shall be deemed to be the projection of the cantilever.

† Fixed seating implies that the removal of the seating and the use of the space for other purposes is improbable.

resting on, the lower layer. The bars in each layer must be close enough for the concrete and steel to work effectively together, thus justifying the assumption, which is permitted in design, that the bending moments can be calculated on the basis of the elastic theory for thin homogeneous plates. Accordingly, it is common practice to restrict the distance between the main bars to not more than three times the effective depth of the slab (that is, the distance of the bars from the compressed surface of the slab).

It has already been stated that the rectangular section is not the most efficient structurally for reinforced concrete, because the concrete in the tensile zone of the section is usually unable to play any important part in resisting the external loading. However, in the solid slab floor with low percentages of reinforcement, cracking of the slab is usually insignificant for normal working loads, and most of the concrete throughout the slab carries stress and helps to reduce the bending under load. At higher loads the value of the concrete in tension becomes less and less important, so that it would be reasonable, from consideration of the ultimate strength of the slab, to adjust the cross-section of the slab by removing the concrete in the tensile zone except where it is needed to surround the reinforcement and to connect it to the compression zone.

If this is done, the floor becomes of ribbed construction, the slab of which is almost wholly in compression, with a series of ribs in one or two directions in which the reinforcing bars are concentrated. Usually a flat soffit for the floor slab is required, to form a base for a ceiling below, and it is therefore common to design the slab with hollow blocks of concrete or clay in between the ribs, to replace the solid concrete that is structurally unnecessary. If the blocks have a sufficient strength, however, they may be assumed to play a structural role, acting in combination with the ribs and the topping of concrete that is cast *in situ* over them; the tops of the blocks help the concrete topping to resist compression, and the block walls adjacent to the ribs help the ribs to resist shearing forces.

It is becoming more common to make floors of precast concrete beams, usually laid side by side and of box-section, I-section, or inverted U-section. Additional strength may be obtained by casting ribs *in situ* between the beams and an *in situ* topping at least $1\frac{1}{4}$ in. thick over the units. In all these floors, the cross-section is such that much of the unwanted concrete in tension is omitted. A structural disadvantage of this type of floor is that its effectiveness for the lateral distribution of concentrated loads is much less than that of an *in situ* solid slab, ribbed or hollow-block floor. For a solid slab, for example, the bending moment at mid-span due to a concentrated load may be assumed to be resisted by an 'effective width' of slab equal to the sum of the actual width of the loading and three-fifths of the span. For a precast floor, however, the effective width must not be taken to exceed the load width by more than the width of three precast units and joints when there is no topping, or the width of four precast units and joints where there is a topping of at least $1\frac{1}{4}$ in. Even lower values must be taken if the engineer is not satisfied that load will be effectively transferred between the units.

Floors of composite construction have been developed, which are of high structural efficiency. In some of these floors, precast and *in situ* concrete elements are combined in the most suitable way for satisfying the functional requirements as to strength, stiffness, sound insulation and fire resistance. There is no great difficulty, in design or in construction, in ensuring proper interaction between all parts of the flooring system. In another composite floor, the filler-joist slab, structural steel I-beams are embedded in a concrete slab. Although this system is theoretically rather inefficient in the use of material, in that the top flange of the steel beam usually contributes little to the ultimate strength of the floor, it has proved economical in practice for heavily loaded floors.

In some buildings, particularly where floor loads are heavy, it is convenient and economical to use 'flat slab construction,' in which the beams are omitted, the slabs themselves transmitting the loading direct to the columns. In order to avoid very high local stresses at the column/slab junction it has been usual to provide flared column heads, which give increased support to the slab and have resulted in the term 'mushroom construction' for this system. However, there is a tendency nowadays, for architectural reasons, to avoid these special column heads. The slab itself can be a solid slab, or of ribbed or hollow-block construction.

The flat slab is part of a three-dimensional structure in which loads are transmitted in all directions by the slab, and the columns and slab act together as a space framework. The slab is reinforced either in two directions, parallel to the edges of the panels, or in four directions, i.e. parallel to the edges of the panels and parallel to the diagonals of the panels. The detailed analysis of the structural behaviour of the flat-slab system is very complex, and the designer has the choice of two simplified approaches. In the first, some simple empirical rules are used for the bending moments to be resisted at the various critical sections; however, this method is applicable only to slabs within a restricted range of dimensions and panel shapes. In the second approach, the structure is considered to be divided into two series of frame-works parallel to the lines of columns in the two directions at right-angles, each frame consisting of a row of columns and strips of slab with a width equal to the distance between the centre-lines of the panels on each side of this row of columns. The bending moments are calculated for the mid-span of a panel and for the section at the column support, using in each calculation the appropriate worst condition of imposed loading, and these bending moments are distributed across the sections according to simple empirical rules.

The foregoing comments on floor types are concerned with reinforced concrete or similar forms of construction. These represent the majority of floors designed for large multi-storey buildings. In housing, the traditional timber floor is rarely 'designed' in a structural engineering sense; the joist sizes and the thickness of floor boards that are satisfactory have been developed as a result of long experience. The primary criterion of acceptance has been reasonable stiffness, and this usually requires that the scantlings are such that the stresses induced at working loads are well below those permissible in relation to the possibility of collapse of the floor. In times of acute shortage of timber, engineering principles have been invoked to show that smaller sections of timber than have been commonly used are quite adequate for floors in dwellings; however, the degree of flexibility that can be assumed to be tolerable depends very much on the opinions of the occupants, and it seems likely that many people would not be satisfied with the extremely economical systems that have sometimes been suggested.

Strength of reinforced concrete beams and slabs

With modern methods of design, based on an appropriate load factor against failure, it is necessary to be able to calculate the ultimate strengths of structural members. The calculation of this strength for a reinforced concrete structure is often a much easier task than the determination of the stress conditions at working loads. For beams and slabs, it is necessary to determine, for the type of loading considered, the way in which the bending is distributed throughout the system, and also the ultimate resistances to bending (called the ultimate 'resistance moments') that can be developed at the critical sections where the bending moments are highest.

The engineer can calculate the ultimate resistance moments for a particular cross-section without great difficulty if he knows what basic assumptions he should make with regard to:

the stress-strain characteristics of the concrete in compression

the stress-strain characteristics of the reinforcement

the variation in strain across any cross-section.

The form of the stress-strain relationship for concrete in compression has been the subject of continual investigation and discussion from the earliest days of reinforced-concrete construction. Initially the problem was largely concerned with the determination of the modulus of elasticity, which in the design calculations affected the estimated stresses, particularly those in the concrete. Later, the effects of creep of the concrete were shown to be of such importance that the modulus of elasticity was both difficult to define and of little direct value in the analysis of the behaviour of structures. The use of 'effective' moduli, which include some allowance for creep, was then introduced; it was found that they could be of value both for estimating probable limits for the stresses at working loads and also, when suitable criteria were adopted for the maximum concrete stresses, for calculating ultimate strengths of beams and frameworks. The maximum concrete stresses chosen, however, were known to be fictitious and it has become clear that a more rational approach is necessary before any real advance can be made in our methods of strength calculation.

In recent years many research workers have suggested forms for the stress-strain relationship for concrete, and have considered the effect of the relationship chosen on the estimated strength of reinforced concrete, particularly of simple beams. The form of relationship shown in Fig. 2.1a seems to be reasonable on the basis of present data.

The stress-strain relationship for ordinary mild-steel reinforcement is fairly constant, and it is usually sufficient to assume that the stress is proportional to the strain up to the yield point, with a modulus of elasticity of 30×10^6 lb per sq. in., and that the yield-point stress is maintained for increasing strains up to the ultimate capacity of the concrete. The stress-strain relationships for other reinforcement must be established for each type of steel.

Bernouilli's simple hypothesis that the strains vary linearly across any section ('plane sections remain plane') cannot be exactly true in a cracked member, owing to slip between the concrete and steel at cracks. Nevertheless, experimental evidence has shown that this hypothesis is usually approximately satisfied and can be accepted as a general basis for design calculations, including the estimation of ultimate strengths. Thus, the strain changes steadily from a maximum compression at the top of the beam, through zero at a particular level (referred to as the neutral axis of the section), to a maximum tensile deformation at the bottom of the beam (this tensile deformation being of importance only as regards the stresses developed in the tensile reinforcement).

Since the strain is proportional to the distance from the neutral axis, the stress-strain diagram in Fig. 2.1a may be regarded as the distribution of

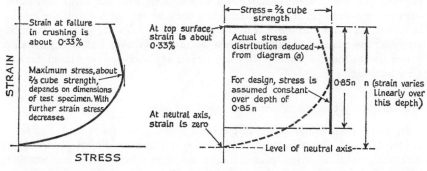

(a) Stress-strain diagram for concrete   (b) Equivalent rectangular stress distribution for compressive zone in beams

FIG. 2.1

Stress–strain conditions for concrete in compression in beams

stress in the compressive zone of a beam. It will be observed that at failure, the stress at the top of the beam is a little less than the maximum stress developed in the concrete, and also that the stress is almost uniform over much of the depth of the compressive zone. Indeed, for practical purposes it is reasonable, and sufficiently accurate, to assume that the stress in the concrete in compression is uniform, as shown in Fig. 2.1b. With this modification, the calculation of the ultimate resistance moments of beams and slabs (spanning in one direction) is very simple and quick.

If reinforcement is provided in the compressive zone, it is usually reasonable to assume that, at failure of the beam, this reinforcement will have reached its yield stress. It is easy to check this from the strain conditions in the beam, which are established in the calculations.

Two conditions of primary failure may occur in a beam or slab. In the first, with increasing load the tensile reinforcement reaches its yield strength before the concrete in compression has developed its full strength; plastic deformation of the steel without increase in its stress leads to higher strains in the concrete and the resistance moment increases until the ultimate conditions shown in Fig. 2.1*a* are reached. In the second, crushing of the concrete occurs before the tensile reinforcement reaches its yield strength; the maximum compressive force in the concrete corresponds to the distribution shown in Fig. 2.1*a* with a depth to the neutral axis of about three-fifths of the depth to the tensile reinforcement, or to the distribution shown in Fig. 2.1*b*, with a depth of uniformly-stressed concrete of one-half of that to the tensile reinforcement.

Two other forms of failure may occur instead of those mentioned above. These are *failure in shear*, by diagonal cracking of the concrete and yielding of any shear reinforcement crossing the diagonal cracks, and *failure in bond*, whereby the bars slip through the concrete. Present knowledge of the resistance of reinforced concrete to failure in diagonal tension or by slip of the reinforcement is inadequate for the formulation of any generally satisfactory method for calculating this resistance. For the time being, therefore, it appears that the present design rules for checking that the shear and bond stresses are within certain specified limits must be retained. From the results of recent experimental work it appears that these rules are not a very good guide to the margin of safety against secondary failure, but it is probably better not to modify them until they can be replaced by recommendations on a load-factor basis.

Redistribution of moments in continuous beams and frames

In recent years much attention has been given, particularly by J. F. Baker, at Cambridge University, to the design of steel frameworks on the basis of the ultimate conditions when 'plastic hinges' are developed in sufficient number to transform the framework into a mechanism. The design of reinforced concrete frameworks along similar lines has been studied by A. L. L. Baker.

It is over twenty years since tests were made at the Building Research Station which demonstrated the great value of moment redistribution in reinforced concrete. The results of one of the tests, on a two-span continuous beam, are summarized in Fig. 2.2. In this test, equal loads were applied in each span at a distance of 1 ft 8½ in. from the central support, the length of span being 5 ft 6 in. The beam was T-form with a flange 15 in. wide and 2½ in. thick, and a rib 4¼ in. wide. The beam had an overall depth of 9 in. and was reinforced with two ⅜-in. top bars for resisting the negative moments over the central support and four ⅜-in. bars at the bottom for resisting the moments in the span. The bars were of mild steel and the concrete of high ultimate strength (6800 lb per sq. in.).

The initial distribution of bending moment was similar to that predicted on the basis of the elastic theory. At yield of the bars at the section over the central support there was a marked drop in the moment at this section, but subsequently, with further increase in load, the moment was maintained at the value corresponding to the development of the yield stress in the continuity bars. The loading was continued until the full strength of the span section was reached, at a load of over five times that at which steel yield commenced over the central support.

The behaviour of this beam is very similar to that which would be expected from the assumption that reinforced concrete is an elastoplastic

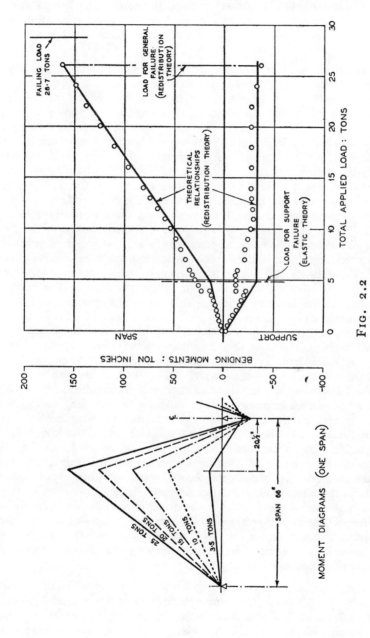

Fig. 2.2

Moment redistribution in continuous beam, primarily due to yielding of the continuity steel

material, and it will be observed from Fig. 2.2 that the formation of a 'plastic hinge' is well established. In other tests, on continuous beams and on portal frames, important increases in load accompanied redistribution of moments, but the formation of a plastic hinge was not usually so clearly indicated.

The practical value of moment redistribution in reinforced concrete is somewhat different from that in structural steelwork. In a steel framework it is impractical or uneconomic to arrange that the section moduli at all sections conform to the distribution of moments corresponding to the elastic theory. It follows that, at yield at one section, there is a reserve of strength at other sections and the theory of plasticity is invoked in order to assess the ultimate strength of the structure. In a reinforced concrete framework, however, there is no great difficulty in adjusting the cross-sections of the members, and their reinforcement, so that the distribution of strength throughout the framework is reasonably in accordance with the bending-moment distribution; if this were done, there would be very little redistribution of moments even if the load were increased to failure, and there would be no necessity for a special design method based on redistribution. Nevertheless, even if a reinforced concrete framework is not designed according to a theory based directly on moment redistribution, a knowledge of this property allows simplification of design calculations. For example, the analysis of the bending moments in a particular member of a multi-storey framework depends on the stiffness characteristics of all the members. These characteristics cannot be defined with great precision owing to the uncertain degree of cracking, and the analysis of the effect of *all* the members on the particular member being studied (and every member must be so studied in turn in the design procedure) is a considerable task for a large framework. However, it is in practice sufficient to use simple approximations for the stiffness characteristics and to estimate the bending moments by considering only a part of the framework at a time, as recommended in the Code of Practice CP 114 for reinforced concrete. From the knowledge of redistribution of moments that can occur, it can be assumed that the errors involved in the estimate of bending moments with this simplified design approach would be largely compensated for by the readjustment of moments throughout the system before failure. Acknowledgment of this effect is also justification for some modification in the distribution of reinforcement where this is helpful, as in the reduction of congestion of bars at beam/column junctions, and can often lead to appreciable economies when (as is usual) the framework is required to have satisfactory resistance to more than one arrangement of loading.

Allowance for the effects of redistribution of moments in this indirect way can be of great value in producing simplicity in design, and in effecting savings of material, but it is possible that in certain circumstances greater economy might be obtainable if there were available a direct design method based on these effects. In developing such a method, there are several difficulties, perhaps the most important of which are that redistribution of moments is often accompanied by excessive cracking of the concrete, and that the relationship between moment and curvature at local zones of incipient failure is very uncertain. The first difficulty is to some extent avoided if the design is such that no redistribution of moments occurs at working loads; the second difficulty will no doubt be removed as a result of further research, and A. L. L. Baker has already put forward suggestions for the limiting local curvatures that may be assumed in combination with a length of member over which these curvatures are operative.

The strength of two-way slabs

Tests on two-way slabs under uniformly distributed loading and concentrated loading have shown that:

(i) at working loads the slabs deform in accordance with the theory of the elastic plate;

(ii) at higher loads there is considerable redistribution of moments so that the ultimate load is sometimes twice that calculated on the basis of the bending moments deduced from the elastic theory.

With panels fixed at, or continuous over, their edges, the effects of moment redistribution can be particularly important. As a result of inelastic deformation, the relationship between the moments in the span and those over the supports changes; the distribution of tensile force in the reinforcement crossing any section tends to become more uniform; and, if the slab is relatively weak in one direction, there is a change in the proportion of load effectively supported in the two span directions. Each of these effects leads to an increase in the strength of the slab.

In recent years, allowance has been made in design for the effects of redistribution of moments, by modification of the bending moment coefficients to be assumed at critical sections of a slab. However, in a load-factor method of design, a more direct estimate of the strength of a slab can often be obtained by the use of the yield-line theory of slab failure which has been developed, particularly by Johansen. As a very simple example, consider a uniformly loaded square slab simply-supported along its four edges (Fig. 2.3). It is known from experiments that, at failure of the slab, there is a concentration of large curvature and heavy cracking along the diagonals of the slab, and the sections crossing these lines tend to develop their full strength, corresponding usually to the yield stress in the reinforcing bars. Hence the lines are referred to as 'yield-lines' or 'fracture-lines'. For the large deflections at incipient failure of the slab, it is assumed that the four parts of the slab into which it is divided by the yield-lines remain plane, additional deflection resulting only from the local curvature at the yield-lines, whilst each part of the slab rotates about the outer edge.

If reinforcement is disposed uniformly across the slab in each direction, so that the ultimate strength of any section, normal to the reinforcement, is M per unit width, the failing load S of the slab can be calculated by considering the equilibrium of any one of the slab parts. Taking moments about the slab edge:

$$ML = \frac{S}{4} \times \frac{L}{6}$$

or $\qquad S = 24\ M.$

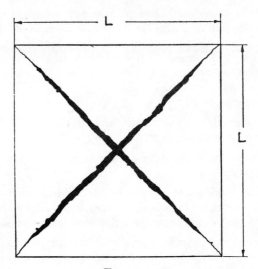

FIG. 2.3

Basic pattern of major cracks indicating 'yield lines'
or 'fracture lines' for a square slab simply-
supported on all edges by very stiff beams

It is clear from this example that the strength of a slab can be determined
very easily if the pattern of major cracks or yield lines can be deduced from
the known conditions of loading and support. Rules for obtaining this
pattern have been formulated by Johansen, and the method is already being
adopted for design purposes in the Scandinavian countries.

The interaction between slab and beam

The Code of Practice CP 114 recommends a very simple rule for determining the amount and distribution of the load transferred by the slab to its
supporting beams, as shown in Fig. 2.4. This rule can be used whatever

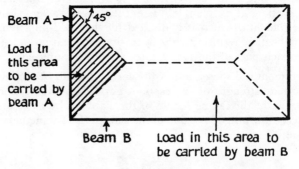

FIG. 2.4

Distribution of load between beams supporting floor

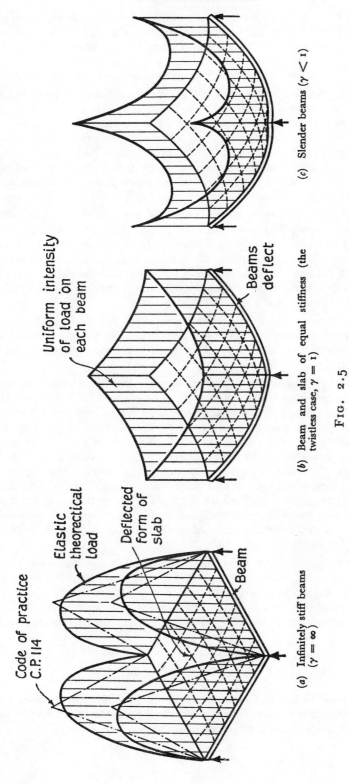

FIG. 2.5

Uniformly loaded square slab supported by beams on all four edges. Distribution of vertical load transmitted to the beams

(a) Infinitely stiff beams ($\gamma = \infty$)

(b) Beam and slab of equal stiffness (the twistless case, $\gamma = 1$)

(c) Slender beams ($\gamma < 1$)

Code of practice C.P. 114

Elastic theoretical load

Deflected form of slab

Beam

Uniform intensity of load on each beam

Beams deflect

relationship exists between the flexibility of the slab and the flexibility of the beams. However, analytical and experimental studies at the Building Research Station by Wood have shown clearly that the actual intensity and distribution of beam loads are considerably dependent on the relative stiffnesses of beam and slab, and on whether plasticity is present or not.

Considering first the approximately elastic behaviour of a combined beam–slab system at working loads, the slab being assumed to be square and uniformly loaded, the effect of modifying the beam stiffness can be seen in Fig. 2.5. When the beams are very stiff, the conditions are similar to those for a slab supported on walls, and the support reactions are as shown by the hatched areas in Fig. 2.5a. The triangular distribution assumed in the Code of Practice is indicated in the figure, and is a reasonable approximation to the actual loading.

When the beam stiffness is reduced, the load from the slab is distributed more uniformly along the beam until $\gamma = 1$, where γ denotes the ratio of the combined stiffness of two opposite beams to that of the full width of slab between them. For this condition, the reaction between slab and beam is uniform over the whole span as shown in Fig. 2.5b; and the slab behaves as if made of independent strips, each with the same deflection curve, without interference from adjacent strips.

When the beam stiffness is still further reduced, the load on the beam tends to become concentrated at its ends as shown in Fig. 2.5c. It is clear that the actual load distribution may be quite different from that at present assumed in design.

With regard to conditions at failure, experiments have been made on 6-ft square slabs supported on all four edges by encased steel girders (Plate 2.1). The effect of varying the relative strengths of slab and beam is shown in Plate 2.2 With a strong beam giving a rigid support to the slab, the major cracking occurs along the diagonals (Plate 2.2a). With a much weaker beam (Plate 2.2b), the cracking at failure forms a 'rectangular' pattern, the main cracks passing through the centres of the beams. Clearly there is some combination of strengths of slab and beam at which the form of cracking or yield-line pattern changes from the diagonal to the rectangular. Attempts to find this relationship experimentally resulted in the mode of failure shown in Plate 2.2c, in which radial pattern of cracking has developed, with a final Y-form for the major cracks.

These investigations have shown that far more data are necessary before design can be based fully on the effects of composite action between the various elements of a structure. However, it is hoped that these effects can be gradually allowed for in Codes of Practice, the load factor being suitably reduced as knowledge of the real behaviour of structures increases.

DIMENSIONAL STABILITY

The dimensional stability of floors is concerned mainly with the effects of changes in moisture content, particularly drying shrinkage, and with the deflections of floors under the imposed loading.

Effect of moisture changes

In suspended concrete floors the effects of shrinkage of the structural concrete are usually unimportant and the only relevant design provision is the need to introduce at least 0·15 per cent of distribution reinforcement at right-angles to the main bars is solid slabs spanning in one direction. Even this small amount of distribution steel is not wholly for controlling shrinkage; it is partly required to resist local longitudinal bending due, for example, to concentrated loads. Drying shrinkage in a concrete screed, however, can be a serious matter, contributing to cracking and failure in adhesion of the screed and of any floor finish laid over it. The control of drying shrinkage in floor screeds and finishes is dealt with in Chapter 4; the special case of the floating floor is discussed on p. 42.

Timber has a relatively high moisture movement across the grain, and consequently timber components in a building are liable to appreciable changes in dimensions as the moisture content of the timber changes. It is important therefore that the timber should, at the time of fixing, be seasoned to a moisture content that is appropriate to the conditions at which equilibrium will ultimately be reached in the building. Ideally, the timber should be pre-conditioned to its ultimate moisture content and should be maintained in this condition between the time of fixing and the time of occupancy. This is hardly practicable in house construction, and hence there is always risk of some change of dimensions and also of warping or twisting. These effects can be minimized or concealed by attention to detailing.

Particular attention should be paid to timber floors supporting plaster ceilings. It is important to use adequately seasoned timber, to keep timber dry during building operations, to use sufficient binders, and to use herring-bone strutting between the floor joists instead of solid strutting. With insufficient binders, ceiling joists can twist as they shrink, causing cracking of the ceiling. With solid strutting between the joists, the shrinkage of the joists tends to free them from the struts; this increases the differential loading of joists, and exaggerated local deflections may cause cracking of the ceiling. Herring-bone strutting is tightened by the shrinkage of the joists, but there is still a risk of cracking at the junction of the ceiling and the walls and it may be necessary to conceal this by providing pre-formed coving at the junction.

Deflection of floors

The requirement that a floor should not deflect excessively under load is difficult to express in quantitative terms. Byelaws usually refer merely to the need to avoid 'undue deflection', and it is left to the Codes of Practice for various types of construction to deal with the matter more explicitly.

In the B.S. Code CP 112 (1952), 'The structural use of timber in buildings', the basic requirement as to stiffness and deflection is stated as follows: 'The dimensions of all flexural members should be such as to restrict deflections within limits appropriate to the type of structure, having particular regard to the possibility of damage to surfacing materials, ceilings, partitions and finishings and to functional needs generally in addition to aesthetic requirements.' This statement gives some indication as to what to consider when deciding whether the deflection is 'undue', but clearly the magnitude of tolerable deflection varies widely in relation to the particular circumstances. To help the designer further, therefore, the Code adds a simple qualification: 'in the case of floors, this requirement may be assumed to be satisfied if the deflection of the supporting members when fully loaded does not exceed 0·003 of the span.' This is the kind of rule-of-thumb that has been applied to the limitation of deflection for floors, beams and girders in buildings and bridges for many years with reasonably satisfactory results. It is based on practical experience rather than on theoretical principles.

The B.S. Code CP 114 (1957), 'The structural use of reinforced concrete in buildings', introduces a similar basic requirement for the stiffness of reinforced concrete members: 'Reinforced concrete should possess adequate stiffness to prevent such deflection or deformation as might impair the strength or efficiency of the structure, or produce cracks in finishes or partitions.' However, in attempting to give quantitative data to guide the designer, the Code does not refer to a permissible deflection/span ratio. There is always the difficulty with a limitation in these terms that the deflection must be calculated (unless a prototype of the flooring system can be tested), and the calculations are liable to serious error. The deflection/span ratio for a beam or slab can be shown, however, to be roughly proportional to the stress in the tensile reinforcement and to the ratio of the

TABLE 2.2

Maximum values of span/depth ratio of beams and slabs

	Ratio of span to overall depth
Beams	
Simply-supported beams	20
Continuous beams	25
Cantilever beams	10
Slabs	
Slabs spanning in one direction, simply-supported . . .	30
Slabs spanning in one direction, continuous	35
Slabs spanning in two directions, simply-supported . .	35
Slabs spanning in two directions, continuous . .	40
Cantilever slabs.	12

span to the depth of the member, and to be dependent on the conditions of support at the ends of the span. Accordingly, the Code introduces the following method of complying with the basic stiffness requirement. 'For all normal cases it may be assumed that this condition is satisfied for beams and slabs if the ratio of span to overall depth does not exceed the values given in Table 13.' This table referred to in the Code is reproduced here (Table 2.2).

Cracking of reinforced concrete beams and slabs

Bending of a beam or slab under load stretches the concrete and steel in the lower part of the section (or in the upper part over supports in continuous systems). At low loads the tensile stresses developed in the concrete can be withstood. But the tensile strength of concrete is low, only about one-twelfth or less of the compressive strength, and at working loads it is to be expected that some cracking will have occurred, particularly

Test on composite slab–beam system

PLATE 2.1

c*

(a) System with stiff beams

(b) System with flexible beams

(c) System with a beam stiffness giving an intermediate pattern of cracking

Modes of failure of slab–beam systems

PLATE 2.2

in beams. This is unimportant structurally but, with the present trend towards higher permissible stresses and utmost economy of materials, it is as well to understand the mechanism of the process and the factors that affect the width of individual cracks.

At low loads, before cracking starts, the tensile reinforcement and the concrete immediately surrounding it stretch by the same amount, a primary requirement of reinforced concrete being that there must be a good bond between the two materials. The stresses developed are proportional to the moduli of elasticity; that for steel is about ten times that for concrete and hence, before cracking, the steel stress is about ten times the stress in the adjacent concrete. Since the tensile strength of concrete is unlikely to be more than about 400 lb per sq. in., the steel stress is always very low before cracking starts; indeed the reinforcement has little effect on the load at which cracks occur.

When a crack develops, the maximum steel stress increases more rapidly with applied load, since most of the tension at the cracked section is borne by the reinforcement. Immediately on each side of the crack, the stress in the concrete is zero but, because of the bond between the concrete and steel (which is broken only close to the crack), it increases steadily with distance from the cracked section. As the imposed load on the beam is increased, a stage will be reached at which the stress in the concrete again attains the tensile strength of the concrete, at some distance from the first crack, and a second crack opens there. This process continues until a series of more or less equally spaced cracks has developed over the length of beam subjected to heaviest bending (i.e. in the middle of the span, or on the top of the beam over supports). In practice, it is the aim of the designer to ensure that, should cracking be unavoidable, it should be distributed as many closely-spaced fine cracks rather than concentrated in one or two wide cracks.

The width of a crack (ignoring subsidiary effects such as shrinkage) is clearly the difference between the elongations of steel and concrete between successive cracks. The elongation of the concrete is very small compared with that of the steel, particularly at high stresses. The stress in the steel is a maximum at a crack and decreases between cracks; however, for practical purposes the elongation of the steel may be assumed to be proportional to the stress in the steel at the cracked section. Hence the widths of the cracks are proportional both to the steel stress f_s, and to the distance between cracks.

The distance between cracks, being the distance required to build up the concrete stess to its ultimate strength by the action of the bond between the concrete and its reinforcement, increases with the tensile strength of the concrete f_{ct} and with the diameter d of the reinforcing bars, and decreases with increasing strength τ of the bond and with increasing proportion of steel r (r is the ratio of the areas of steel and concrete in tension).

Thus the widths of cracks can be expressed approximately by the equation:

$$\text{Crack width} = C\,\frac{f_{ct}}{\tau}\,\frac{d}{r}\,f$$

The value of the constant C has yet to be established by further research, so this equation cannot be used at present for quantitative calculations of crack widths. However, the equation shows that limitation of stress may sometimes be necessary to restrict cracking; that for a given area of tensile reinforcement it is better to use several bars of small diameter rather than a small number of large bars; and that the use of bars of special surface characteristics, giving a high bond strength, helps to distribute the cracks.

SOUND INSULATION

The lowest floor of a building, whether of suspended or of solid construction, raises no problem of sound insulation other than the possible transmission to the structure of vibrations from machinery; any contribution to indirect airborne sound transmission between adjoining rooms on this storey is usually small. Any of the upper floors may provide a problem of direct sound insulation. It should be noted that airborne sound transmission occurs in both directions, upwards and downwards, whereas impact sound transmission occurs only downwards; therefore in the top storey of a building there is no problem of impact sound, but only one of airborne sound, from the rooms below.

The two main types of floor construction, so far as sound insulation is concerned, are concrete-slab floors and wood-joist floors. The former include hollow-pot and precast concrete beam floors, while steel or concrete joists with boarded floors and plaster ceilings are grouped with wood-joist floors. Concrete-slab floors give much better sound insulation than joist floors, even without special treatment, and it is much easier to improve them to give a still higher standard of insulation.

As with walls, the airborne sound insulation of a plain concrete slab floor is largely determined by its weight (Fig. 2.6). A floor weighing 50 lb/sq.ft will give an insulation of about 45 dB; one weighing 100 lb/sq.ft

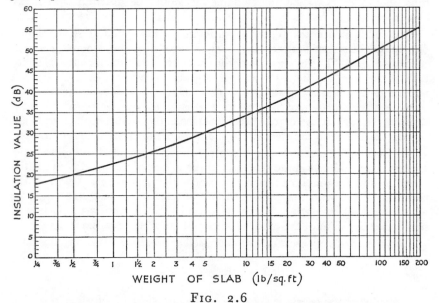

FIG. 2.6

Dependence of sound insulation on weight of a slab. (The curve shows the average insulation value over the frequency range 100–3200 c/s)

will give about 50 dB. A reinforced concrete slab 4 in. thick with floor finish and plastering will weigh at least 50 lb/sq.ft, giving 45 dB insulation; an 8-in. reinforced concrete slab will give 50 dB.

It is possible by various means to obtain an increase of about 5 dB airborne insulation over and above that due to weight, though not necessarily above a maximum insulation of about 50 dB. The methods are (a) a floating floor, (b) a suspended ceiling, and (c) a lightweight screed; these constructions are described in some detail later.

Increasing the weight of a concrete floor does not improve the impact sound insulation, except to a limited extent at low frequencies. Nor, with the notable exception of the floating floor, will the alternative methods for improving airborne sound insulation add significantly to the impact insulation. The floating floor improves both airborne and impact insulation; it is the only known method that will do so, and moreover it is the only simple *structural* method known of improving impact insulation. The other, non-structural, method of improving impact insulation is a soft or resilient floor finish or floor covering, such as cork or rubber, or (best of all) carpeting. Thick cork or rubber finishes give about the same improvement of impact

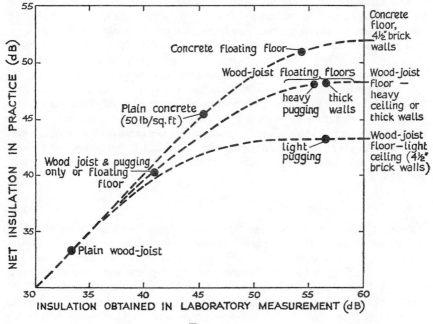

FIG. 2.7

Net airborne sound insulation of floors, where there is indirect transmission via supporting walls. The insulation in practice is reduced below the value obtained by laboratory measurement, by an amount that depends on the construction of both floor and walls. It will be seen that the maximum values achievable in practice are:

for a concrete floor	52 dB
for a wood-joist floor with heavy ceiling (or with thick walls) .	48 dB
for a wood-joist floor with light ceiling	43 dB

insulation as a floating floor; carpet on underfelt gives a very much greater improvement. But none of these floor finishes adds to the airborne sound insulation of the floor.

The wood-joist floor is a more complicated structure, acoustically, than the concrete slab floor, and its behaviour as regards sound transmission is different. Even so, weight is important, especially that of the ceiling. The airborne sound insulation of a wood-joist floor tends to be greater than its weight would lead one to expect, but it is still much less than that of a heavy concrete floor. Moreover, with wood-joist floors, the indirect sound transmission via the surrounding walls is greater than with concrete floors, because of the different degrees to which the walls are stiffened or restrained by the two types of floor. If wood-joist floors have heavy lath-and-plaster ceilings, and especially if these ceilings are loaded with heavy pugging, their stiffening effect on the walls is increased, and indirect transmission of sound is reduced; the walls can also be stiffened by making them thicker. Figure 2.7 shows the extent to which the inherent sound insulation of a floor (as measured in the laboratory) may be reduced by indirect sound transmission via the walls of the building.

The standards of sound insulation demanded of floors may differ widely in different classes of building. The investigation of sound insulation by the Building Research Station has been concerned mainly with dwellings, and this work has resulted in the grading system for flats already described in Volume 1. When discussing forms of construction for sound insulation, it is necessary to relate them to some standard of effectiveness, and the grades of performance defined for flats, namely Grade I and Grade II, will be used here for that purpose. It should be borne in mind, however, that a form of construction condemned in respect of such a standard may be quite satisfactory in some other situation where the noise problem is different.

The methods of constructing floors for sound insulation (based on Grades I and II) will now be dealt with, first for concrete floors, then for wood-joist floors.

CONCRETE FLOORS

Various types of concrete floor construction are listed in Table 2.3 with the grade of insulation that each is likely to provide in practice. The basic construction is assumed to be either a solid reinforced concrete slab not less than 4 in. thick, or a slab formed with hollow concrete beams or with concrete beams and hollow clay infilling blocks, with an average total weight of the floor of not less than 45 lb per sq. ft. The gradings apply also to concrete floors of the trough-soffit type with a flat board or plaster ceiling underneath, provided that they have the stipulated weight.

It will be seen from Table 2.3 that it is possible to obtain Grade I or Grade II insulation by the following methods of construction:

Grade I (see also Fig. 2.8)
    Concrete floor with a floating concrete screed
    Concrete floor with a floating wood raft
    Concrete floor with suspended ceiling and a soft floor finish or
      covering

Concrete floor with 2-in. lightweight screed with a dense topping and a soft floor finish or covering

Heavy concrete floor (6-7 in. solid slab) with a soft finish or covering.

Grade II

Concrete floor with a soft floor finish or covering.

Each of these methods of construction will now be considered in more detail.

TABLE 2.3

Grading of concrete floors in flats

Construction	Sound insulation grading		
	Airborne	Impact	Overall
Concrete floor (reinforced-concrete slab or concrete and hollow-pot slab) weighing not less than 45 lb/sq. ft, with hard finish	Grade II	4 dB worse than Grade II	—
Concrete floor with finish of wood boards or ¼-in. linoleum or cork tiles	Grade II	Grade II	Grade II
Concrete floor with finish of thick cork tiles or of rubber on sponge rubber underlay	Grade II	Probably Grade I	Grade II
Concrete floor with floating concrete screed and any finish	Grade I	Grade I	Grade I
Concrete floor with floating wood raft	Grade I	Grade I	Grade I
Concrete floor with suspended ceiling and hard finish	Probably Grade I	2 dB worse than Grade II	—
Concrete floor with suspended ceiling and wood board finish	Probably Grade I	Grade II	Grade II
Concrete floor with suspended ceiling and finish of thick cork tiles or of rubber on sponge-rubber underlay	Probably Grade I	Grade I	Probably Grade I
Concrete floor with 2-in. lightweight concrete screed and hard finish	Probably Grade I	4 dB worse than Grade II	—
Concrete floor with 2-in. lightweight concrete screed and finish of thick cork tiles or of rubber on sponge-rubber underlay	Probably Grade I	Probably Grade I	Probably Grade I
Concrete floor weighing not less than 75 lb/sq. ft (reinforced concrete slab 6–7 in. thick) with hard finish	Grade I	4 dB worse than Grade II	—
Concrete floor weighing not less than 75 lb/sq. ft, with finish of thick cork tiles or of rubber on sponge-rubber underlay	Grade I	Grade I	Grade I

Floating floors

Wood-raft floating floors (on concrete). The wood-raft floating floor consists simply of floor boarding nailed to battens to form a raft which rests on a resilient quilt laid over the structural floor slab. *The battens must not be fixed in any way to the slab.* For structural reasons the floor boards should preferably be tongued and grooved, and lot less than $\frac{7}{8}$ in. thick, though $\frac{5}{8}$-in. tongued and grooved boards have been used and have proved satisfactory for sound insulation. The battens, which are usually spaced at 16-in. centres, should be $1\frac{1}{2}$ or 2 in. deep and not less than 2 in. wide, in order to spread the load over a sufficient area of the quilt.

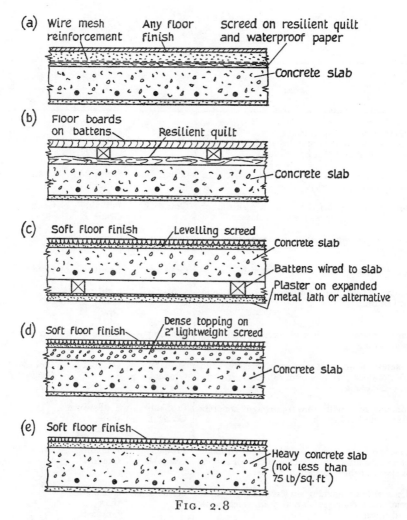

FIG. 2.8

Grade I concrete floors: concrete slabs not less than 54 lb/sq. ft, with (a) floating screed, (b) floating wood raft, (c) suspended ceiling and soft finish, (d) lightweight screed and soft finish; or (e) heavy concrete slab with soft floor finish

The resilient layer is a very important feature of the floating floor, and only the most suitable materials should be used. Glass wool and mineral wool are in most common use for resilient layers; quilts of the long-fibre type have been found the most satisfactory. Other materials are sometimes suggested, but at present none is known of comparable cost that appears to have such generally suitable properties as the glass-wool and mineral-wool quilts. A nominal quilt thickness of 1 in. at a density of 5–6 lb per cu. ft is recommended, but lower densities down to 3 lb per cu. ft may be used provided that the quilt does not compress to less than $\frac{3}{8}$ in. under the battens of a wood-raft floor. Thicker quilts give better insulation but they may allow too much movement of the floating floor. Bitumen-bonded mats are the cheapest form of glass-wool or mineral-wool quilt, and they are often used on this account, but paper-covered plain wool quilts are nevertheless preferred because of their better performance for impact sound insulation and because they are less susceptible to damage from the slight rocking movement of the raft battens when the floor is walked on.

Most resilient quilts are obtained in rolls 3 ft wide. They should be laid with the edges closely butted but not overlapping. The quilt should normally be turned up a little against the surrounding walls as a means of separating the floating floor from the walls; this separation is important, but turning up the quilt is not essential if the gap can be otherwise ensured. The skirting should be fixed only to the walls, not to the floor.

Softwood is generally used for floating floors in dwellings. Hardwood involves special precautions because it is usually supplied kiln-dried to a low moisture content; subsequently, when the building is completed and in use, the wood may take up moisture and swell, and the floating raft, being unrestrained, will buckle. A hardwood floating raft, therefore, should be constructed with the wood at a higher moisture content than that at which it is usually supplied; a hardwood with a comparatively low moisture movement is to be preferred, such as teak, guarea, African mahogany, makoré, muninga, East African camphorwood, Rhodesian teak, ayan, kobrodua, iroko or opepe. The use of narrow boards increases the number of joints, which helps to accommodate any swelling or shrinkage movement. Battens for hardwood floating floors should not be less than 2 in. by 2 in., to resist buckling. The floating floor should not be placed in position until the structure, especially the floor slab, has dried out.

Concrete-screed floating floors. This type of floating floor consists of a layer of concrete not less than $1\frac{1}{2}$ in. thick (2 in. thick or more is better), resting on a resilient quilt that is laid over the structural floor slab and turned up against the surrounding walls at all edges. As with wood-raft floating floors, the resilient quilt is usually of glass wool or mineral wool, preferably of 1-in. nominal thickness at a density of 5–6 lb per cu. ft. The quilt compresses to $\frac{3}{8}-\frac{1}{2}$ in. under the load of a floating screed. Paper-covered quilts of plain wool give better insulation than bitumen-bonded mats; nevertheless, the latter have been extensively used under floating concrete screeds because they are cheaper, and in many instances they have proved satisfactory. Waterproof building paper is laid over the quilt to prevent wet concrete running through it; if the quilt is supplied with its own covering of waterproof paper, it may be sufficient to provide extra waterproof paper in narrow strips (say 6 in. wide) covering the joints in the quilting only. It is usual to provide wire-mesh reinforcement (e.g. ¾–2 in. mesh chicken wire) for the floating screed, and this is normally laid directly on the waterproof paper. Besides reducing the risk of cracking of the floating screed, the wire netting protects the building paper and the quilt from mechanical damage during the operation of placing the concrete; any such damage might well result in the concrete making direct contact with the structural slab, which would spoil the insulation of the floating floor. However, the wire mesh can be omitted from screeds 2 in. thick or more, if sufficient care is taken not to damage the quilt. A suitable mix for the concrete screed is 1 : 2 : 4, cement : sand : gravel aggregate, with an aggregate size of not more than ⅜ in.

Concrete-screed floating floors may not be suitable for rooms larger than about 200 sq. ft, or 250 sq. ft at most, or with a greater length than 15–20 ft. This is because a slight 'dishing' or curling up at the corners invariably occurs with floating floors, because the top surface dries more quickly than the rest and there is no bond with the sub-floor. This curling is not noticeable in small rooms; however, in large rooms the risk of cracking from drying shrinkage makes it necessary to sub-divide the floating screed into bays, and the curling of these separate bays can lead to difficulty with many types of floor finish. To minimize curling, the driest mix that can be satisfactorily laid should be used, and curing should be as long as possible.

Screeds based on calcium sulphate plaster are also in use. These do not shrink significantly on drying, and their use therefore does not call for the above precautions and restrictions on room size.

Partitions on floating floors. Partitions (apart from such short lengths as the sides of cupboards) should not be built on top of floating floors, which should be self-contained within each room. Building heavy partitions on floating floors may overload the resilient quilt and reduce its insulating properties; moreover, the movement of the floating floor may cause cracking of the partitions.

Pipes and conduits in floating floors. It is often necessary for services, such as electric conduits, gas pipes and water pipes, to traverse a concrete floor. Whenever possible these pipes should be accommodated within the thickness of the floor or the levelling screed, but sometimes they have to be laid on top of the slab and contained within the depth of a floating floor. This is more likely to occur with a floating concrete screed. A floating wood raft requires a very level surface as a base, and therefore usually calls for a levelling screed, in which the pipes can be embedded. However, pipes or conduits need not cause trouble with a floating screed provided that they:

do not extend more than about an inch above the base,

are properly fixed so as not to move while the floating screed is being laid,

are haunched up with mortar on each side to give continuous support to the resilient quilt.

When two pipes cross, one of them should be sunk into the base slab. The resilient quilt should be carried right over the pipes. If a wood-raft floating floor is being used, and the pipes have to be laid above the slab, the pipes can be readily accommodated parallel to and between the raft battens, but in the other direction the battens will have to be notched over them; the battens must be thick enough to allow for notching.

Floor finishes and coverings

In present-day flats and in many other classes of building, hard floor finishes, such as thermoplastic tiles and pitchmastic, are commonly used. Finishes of this type make virtually no contribution to the sound insulation of a floor. Ordinarily, no floor finish adds anything to the airborne sound insulation, but the impact sound insulation can be considerably improved by means of a finish that is sufficiently soft or resilient. Thus, it is possible to raise most floors up to Grade I, *for impact insulation only*, simply by adding a finish or covering that is soft enough. Thick fitted carpet or underfelt, for instance, will nearly always give Grade I impact insulation. If, therefore, a plain concrete floor that is heavy enough to have an airborne sound insulation of Grade I, say 6–7 in. reinforced concrete, is fitted with a carpet, an overall insulation Grade I is achieved. Other floor finishes giving Grade I impact insulation when applied to a plain concrete floor include rubber flooring on a sponge-rubber underlay, or cork tiles $\frac{5}{16}$ to $\frac{3}{8}$ in. thick. A floor finish on concrete of $\frac{3}{16}$–$\frac{1}{4}$-in. cork tiles, or $\frac{1}{4}$-in. linoleum or soft rubber, would be expected to give Grade II impact insulation, so that any normal concrete floor weighing 45 lb per sq. ft or more with a floor finish of this type would have an overall sound insulation of at least Grade II.

Lightweight concrete screeds

A limited amount of experience has been gained with lightweight concrete sandwiched between the floor finish and the structural floor slab without a resilient quilt. In many instances this construction has given Grade I airborne sound insulation, but the impact insulation is usually no better than that of a concrete floor with the same floor finish. Thus, a resilient floor finish of the kind already described will be necessary to give the floor an overall insulation rating of Grade I. This method is therefore comparable for sound insulation to the use of a heavy concrete floor (6–7 in. reinforced concrete), but there is of course a small saving in weight. It has not yet been possible to investigate fully all the details of the construction, but the essential requirements would appear to be as follows:

the density of the lightweight screed should be not more than 70 lb per cu. ft,

the thickness of the lightweight screed should be not less than 2 in.,

an impervious or airtight layer should be provided above the lightweight screed.

The provision of an airtight layer sealing the top of the lightweight screed appears to be important. A dense concrete topping is often required above a lightweight screed to ensure a satisfactory base for the floor finish, and this topping will of course seal the screed. Wood boards nailed direct to the screed do not form a satisfactory seal, even when tongued and grooved.

It is not yet known whether some types of lightweight concrete screed are better than others, assuming that the density requirements are met. The strength of the screed must, however, be sufficient to restrain the tendency of the dense topping to curl and hence to crack under load; very light aerated or vermiculite concretes are suitable.

Suspended ceilings

Suspended ceilings are comparable with lightweight screeds in that they are chiefly of benefit against airborne sound. They can be used to raise the sound insulation of a normal concrete floor up to Grade I, provided a soft floor finish is also used to give the necessary improvement in impact insulation. Not all the suspended ceilings that have been measured have given a satisfactory improvement of sound insulation, and the requirements for a successful system of construction are not fully known. The following features would appear to be important:

the ceiling membrane should be moderately heavy, say, not less than 5 lb per sq. ft

the membrane should not be too rigid

the ceiling should be airtight, to eliminate direct sound penetration via air-paths, such as would occur with open-textured materials or with open joints

the points of suspension from the floor structure should be as few and as flexible as possible

the air space should be fairly deep—preferably not less than 6 in.

In spite of their usefulness for sound absorption, ceilings of soft insulating fibreboard alone are not recommended for sound insulation because of their light weight and porous nature. Plastering on expanded metal or on ceiling boards, provided the total weight is not less than the 5 lb per sq. ft mentioned above, and provided the whole membrane is supported by light hangers, is usually satisfactory. The air space above the ceiling may range in depth from 1 in. to 12 in. or more, but the deeper the better. Any air space can be made more effective by lining it with sound-absorbent material such as mineral wool or glass wool quilt. If heavy mineral wool is used and is laid on top of the ceiling it has a 'damping' effect on ceiling vibrations which may have additional benefit for sound insulation. The floor finish required to raise the impact insulation to Grade I, and therefore to make the floor Grade I overall, is the same as those already described for heavy plain floors and for floors with lightweight screeds, namely cork tiles $\frac{5}{16}$–$\frac{3}{8}$ in. thick, rubber on sponge-rubber underlay, or thick carpeting.

WOOD-JOIST FLOORS

As stated earlier, the sound insulation of wood-joist floors depends, far more than that of concrete floors, on the amount of indirect or flanking sound transmitted via the walls. Flanking transmission always has some effect on the overall insulation, but if the sound energy passing up or down the walls is greater than the energy passing through the floor, then it is the walls and not the floor that will actually control the sound insulation between the rooms. Once the floor has been given enough insulation to ensure that the amount of sound transmitted through it is no more than that going down the

TABLE 2.4
Grading of wood-joist floors in flats

Construction		Sound insulation grading		
		Airborne	Impact	Overall
Plain joist floor with plasterboard and single-coat plaster ceiling (no pugging)	Thin walls	8 dB worse than Grade II	8 dB worse than Grade II	—
	Thick walls	4 dB worse than Grade II	5 dB worse than Grade II	—
Plain joist floor with plasterboard and single-coat plaster ceiling and 3 lb/sq. ft pugging on ceiling	Thin walls	4 dB worse than Grade II	6 dB worse than Grade II	—
	Thick walls	Possibly Grade II*	Possibly Grade II*	Possibly Grade II*
Plain joist floor with heavy lath-and-plaster ceiling (no pugging)	Thin walls	Probably 4 dB worse than Grade II*	Probably 6 dB worse than Grade II*	—
	Thick walls	Grade II	Grade II	Grade II
Plain joist floor with lath-and-plaster ceiling and 17 lb/sq.ft pugging on ceiling	Thin walls	Grade II	Grade II	Grade II
	Thick walls	Grade II or possibly Grade I*	Grade II	Grade II
Floating floor and plasterboard and single-coat plaster ceiling (no pugging)	Thin walls	4 dB worse than Grade II	3 dB worse than Grade II	—
	Thick walls	Possibly Grade II*	Possibly Grade II*	Possibly Grade II*
Floating floor with single-coat plaster plasterboard ceiling and 3 lb/sq.ft pugging on ceiling	Thin walls	2 dB worse than Grade II	2 dB worse than Grade II	—
	Thick walls	Grade II or possibly Grade I*	Grade II or possibly Grade I*	Grade II or I*
Floating floor with heavy lath-and-plaster ceiling (no pugging)	Thin walls	2 dB worse than Grade II	Grade II	—
	Thick walls	Grade II or I†	Grade I	Grade II or I†
Floating floor with lath-and-plaster ceiling and 3 lb/sq.ft pugging on ceiling	Thin walls	Possibly Grade II*	Grade II*	Possibly Grade II*
	Thick walls	Grade II or I†	Grade I	Grade II or I†
Floating floor with lath-and-plaster ceiling and 17 lb/sq.ft pugging on ceiling	Thin walls	Probably Grade I	Probably Grade I	Probably Grade I
	Thick walls	Grade I	Grade I	Grade I

* Assumed from other measurements
† May give Grade I with very thick walls

walls, further treatment of the floor will be of little value unless the amount of sound transmitted by the walls can be reduced correspondingly. This means reducing the vibration of the walls, either by making them thicker, or by making the floors heavy enough and stiff enough laterally to restrain vibration of the walls. Concrete floors restrain the walls sufficiently; ordinary wood-joist floors do not. A special type of wood-joist floor construction will be described which does in fact restrain thin walls sufficiently to make them as resistant to sound transmission as much thicker walls that are not similarly restrained. But most other wood-joist floors have little effect in stiffening the walls, and the maximum net sound insulation is then dependent on the thickness of the walls, even though the floor may have potentially higher insulation. Therefore in giving insulation values for wood-joist floors, it is also necessary to specify the wall system. This has been done in Table 2.4 which gives the sound-insulation grading of a number of types of wood-joist floor construction, both with thin and with thick walls. To be classed as a thick-wall system, two or more of the walls below the floor must be at least 9 in. thick; the walls above the floor need not be as thick. Metal anchorages connecting floor joists to walls, sometimes employed to give lateral support to the walls, do not impart sufficient stiffness to give any improvement of sound insulation.

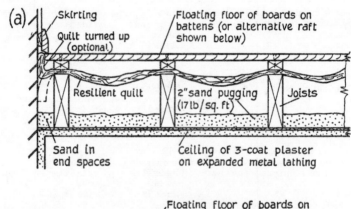

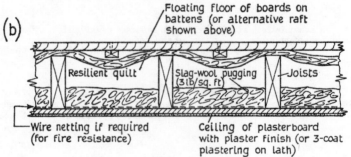

FIG. 2.9

Insulated wood-joist floors (a) with heavy pugging, (b) with light pugging (mainly for use with thick walls)

An untreated wood-joist floor is much worse for sound insulation than an untreated concrete floor. In fact, the insulation of the untreated wood-joist floor is well below any standard that is likely to be acceptable in flats, but it is usually sufficient for houses in one occupation, especially if the ceiling is made moderately heavy, say, not less than 5 lb per sq. ft. Another disadvantage is that treated wood-joist floors are more liable than treated concrete floors to be wrongly constructed in matters of detail. But there may of course be reasons for preferring wood-joist floors in some flats, such as conversions in old houses.

Basically, there are only two forms of treatment for wood-joist floors that provide a marked improvement of sound insulation. These are illustrated in Figs. 2.9 *a* and *b*. Of these, the first is better because it is less dependent on wall thickness.

Wood-joist floors with thin walls

When the walls are thin (i.e. $4\frac{1}{2}$-in. brick or less) the sound insulation of most wood-joist floors, including that shown in Fig. 2.9*b*, will fall short of Grade II by at least 2 dB, because of transmission by the walls. To be more effective, the floor must be heavy enough and stiff enough laterally to hold the walls effectively—in the manner of a concrete floor. The only satisfactory method known at present to achieve this is the construction shown in Fig. 2.9 *a*. This comprises a ceiling of expanded-metal lath and 3-coat plaster, loaded directly with a pugging of 2 in. of dry sand (or other loose pugging material having at least the same weight, namely, 17 lb per sq. ft), and a properly constructed floating floor. It is important that the pugging should be supported by the ceiling; if it is supported independently the insulation will be less. The metal lathing must be securely fixed to the joists, as it has to support the weight of the sand pugging as well as the plastering. The sand must cover the whole ceiling, including the narrow spaces between the end joists and the walls; it should be dry when it is placed in the floor. Sand containing deliquescent salts must, of course, be avoided.

Wood-joist floors with thick walls

When the walls are thick (i.e. at least two of the walls below the floor are not less than 9-in. brick), the lighter form of wood-joist floor construction (Fig. 2.9 *b*) can be used instead of the heavy one just described, to obtain at least Grade II insulation; however, the heavier construction is still to be preferred, because with thick walls it can be relied on to give Grade I insulation. In the lighter form of construction, the floating floor remains an essential feature but the pugging is reduced to a weight of not less than 3 lb per sq. ft ; the ceiling supporting it can therefore be of plasterboard with a single-coat plaster finish. It is even more important than before that the pugging should be supported direct on the ceiling and not independently. Wire netting separately stapled to the joists is sometimes inserted above the ceiling to retain the pugging in position, in order to ensure that the floor attains a full half-hour fire resistance ; the netting must not prevent the pugging from bearing fully on the ceiling. Alternatively (and preferably for sound insulation) the same fire resistance can be achieved by increasing the thickness of the plaster finish on the plasterboard ceiling to $\frac{1}{2}$ in. The pugging material normally recommended is high-density slag wool (12–14 lb per cu. ft), 3 in. thickness being required to give the minimum weight of 3 lb per sq. ft. Other pugging materials can be used, provided they are of the loose wool or granular type and the thickness used is sufficient to give the stipulated weight; very lightweight materials, such as glass wool or exfoliated vermiculite, are not suitable.

Floating floors for wood-joist floors

The floating floor consists of floor boarding nailed to battens to form a raft, which rests on a resilient quilt draped over the joists. The raft must not be nailed down to the joists at any point and it must be isolated from the surrounding walls, either by turning up the quilt at the edges (which is the better practice), or by leaving a gap round the edges to be covered by skirting. The floor boards should not be less than $\frac{7}{8}$ in. thick, preferably tongued and grooved; the battens should be 2 in. wide and at least 1 in. deep—it is better if they are $1\frac{1}{2}$ in. or 2 in. deep. They should be parallel with the joists, because, with battens laid cross-wise, the bearing area is too small and the quilt is overloaded; the loads transmitted from the raft should be distributed over the whole upper surface of the joists.

There are two common methods of constructing the raft. One, shown in Fig. 2.9a, is to place the battens on the quilt along the top of each joist and to nail down the boards to the battens in the normal way. The other method, shown in Fig. 2.9b, is to prefabricate the raft in separate panels as long as the room and 2–3 ft wide, with the battens across the panels and positioned so that they will lie between the joists; the battens should project a few inches beyond the sides of the panels, so that the panels can be screwed together after laying to form a complete raft.

Because the flooring is not nailed down to the joists, particular care must be taken to level up joists that are to carry a floating floor; in particular, end joists must not be lower than the others, as this produces a tendency for the floating raft to tip and for furniture next to the walls to rock.

Resilient layers. The requirements regarding quilts for floating wood-joist floors are no different from those already described for concrete floors. Glass-wool and mineral-wool quilts are preferred, and they should have a nominal thickness of 1 in., preferably with a density of 5–6 lb per cu. ft, giving a weight of about $\frac{1}{2}$ lb per sq. ft exclusive of the paper covering; however, lower densities, down to 3 lb per cu. ft, can be used provided the quilt beneath the battens does not compress to less than $\frac{3}{8}$ in. when the design load of the floor is applied. It is good practice to turn up the quilt all round the edges against the walls, though this is not essential if the floating floor does not touch the walls; the gap is normally covered by a skirting fixed to the wall only.

Partitions on floating floors. A practice that is sometimes adopted, particularly for two-storey dwellings, is to build the internal partition walls up to first-floor level only, and then to construct the wood-joist floor continuously over the whole area of the dwelling, building the upper partitions on top of the floorboards. This method has sometimes been used even when there is a floating floor, but is not recommended in these circumstances. Partitions should be supported either on the partitions below or on the floor joists, the floating floor being constructed as a separate independent raft within the confines of each room.

Suspended ceilings

An independent ceiling is not very effective as a means of improving the sound insulation of a wood-joist floor. It adds little to the insulation provided by a floating floor and pugging; and, to be of much value used alone, say, for improving the sound insulation of an existing wood-joist floor, a suspended ceiling would probably need to be impracticably heavy. It is true that the airborne insulation at *high* frequencies could be improved by a comparatively light suspended ceiling, but wood-joist floors are mainly deficient in sound insulation at the lower frequencies and more weight is generally required to remedy this deficiency. Suspended ceilings are not of much benefit for impact insulation. If a floating floor is being built it is usually a simple matter to pug the ceiling, and nothing worthwhile is then gained by adding a suspended ceiling. If carpeting or some other soft floor covering is being added to an existing floor to improve the impact insulation, the addition of a heavy suspended ceiling, also, may give a moderate improvement of the airborne sound insulation; but such a floor is unlikely to approach Grade II for airborne sound insulation unless the walls are thick.

FIRE PROTECTION

In the context of fire protection, the term 'suspended floor' refers to any floor that is so raised that fire may break out beneath it. In these circumstances the floor should prevent the fire spreading to other parts of the building or compartment. Byelaws require floors above the lowest storey to have a specific fire resistance ranging from half-an-hour or one hour in domestic and small buildings to two or four hours in large public and warehouse buildings. In certain circumstances a suspended ground floor may also be required to conform. The test requirements for floors are similar to those for walls: the floor must not allow flames and hot gases to pass through it, must not get excessively hot on the upper surface, and must not collapse.

Timber suspended floors

The fire resistance of timber floors depends on the size of the joists, the thickness and jointing of the boarding (whether plain-edged or tongued and grooved) and the type of ceiling, if any, provided below it.

The width of the joists is of more significance than the depth. A 2-in. joist with tongued and grooved boarding will withstand the fire for 20 minutes before collapse; with $1\frac{1}{2}$ in. wide joists the time is reduced to 16 minutes. The corresponding times for plain-edged boarding are 16 minutes and 12 minutes.

Flame penetration through the boards, however, will occur before the joists collapse. Tongued and grooved boarding may delay penetration by some 6 minutes but plain-edged boarding will be penetrated almost immediately. An overlay of plywood not less than $\frac{3}{16}$ inches thick or a continuous layer of glass wool inserted between plain-edged boarding and the joists will make it similar to tongued and grooved boarding in resistance to penetration.

It will be seen, therefore, that the resistance of a timber floor structure to fire depends largely on the degree of protection afforded by the ceiling below it. Table 2.5 shows the time to penetration of a selection of ceiling constructions. To assess the ultimate resistance of the floor in terms of collapse, the time to penetration of the ceiling is added to time to collapse of joists; in respect of flame penetration the times to penetration of ceiling and of boarding are added together.

For many years it was traditional to use timber boarded and joisted floors with a ceiling of wood lath and plaster. The tables show that such a floor, if tested according to B.S. 476, would fail to attain the lowest recognized grading of half-an-hour. As no serious consequences had resulted from its use, a special grading was introduced into building byelaws so that this form of construction could remain acceptable for small houses. This grading, known in England as the 'half-hour modified grade' and in Scotland as the '30-minute qualified period' requires the floor to resist collapse for half-an-hour but the penetration and insulation requirements need only be satisfied for 15 minutes.

In addition to the materials shown in Table 2.5, wood-wool slabs, compressed straw slabs and asbestos insulation board may be used either dry or in conjunction with plaster, to provide fire resistance in timber floors to the half-hour or modified half-hour grades. Where it becomes necessary to raise the grading of a floor from the modified to the full half-hour period the sound-insulation treatments illustrated in Fig. 2.9 (p. 46) will provide the additional protection.

TABLE 2.5

Time for fire to penetrate various ceiling constructions

Description	Time for flame to penetrate the ceiling (min.)
Fibreboard, $\frac{1}{2}$-in. thick, without plaster finish .	8
with $\frac{3}{16}$-in. skim coat of plaster .	10
with $\frac{1}{2}$-in. coat of plaster . . .	20
Plasterboard $\frac{3}{8}$-in. thick, without plaster finish .	10
with $\frac{3}{16}$-in. skim coat of plaster .	13
$\frac{1}{2}$-in. thick without plaster finish .	18
with $\frac{3}{16}$-in skim coat of plaster .	25
Plaster on wood lath	17
Plaster (gypsum) $\frac{5}{8}$-in. thick on metal lath .	41

A fire resistance of one hour may be achieved by fixing expanded metal or perforated plasterboard lath to the underside of the joists and finishing with a lightweight gypsum vermiculite plaster. Alternatively, normal three-coat gypsum plaster may be used when the expanded metal is suspended clear of the joists by steel hangers. If a dry finish is preferred there are special methods of fixing asbestos insulation board to give one-hour fire resistance.

TABLE 2.6

Fire resistance of reinforced and hollow tile floors

Construction and materials	Minimum thickness (in.) including screed, for period of:			
	4 *hours*	2 *hours*	1 *hour*	½ *hour*
Solid slab, T-beam, filler-joist or precast inverted channel sections of *in situ* or precast concrete .	6	5	4	3½
Precast or *in situ* concrete inverted U-section or jack-arch floors where the minimum thickness occurs only at the crowns	6	4	3	2½
Hollow concrete or clay blocks and precast concrete units of box- or I-section . . .	5	3½	3	2½

Where hollow constructions are used the thicknesses relate to the minimum total thickness of solid material in the cross-section.

For all floors, the cover to the steelwork should be :

    (a) For periods of ½, 1 and 2 hours not less than ½ inch

    (b) For a period of 4 hours not less than 1 inch

Where periods of fire resistance greater than one hour are required, the timber floor is generally uneconomical. It can, however be designed to attain up to two hours by using timbers of heavy section in conjunction with thermal insulating layers between the ceiling and the joists, or by the use of asbestos sprayed directly on to the timber.

A number of ceilings fixed below timber floors make use of combustible boards. Where such boards are used without a plaster finish, consideration should be given to their flame-spread characteristics, especially with the ceilings of rooms and passages that afford means of escape for the occupants of the building; this is discussed in Volume 1, pp. 141–2.

Non-combustible suspended floors

Non-combustibility does not of itself ensure fire-resistance. Metals, for example, lose strength rapidly when heated above a critical temperature, and any steel or aluminium used structurally either as beams or as reinforcement in concrete must be insulated. Critical temperatures range from about 550°C for mild steel to as low as 200°C for aluminium and high-tensile wire. Concrete, plaster, mineral wool and certain asbestos products are among the materials that will provide the necessary thermal insulation.

Structural steelwork exposed beneath a floor slab may be protected either by encasing each member individually or by suspending below the structure a ceiling capable of providing in full the required fire resistance.

The fire resistance of solid reinforced concrete slab floors depends on the minimum thickness of the slab and on the thickness of cover to the reinforcement. Plaster ceilings, particularly those of vermiculite plaster, applied directly to the underside of the slab, provide useful protection.

With hollow floors of precast concrete units or clay blocks it is the minimum total thickness of solid material which determines their fire resistance. A structural topping of screed may be included in this thickness but the effect of ceilings, even when applied directly to the soffit, must be ignored.

TABLE 2.7

Fire resistance of prestressed concrete suspended floors

Period of fire resistance (hours)	Thickness of concrete cover to reinforcement (in.)
1	$1\frac{1}{2}$
2	$2\frac{1}{2}$*
4	4*

* Where the thickness of cover is $2\frac{1}{2}$ in. or more, a light mesh reinforcement is required to retain the concrete in position; this mesh should itself have a concrete cover of 1 in.

Table 2.6 shows the floor and cover thicknesses necessary to achieve various periods of fire resistance.

The fire resistance of prestressed concrete floors may be influenced by the type of aggregate, the concrete strength, the bond between the concrete and the steel, the arrangement of the wires, the shape of the section, and the type of construction of which the prestressed unit forms part, but is mainly dependent on the thickness of cover to the steel. Table 2.7 shows the relationship between cover and fire resistance for beams; it is based on Tables 10 and 11 of C.P. 115: 1959. The cover thicknesses recommended in this table will generally be found to be conservative for slab floors, and many of the proprietary prestressed floor systems will, under tests, achieve the same standards of fire resistance with reduced cover because of the considerable effect of soffit finishes on the behaviour of the floor. Surface finishes which, when adequately bonded to the concrete, will effect an increase in fire resistance of approximately 2 hours are:

1-in. vermiculite concrete slabs used as a lining to the mould

$\frac{7}{8}$-in. gypsum-vermiculite plaster

$\frac{3}{4}$-in. sprayed asbestos.

THERMAL INSULATION

Of all the suspended floors in a building, the ground floor is usually the only one that needs to be insulated. Here, heat is lost to the air in the space below and by radiation to the ground. A ground floor over an unventilated crawl-space is likely to transmit heat at a lower rate than if it were in contact with the ground; but with a floor separated from the ground by a walk-way exposed directly to the open air, the benefit of insulation from the ground may be nullified by unusually high convection losses from the exposed surface. The suspended timber ground floor, relying on ventilation to disperse dampness, is a construction between these extremes, for which the following values of thermal transmittance are usually adopted:

Freely ventilated floor of boards on joists, $U = 0.40$.

Covered with parquet, linoleum or rubber, $U = 0.35$.

These are engineering design values, based on the assumptions that the ventilating air and the outside are air at the same temperature and that ventilation is free. In practice, however, the average rates of heat loss can be expected to be somewhat lower than these values. Surface coverings may add little to the inherent thermal resistance of the boards but, by stopping air infiltration through joints and edges, they increase the effectiveness of the floor as a heat barrier and lessen discomfort due to draughts.

If the thermal resistance of the floor itself is improved by additional insulation, the influence of ventilation below it is reduced, since less heat is fed into the ventilated space by the floor. A few such improvements are shown in Table 2.8, with the corresponding U-values calculated on the design assumptions mentioned.

TABLE 2.8

Insulating material	Method of application	U-value ($Btu/ft^2h°F$)
1-in. insulating fibre-board	Two $\frac{1}{2}$-in. boards glued together, nailed to the joists and covered with 1-in. floor boards	0·19
$\frac{1}{2}$-in. insulating fibre-board	Boards cut to fit between joists, supported on and nailed to wooden fillets	0·20
Aluminium foil (double-sided, paper-reinforced)	Foil draped over joists and stapled or tacked before floor boards are fixed	0·25
Mineral-wool quilt, 1 in. thick	Quilt draped over joists and secured by timber fillets before floor boards are fixed	0·15

Intermediate floors

With intermediate floors, special attention to thermal insulation is rarely necessary. It may need to be considered, however, where a floor penetrates the insulation of an external wall, as at a projecting or a re-entrant balcony.

Here, where abnormal exposure may cause excessive local heat loss or local cooling of the slab sufficient to encourage condensation, insulation of the exposed part of the slab can be beneficial.

A floor-heating system may call for insulation below the heating panels. This is discussed in Chapter 5.

DURABILITY AND MAINTENANCE

Surface wear and the behaviour of floor coverings are discussed in Chapter 4. This section is concerned with deterioration in the structure and decking of suspended floors.

Timber ground floors

Dampness is the main cause of deterioration in suspended timber ground floors. Moisture can gain entry to the timber in two ways: it may pass by capillary paths through porous materials briding between the ground and the timber, and it may be absorbed by the timber from humid air. Timber ground floors have to be designed so that the water entering in these ways does not produce a moisture content in the timber greater than 20 per cent, otherwise rotting is liable to occur.

The need for preventing direct contact between timber and brickwork or concrete through which ground moisture can rise has been appreciated for many years. The floor joists should be supported entirely on wall plates resting on sleeper walls, with a damp-proof membrane between the wall plates and the sleeper walls. Preferably, the ends of joists should be carried on independent sleeper walls, and not be embedded in the structural walls. If, however, the joists have to be let into the walls, special precautions should be taken at their ends. A brush coating of preservative should be applied and the ends of the joists should be wrapped in bitumen felt.

With solid external walls, the most vulnerable piece of timber in a ground floor is the skirting board that links the floor and wall. This is usually fixed directly to the structural wall which, although it is above the wall damp-proof course, may be sufficiently damp to encourage rotting. The skirting is usually painted on the face but is often bare at the back, or at most covered with a single coat of primer. For this reason moisture can travel from the wall into the skirting far more readily than it can escape from the wood into the air. Fungal attack in these circumstances is usually caused by the wet-rot fungus *Coniophora cerebella*, which will not spread to the floor timbers as a whole unless these also are damp. This trouble should not occur with a cavity wall.

In the absence of direct contact with damp materials, the floor timber may still pick up moisture from damp air in the space below. If this space is insufficiently ventilated, the air in it may become nearly saturated with water vapour from the ground, especially if only a weak and porous concrete has been used as a site covering. Below an unheated room in winter, condensation may then occur. Even without actual condensation, however, the timber may absorb sufficient moisture from saturated air for fungal attack to occur, especially if the upper surface of the floor is sealed, as by a covering of linoleum, so that the timber cannot dry out in that direction.

The main precaution against moisture building up in this way is to ventilate the space beneath. The current recommendation is that this space should be not less than 3 in. deep, and any walls that might impede the flow of air should be in honeycomb construction. Vents should be provided in at least two external walls on opposite sides of the building; if possible they should be provided in all walls. Where there are obstructions caused by solid floors, hearths, etc., which might produce stagnant zones in the underfloor space, pipes should be provided to ensure a through draught. The standard recommended for the area of external vents is that they should provide $1\frac{1}{2}$ sq. in. of open area for every foot run of external walling. These vents should be well clear of the ground and free from obstructions. For economy, the ground floor is sometimes constructed at a level that does not permit of ventilation in this way; the vents are then either sloped downwards through the wall or are fixed below ground level with a curb around them. In either case, water is liable to gain entry through the vents into the underfloor space. The practice is a bad one; the small economy effected does not compensate for the risks involved.

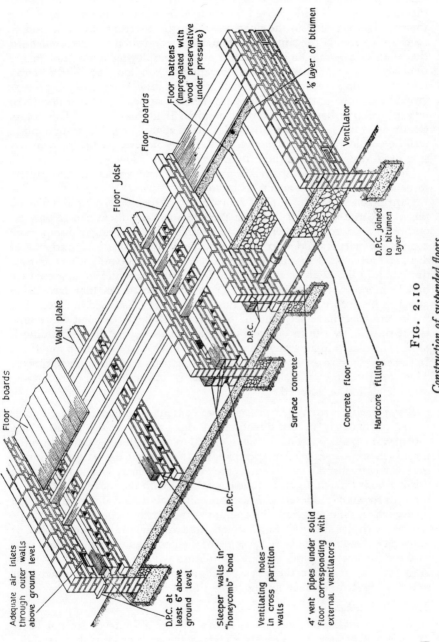

Floor boards

Floor battens (impregnated with wood preservative under pressure)

Floor boards

Floor Joist

½ layer of bitumen

Ventilator

Wall plate

D.P.C. joined to bitumen layer

Floor boards

D.P.C.

Surface concrete

Concrete floor

Hardcore filling

Adequate air inlets through outer walls above ground level

D.P.C. at least 6" above ground level

Sleeper walls in "honeycomb" bond

Ventilating holes in cross partition walls

D.P.C.

4" vent pipes under solid floor corresponding with external ventilators

FIG. 2.10

Construction of suspended floors

Given full ventilation of the under-floor space, the floor boarding must be tongued-and-grooved if draughts are to be avoided in the room above. This is not needed if an impervious floor finish is to be provided, but nevertheless the tongued-and-grooved boarding gives a much flatter surface than square-edge boarding to the floor on which the covering has to be laid.

As an additional precaution, particularly on wet sites, it is recommended that the site concrete be of structural quality employing a mix not leaner than, say, 1 : 2 : 4. In Scotland, where climatic conditions are likely to lead to greater dampness, much more stringent precautions are taken to prevent ground moisture getting into the space beneath suspended timber floors. An oversite coating based on bitumen or pitch is normally used. This solum treatment is the subject of a British Standard 2832 : 1957. The system might well be considered in construction south of the Border, particularly on wet sites or in districts where the rate of evaporation is low.

Figure 2.10 illustrates various constructional features designed to protect suspended timber floors against rising damp.

Care taken to protect timber floors from dampness may be nullified by pieces of waste wood left lying on the site concrete; these can initiate an outbreak of dry rot. Another source of trouble is the bridging of damp-proof courses by mortar droppings. In one particularly bad case an outbreak of dry rot had started in the vicinity of a cavity party wall, where mortar droppings in the cavity were expected to do little harm and so no great care had been taken to avoid them. The treatment of floors that have been attacked by dry rot or other fungi has already been discussed in Chapter 1.

Ground floors have been known to suffer attack by beetles, but the trouble is not sufficiently rife to warrant defensive measures unless the building is to be constructed in an area that is known to have a large beetle population. In these circumstances, it would be worth using pressure-impregnated timber. The preservative used should be one that is non-staining and inodorous; creosote should be avoided.

Dimensional changes. When the moisture content of timber rises the timber swells, particularly in the directions at right-angles to the grain. Thus, the movement of a boarded floor in a direction across the boards can be quite large; the pressure exerted has been known to push out the walls of a building. Normally a small gap is left at the edge of the floor, to be covered by a skirting board. Such a gap is sufficient to cope with the movement likely to occur in rooms of moderate size, as in dwellings, but special precautions will be needed with large floors. The amount of movement to be expected can be assessed with the aid of Forest Products Research Laboratory Leaflet No. 9; allowance should be made at the edges of the floor and at any openings such as those for heating pipes. Where a building is likely to be left vacant for long periods, or where there is a possibility of flooding of the under-floor space, a bigger allowance for movement must be made.

Timber intermediate floors

In most buildings timber floors above ground floor level are not likely to remain damp for long periods except at the ends of joists that are built into external walls. A minimum treatment for these joist ends is to provide a brush application of preservative; a wise course is to wrap them also in bitumen felt. The latter course is recommended particularly for solid walls;

with cavity walls, preservative treatment alone should be adequate. Joist ends that have not been given sufficient protection can be safeguarded to some extent by drilling a hole from a point as near as possible to the end, downward and at an angle towards the end, and injecting fungicide into this hole.

Deflection of suspended timber floors is sometimes responsible for the cracking of ceilings. In traditional construction it was customary to provide herring-bone struts between the joists to minimize distortion. This is rarely done now. Moreover, following the timber shortage just after the last war, joist sizes were much reduced. Both these factors are likely to have encouraged movement of the joists and consequent cracking of rigid ceilings fixed to them. Now that timber is in plentiful supply, reversion to the old standards for joist sizes, and to herring-bone strutting, should be considered when a crack-free ceiling is required.

Suspended concrete floors

Structural concrete is usually so dense that water vapour diffuses through it only very slowly, and consequently it is not always necessary to ventilate the air space beneath a suspended concrete ground floor. It would be unwise, however, to assume that precautions to minimize dampness can always be omitted. They may still be required if the upper surface of the concrete is sealed by an impermeable floor finish or covering that is sensitive to moisture. If such a floor is colder than the ground below, moisture will tend to distil from the ground to the concrete and to condense at the upper, cold, surface of the concrete, where it may affect the floor covering. In such circumstances there is good reason to cover the ground with an impervious bitumen coating. In extreme cases, or when water is likely to find its way through the floor into the space below, ventilation should be provided.

The protection of concrete against attack by chemicals has already been discussed (p. 7). It is particularly important to prevent such attack in suspended floors, because there may be a risk of collapse after only a small part of their strength has been lost. Wherever there is a risk of concrete or steel being attacked, a protective membrane should be provided above the structural members. This would normally take the form of a bitumen or asphalt layer, but where oil is present p.v.c. sheet is better. Guidance on the choice of finish for floors that must resist chemical attack is given in Chapter 4.

Steel-and-concrete floors

Composite steel-and-concrete floors occur in two common forms: the beam-and-slab floor, in which steel beams support concrete slabs, and the filler-joist floor, in which the steel beams are embedded in concrete. The protection required by the steelwork has been discussed on p. 8; however, special precautions may be needed with a filler-joist floor when, to save weight, lightweight concrete is employed. Here, reliance cannot be placed on the lightweight concrete to offer full protection from corrosion to the steel joists. Though now prohibited, it was at one time common to use clinker aggregate, which is itself corrosive to steel, and the concrete then actively encouraged corrosion. Unless the concrete surrounding the joists is dense, additional protection to the steel, such as a heavy bitumen coating, should be provided.

Chapter 3

SOLID FLOORS ON THE GROUND

In the past, solid ground floors were commonly of natural stone flags or of clay bricks. Today, concrete is almost invariably used for the foundation layer or sub-floor, and it may also provide the finished surface.

The concrete is generally laid on a bed of hardcore, which reduces the capillary rise of ground moisture and can be used to provide a level surface. The hardcore may consist of rubble or other inert material of coarse grading. It should not contain any appreciable amount of soluble salts; sulphates, particularly, must be avoided. Further, it should not be liable to swell or to crumble when wet.

Under-burnt colliery shale used as hardcore has been known to expand and to cause heaving in concrete floors cast on it. A well-burnt shale, recognizable by its red colour, should give no such trouble. Even when well burnt, however, colliery shale may contain sulphates; on wet sites, these have been carried up into the concrete, which they have attacked, and the resulting expansion of the slab has pushed outwards the external walls of the building. It is recommended that, on wet sites, waterproof paper or other impermeable sheeting should be laid over the shale before the concrete is placed. The same precaution is advisable if much gypsum plaster is present in brick rubble used as hardcore.

Hardcore should be well consolidated before concrete is laid on it.

Cracking may occur in a concrete solid floor either through shrinkage or because the slab is not evenly supported over its area. Shrinkage cracks are liable to form in large concrete floor slabs, especially in the absence of reinforcement. To minimize this, and to ensure that any cracking that does occur is along regular lines, it is advisable to lay the concrete in relatively small areas at a time. One way is first to lay alternate squares of about

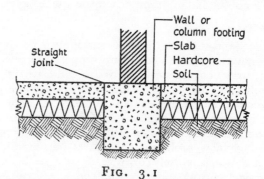

FIG. 3.1

Joint of floor slab and wall or column base: slab rests only on hardcore

10 yd side, and to lay the intermediate squares after the initial shrinkage of these has taken place. Avoidance of cracking in floor finishes is discussed in Chapter 4.

To avoid cracking through unequal settlement it is advisable to form a straight vertical joint where a floor slab meets a wall or column base, to ensure that the slab rests only on the hardcore and not on the foundation of the wall or column (Fig. 3.1).

The concrete will usually be of 1 : 2 : 4 mix and laid not less than 3½ in. thick, even in domestic work. The surface finish should be suitable as a base for the floor finish to be applied later (*see* p. 74).

Exclusion of moisture

A damp-proof membrane is usually required in a solid ground floor, to prevent rising dampness from affecting the floor finishes.

Until recently, the standard recommendation was to sandwich an ⅛-in. layer of bitumen or pitch, poured hot, within the concrete. This means that the concrete must be laid in two layers, each being brought to a smooth surface, and that the full depth of the concrete is not available to act monolithically to minimize curling as the slab dries out. In future, this method is likely to be superseded by the use of thin synthetic-resin foil or film; for instance, polyethylene film, 0·0075 in. thick, delivered to the site in roll form, has been successfully used as a damp-proof membrane. This has the great advantage that it can be laid directly on the rolled and blinded hardcore, so that the concrete slab can be laid in one operation.

A number of factors will influence the location of the damp-proof membrane. If it is placed within or below the concrete floor, enough time must be allowed for the concrete to dry out before any moisture-sensitive finish is laid. This delay will be avoided, of course, if the damp-proof membrane is on top of the concrete; it will then need to be of asphalt or pitch mastic,

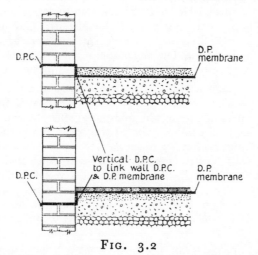

FIG. 3.2

Joint between damp-proof membrane and d.p.c. in walls

$\frac{1}{2}$ in. thick (if the mastic is to form the floor *finish*, it needs to be laid at least $\frac{5}{8}$ in. thick, *see* p. 67). If the concrete slab itself must be kept dry, or protected from sulphates in hardcore, the membrane will of course be placed underneath it. The position of the membrane in relation to floor-heating elements is discussed in Chapter 5.

Wherever the damp-proof membrane is located, it needs to make a watertight joint with the damp-proof courses in adjacent walls. Typical details are shown in Fig. 3.2.

In basements, the waterproof construction may have to withstand the pressure of a head of water. The traditional practice has been to 'tank' the basement with a continuous membrane of asphalt located under the structural floor and behind the structural walls. With this system, if any defects occur, repair may be very difficult. Because of this, a new practice is gaining acceptance, in which reliance is placed on walls of high-quality concrete without any tanking; a Code of Practice is in preparation.

Heat insulation

Floors of hardcore and concrete laid direct on the ground do not lose heat in the same way as walls and roofs. The ground acts to some extent as an accumulator of heat, and in fact most of the heat loss occurs within a few feet of the edges adjacent to the external walls. Consequently, the average heat flow is dependent on the size and shape of the floor. Typical values in terms of thermal transmittance (U) are quoted in the Guide to Current Practice, issued by the Institution of Heating and Ventilating Engineers; they are used in exactly the same way as are the U-values of walls and roofs. For the solid floor of a small dwelling, a U-value of 0·2 Btu/sq. ft h °F is usually adopted in practice; this value is reduced to 0·15 by the addition of a surface finish of wood blocks.

The relatively high thermal performance of the solid concrete floor is a feature of its position rather than of its specific construction, and it is obtained without special effort. From the standpoint of heat conservation alone, further improvement might not be justified, and insulation could perhaps be used to better effect elsewhere; however, additional surface insulation has the incidental benefits of making the floor warm to the touch (*see* Chapter 4), and of responding quickly to intermittent heating.

As heat loss through a solid floor is most rapid at the edges, it may be expected that the floor surface temperature of a heated building will be lowest at the corners and along the margins against the exposed walls. The very few complaints of condensation at the edges and corners of rooms in traditional dwellings do not suggest a need for edge or marginal insulation, but where the wall construction is thin, as with light cladding or curtain walling, and also where the floor is part of a raft foundation projecting beyond the perimeter of the superstructure, some extra insulation may be needed. The published U-values for solid floors refer to constructions surrounded by 9-in. brickwork, and higher values would apply with thinner walls.

The provision of edge insulation for solid floors is described, in relation to floor heating, in Chapter 5.

Chapter 4

FLOOR FINISHES

PROPERTIES

FLOOR finishes, except in a few special constructions, do not contribute to the strength of the floor; they are used for one or more of three reasons:

> to protect the structural floor from wear or corrosion
> to provide an attractive appearance
> to increase the comfort or safety of the user.

Which of these primary functions is considered to be the most important will depend on the proposed use. In a factory, for example, protection and safety are the first requirements, with good appearance and comfort to be sought wherever possible. In a home, good appearance and comfort will be more important.

Any given finish must provide the desired balance of properties, and must be sufficiently durable; it will be expected to last for a period commensurate with its initial cost, the cost of its replacement, and any costs arising from disorganization associated with its replacement. In other words, good value is required.

A variety of influences affect the life of a floor finish. Most important is the ever-present abrasive action of traffic; other factors include the action of liquids in producing dimensional changes, erosion and corrosion, the impacts of falling objects, and the dents caused by heavy loads. Thus there is a series of secondary requirements that the finish must fulfil, which will depend on the conditions of service. These must be considered in relation to the three primary functions—protection, appearance, and comfort—because the life of a finish is the period during which *all three* continue unimpaired. For example, a printed linoleum protects no less and is as comfortable after the pattern has worn off but its appearance may no longer be acceptable; on the other hand mastic asphalt, with no change in appearance or comfort, is no longer useful if a defect allows corrosive liquid to penetrate to the structure.

To summarize, the properties required of a floor finish are:

(1) Attractive appearance

(2) Comfort and safety—

>   Freedom from slipperiness
>   Warmth
>   Quietness
>   Resilience

(3) Durability—
    Resistance to:
        abrasion
        water and other liquids
        indentation
        impact
        sunlight
        moulds and fungi
        high temperature or fire.

There is a wide variety of materials available for floor finishes, and each should be evaluated in relation to the above requirements so that its suitability for any particular type of use may be assessed. Quantitative evaluation is difficult and few laboratory tests are available. The materials must therefore be assessed largely on the basis of experience. To simplify the evaluation, two types of use are distinguished: *domestic*, where only foot traffic is involved, and *industrial*, where truck traffic is also a factor. The materials are compared separately in Tables 4.1 and 4.2 on this basis, using a 5-point scale of values, from 'very good', through 'fair', to 'very poor'. The scales used are not the same in these two tables, which are not to be compared. Table 4.3 compares the resistance of various flooring materials to attack by industrial liquids. The factors covered by these tables will now be considered in more detail, and some information will then be given about each type of finish.

Appearance. Any rating of the appearance of a floor finish must be largely a matter of individual judgment, and all that can be done here is to indicate the range of colours and patterns available.

Slipperiness. Measurements of the forces applied to the floor surface by the feet of users have indicated that a coefficient of friction between footwear and floor finish greater than 0·4 will ensure freedom from slipperiness. Few materials fall below this value when they are new, but in time a floor may become slippery through the polishing action of traffic, the presence of water or oil, or the use of too much wax polish. Any evaluation of slipperiness must therefore take account of these factors and is best based on experience as well as on measurement.

The requirement of freedom from slipperiness may conflict with the need in many industries for a smooth hygienic floor, which will often be wet and will then be even more slippery to rubber boots.

Warmth. The term 'warmth' is here used to refer to the subjective experience of the user. A floor finish has no great effect on the total heat loss from a room; only about 15 per cent of the heat lost passes through the ground floor, and the difference between the effects produced by the best and worst floor finishes can amount only to about 3 per cent of the total heat loss. But it is everyday knowledge that to bare feet a concrete surface feels cold and a carpet feels warm. What produces this effect is the rate at which the skin loses heat to the surface, and this can be related to the thermal constants of the finish.

When the feet are shod the conditions giving rise to sensations of coldness or of warmth are more complex, and they may vary from one person to another. Probably the temperature of the air in the room and the occurrence of draughts along the floor are important.

Quietness. Floor finishes, other than high resilient materials such as sponge rubber and cork, have little effect on transmission of airborne or impact sound through a floor structure (*see* p. 43). Also, except for carpets, they have little value as sound absorbers.

The problem of comparing the **amounts** of noise generated by impacts on different floor finishes has not been studied in any detail; it is well known that there is a very wide range. The values given in Table 4.1 are based on experience of floors in use.

Resilience. Under this heading are included all those properties of a finish that combine to give it a distinctive 'tread' or 'feel'. This property has not been studied and is not easy to define; little is known about the kind of resilience required in different situations.

Resistance to abrasion. In investigating the properties of flooring materials, probably most effort has gone into measuring 'abrasion resistance', and a large amount of very misleading information is available. This is not a property that can be measured in absolute units, and it has no exact meaning except in relation to a particular abrasion process. No machine for the accelerated testing of floors can give results of value unless it reproduces the process of abrasion that occurs in actual use. None of the many machines used for floor testing in Europe or America does this; only a few can rank different materials qualitatively in the order of their performance in use, and, of these, it is doubtful if any can give a quantitative assessment. The most that can be expected from a machine is a comparison of varieties of the same material—e.g. different samples of timber or of concrete.

At present, therefore, assessment of wear resistance is usually based on practical experience.

Resistance to water and other liquids. The effects of moisture probably cause more damage to floor finishes than any other agency, even abrasion. For this reason, moisture effects are considered separately; liquids other than water are usually met only in particular industrial circumstances.

Water may reach a floor finish or its adhesive from the base slab below or from the atmosphere, or the floor may become wet when liquid is spilt or when the surface is washed.

The exclusion of damp rising from the ground beneath the base slab has already been considered (p. 59). Most floor finishes require a damp-proof course below, either because they themselves are attacked by moisture or because their adhesives come loose from wet concrete. Those not requiring protection are indicated in the tables.

Water incompletely dried out from the concrete of the slab may also damage the floor finish. Both with ground floors and with suspended floors, it is important to allow all water that could reach the floor finish to evaporate before the finish is laid. The time this will take varies greatly with the

TABLE 4.1

Assessment of floor finishes for domestic and similar uses

Type of finish	Colour range	Comfort and safety			Durability			B.S.	C.P.
		Warmth to touch	Quietness	Resistance to slipping	Resistance to wear	Resistance to water	Resistance to indentation		
Timber									
Softwood board	Natural wood shades	VG	F-P	VG*	F	P	G-F	1297	201/2
block		VG	F	VG*	F	P	G-F	1187	201/3
Hardwood block		VG-G	F-P	G*	VG-F	P	VG-F	1187	201/2
board		VG-G	F	G*	VG-F	P	VG-F		201/3
Composition block	Various colours	G	F	G-F	G	G	VG		
Chip board	Natural colours	VG	F-P	G	F	P	VG-F	2604	
Tile and slab									
Clay tile	Various colours	VP	VP	G-F†	VG-G	VG	VG	1286	202
Concrete tile	Various colours patterns and finishes	VP	VP	G-F†	VG-G	VG	VG	1197	202
Sheet									
Cork carpet	Natural, and restricted range of plain colours	VG	VG	VG	G	P	P	810	203
Cork	Grade natural shades, some dyed products	VG	VG	VG	VG-F	P	P		203
Linoleum	Wide range with patterns of many types	G	G-F	G-F	G	P	F-P	810 1863	203
Flexible P.V.C.	Various colours and marble	G-F	VG-G	VG†	VG-F	VG-F	G-F	3261	203
Rubber	Various colours and marble	G	VG	VG†	VG-G	G	G-F	1711	203
Thermoplastic tile	Various colours and patterns	F	F	G	F-P	G	P	2592	203
Vinyl asbestos	Various colours and patterns	F	F	G	G	G-F	F	3260	203

Type of finish	Colour range	Comfort and safety			Durability			B.S.	C.P.
		Warmth to touch	Quietness	Resistance to slipping	Resistance to wear	Resistance to water	Resistance to indentation		
In situ									
Asphalt	Black and dark colours	F	F	G–F	VG	VG	F–P	{1076 1410 1451}	204/4
Cement-bitumen	Black and dark red	F	F	G	G	VG	G–F		
Cement-polyvinyl acetate	Usually yellow and red	G–F	F	G	G	P	G		204/6
Cement-rubber latex	Various colours	G–F	F	G	G	G	G	1201	204/2
Concrete	Restricted range	VP	VP	G–F	VG–F	VG	VG		204/6
Magnesium oxychloride	Various colours and marbles	GF	G–F	G	G	P	VG–G	776	204/5
Pitch	Black and dark red	F	F	G–F	G	VG	F–P	{1375 1783 1450}	
Polyvinyl acetate emulsion	Various colours and marbles	G–F	F	G	F–P	P	F		
Terrazzo	Various colours	VP	VP	G: vP if polished	VG–F	VG	VG		204/3

* except when polished   † except when wet

NOTES:

(1) *Quietness* here is an assessment of the noise generated by traffic: it is not related to noise transmission.

(2) *Wear.* The term is used in the wide meaning to include abrasion, stability, dimensional cracking, cutting, fading etc.

TABLE 4.2

Assessment of floor finishes for industrial use

Type of finish	Resistance				Warmth	Quietness	Ease of cleaning
	Wear	Impact	Indentation	Slipping			
Portland cement concrete, *in situ* .	VG–P	G–P	VG	G–F	P	P	F
ditto, precast .	VG–G	G–F	VG	G–F	P	P	F
High-alumina cement concrete, *in situ* .	VG–P	G–P	VG	G–F	P	P	F
Magnesite . .	G–F	G–F	G	F	F	F	G
Latex-cement . .	G–F	G–F	F	G	F	F	G–F
Resin emulsion cement . .	G–F	G–F	F	G	F	F	G–F
Bitument emulsion cement .	G–F	G–F	F–P	G	F	F	F
Pitch mastic . .	G–F	G–F	F–P	G–F	F	F	G
Mastic asphalt .	VG–F	VG–F	F–P	G–F	F	F	G
Wood block (hardwood) .	VG–F	VG–F	VG–F	VG	G	G	G–F
Wood block (softwood) . .	F–P	F–P	F	VG	G	G	G–P
Metal tiles . .	VG	VG	VG	F	P	P	G–F
Clay tiles and bricks	VG–G	VG–F	VG	G–F	P	P	VG

conditions; the surface should be kept free of stacks of materials and the ventilation should be good. Screeds made with lightweight aggregate take much longer to dry out than do cement-sand screeds. For solid floors on the ground, surface damp-proof layers of mastic have the advantage that they eliminate this problem completely.

Atmospheric moisture may affect floor finishes, notably wood or finishes containing wood, such as linoleum, chipboard and hardboard, and also those based on magnesite. The expansion and contraction of wood blocks with changes of atmospheric humidity is well known. Magnesite floors may, in humid conditions, show beads of moisture on the surface; there is no known cure for this 'sweating', nor are the causes known. None of the other types of finish is particularly susceptible to changes in humidity.

Where a floor is likely to become wet, as in kitchens and with many industrial processes, it is obviously desirable to choose a material not affected by water, and—equally important—one that is not fixed by a water-sensitive adhesive or bedding material.

Other liquids liable to damage a floor finish are the acids, alkalis, salts, oils, and solvents used or produced in many industries. With these, it is important that the floor finish is not itself attacked, and also that it prevents access of any aggressive liquid to the steel or concrete of the sub-floor.

Indentation. It may not matter that a floor finish indents under a load, provided that it recovers when the load is removed; materials vary greatly in their recovery after loading. In a domestic finish, a dent may be objectionable only if it mars appearance. This depends to a large extent on texture and pattern, and there is therefore no depth of residual indentation that can be defined as the maximum tolerable with all finishes.

In an industrial floor, dents may affect truck traffic or they may collect aggressive fluids and become centres of erosion. Again, it is impossible to define tolerable depth. Various indentation tests have been defined in British Standards for such materials as asphalt, linoleum and thermoplastic tiles, but they relate to the quality of the materials rather than to the performance characteristics in actual use.

Impact. Of little account domestically, the effects of impacts of falling materials are of importance in industrial premises and may be very severe, as in foundries and heavy engineering shops, where heavy and often sharp loads are dropped.

The resistance of a floor finish to shattering by impact is affected by the solidity of the bedding; solid bedding will always mitigate the worst effects of impact.

Resistance to sunlight. Some materials change in colour on prolonged exposure to light, especially to direct sunlight. Wood and cork bleach, and some types of plastics become yellow, although the materials may be otherwise unaffected. A test for colour stability is included in the British Standard for polyvinyl chloride materials (in draft).

Resistance to moulds and fungi. Only timber and a few other flooring materials containing cellulose are liable to mould or fungal attack. The effects of the various wood fungi have been described on pp. 10–11. Such organisms may also attack reconstituted timber products such as chip-board.

Mildew affects linoleum, particularly the hessian on which it is calendered. No tests are available for assessing resistance to such attack.

Resistance to high temperature and fire. The temperatures to which a finish is subjected in domestic use, for example around the hearth, below a copper, or over floor heating, are not usually very high. Most materials will withstand them without any change other than some softening.

In industry, much higher temperatures occur, and this may restrict the choice of finish. Many floor finishes will be marked by hot cinders, for example; some will allow flames to spread along them, but none present any severe hazard when used as flooring.

INDIVIDUAL SURFACINGS

Mastic asphalt

Mastic asphalt is prepared from mixtures of bituminous binders and inert aggregate, which may be laid while hot as a jointless floor (B.S. 1076, 1410, 1451) or moulded under pressure into tiles (B.S. 1324 and 1325). It is generally black, but a restricted range of colours can be produced. The jointless flooring is not less than $\frac{5}{8}$ in. thick; the tiles may be $\frac{5}{8}$ to $2\frac{1}{2}$ in. thick.

For special situations an acid-resistant variety is available, and by the use of soft aggregates a spark-proof material can be obtained.

TABLE 4.3

Resistance to industrial liquids

	Water	Satisfactory pH range	Organic acids	Hydro-chloric acid	Sulphuric acid	Nitric acid	Alkali	Sulphate	Mineral oil	Animal oil	Organic solvents
JOINTLESS FLOOR FINISHES											
Portland cement concrete	VG	7-12	P	VP	VP	VP	G	P	G	P	G
High-alumina cement concrete	VG	5-9	G if pH 4·5	VP	VP	VP	F	G	G	F	G
Pitch mastic (depending on grade)	VG	1-11	G	G	F	F	G/F	VG	F	F	P
Mastic asphalt (depending on grade)	VG	1-11	G	G	F	F	G-F	VG	P	P	P
Rubber-latex cement	G	7-12 but better than mixes without latex out-side range	GF	G up to 5% then P	G up to 5% then P	G up to 5% then P	G	F-G	F-G	F	P
Resin-emulsion cement	F	not particularly suitable in wet conditions							G	F	G

	Water	Satisfactory pH range	Organic acids	Hydrochloric acid	Sulphuric acid	Nitric acid	Alkali	Sulphate	Mineral oil	Animal oil	Organic solvents
Portland cement mortar	as above for concrete										
Super-sulphate cement mortar	VG	3-12	G	G up to 0·5%, then P	G up to 1%, then P	F-P	G	G	G	G	G
High-alumina cement mortar	as above for concrete										
Silicate cement	P	0-7	G	G	G	G	VP	G	G	G	G
Sulphur cement	VG	0-10	G	G	G	Dilute, G Concentrated, F	G	G	G	P	G
Rubber-latex cement	as above for jointless flooring, but attack is slower in a thin joint										
Phenol-formaldehyde cement	VG	0-10 greater if specially modified	G	G	Dilute, G Concentrated, F	Dilute, F Concentrated, P	G	G	G	G	G-P
Cashew-nut resin	VG	0-12	G	G	Dilute, G Concentrated, F	10% G 50% F Concentrated, P	G	G	P	P	P
Furane resin	VG	0-12	G	G	G up to 60%	Up to 3-4% cold, 2% hot, G	VG	G	G	G	G

BEDDING AND JOINTING MATERIALS FOR CLAY TILES AND BRICKS

Ranges given as pH=0-x indicate that, apart from specific action by acids that are oxidizing agents, the material resists all concentrations of acids.

Cement-bitumen

Portland-cement mortar gauged with bitumen emulsion is commonly used as a patching compound for factory floors, and to a lesser but growing extent as a floor finish. Only dark colours are available, and the floor finish is laid ⅝ in. thick.

Cement-latex

Jointless floorings prepared from cement and natural rubber latex are used very extensively in ships, both as the wearing finish and as a levelling coat over metal decks. In building, cement-latex is used both for jointless flooring and as a bed and jointing for clay tiles. It can be laid in thicknesses of ¼ in. or more. Its main characteristics are flexibility and strong adhesion to the base—both of which minimize the risk of cracking.

Recently, synthetic and modified rubbers have been used in place of natural rubber latex, and some finishes have greatly improved oil resistance compared with the original material.

Cement–polyvinyl acetate emulsion

Polyvinyl acetate emulsions have been used to mix with Portland cement mortar in the same way as natural latex. The resulting finish is less flexible, more resistant to oil, and less resistant to water than the natural latex equivalent, which it otherwise resembles. It is used in industry in dry situations where resistance to oil is needed.

Chip-board (particle-board)

Compressed wood chips and synthetic resin are formed into boards, which have been nailed to wooden joists to form both the finish and the structure; boards have also been cut to tile size and stuck to concrete bases with bitumen adhesives. The materials are usually ⅝ in. thick.

Clay tiles

Clay tiles are prepared by pressing refined clay and firing in a circular kiln of the type used for pottery. They are commonly divided into three groups—quarries, floor tiles and ceramic mosaic. The division between the first two is not precise and is discussed in the foreword to B.S. 1286, which classifies them as Types *A* and *B* depending on dimensional tolerance. Floor tiles are subdivided into plain colours, vitreous and encaustic. Ceramic mosaics are supplied as pieces up to 1½ in. square mounted on paper in a pattern ready for laying.

Floor tiles, mosaics, and the thinner quarries are used mostly for domestic and similar work; the thicker quarries and paviors, i.e. bricks 9 × 4½ × 1, 1½ or 2 in., are used industrially.

Difficulties arising from differential movement between clay floor tiles and the base on which they are laid can be circumvented by laying on paper or sand.

Composition blocks

Blocks, superficially resembling wood blocks, composed of sawdust, cement and calcium sulphate, and impregnated with linseed oil, are marketed under proprietary names. They are sometimes referred to as 'composition blocks'. They are $\frac{3}{8}$ and $\frac{5}{8}$ in. thick, laid in patterns like wood blocks, but are bedded in cement mortar.

Concrete

Concrete floors are used industrially more than any other type. Several proprietary types of aggregate are now available. For high-quality work the two most important factors are to lay the finish integrally with the base, and to use a low water/cement ratio.

Concrete tiles

A range of concrete tiles is available, varying in the aggregates and pigments used. They vary in thickness from $\frac{5}{8}$ to 1 in., and in size up to 12 × 12 in.

Cork carpet

See linoleum.

Cork tiles

Cork tiles are traditionally prepared by moulding cork granules under heat and pressure, which make the cork resins flow and bind the granules together. Some tiles are now prepared by using resins as binders, using much lower moulding temperatures. The tiles range in thickness from $\frac{3}{16}$ to 1 in., in various sizes up to 36 × 12 in. The edges may be plane or tongued and grooved.

Linoleum and cork carpet

Linoleum, by far the most commonly used floor covering, is prepared from linseed oil, resins, cork and wood flour; cork carpet is similar but only cork is used as filler, in a coarser grading than is used in linoleum. The original linoleum was prepared on a hessian backing (B.S. 810) but now a considerable amount is made, particularly for cutting into tiles, on a bitumen-saturated felt-paper backing (B.S. 1863); this is known as 'felt-backed' linoleum. Another development is 'printed felt-base', a material with a printed paint finish on a backing of bitumen felt. Linoleum is usually 72 in. wide, and 1·8 to 6·7 mm in thickness.

Magnesite (magnesium oxychloride composition) flooring

Magnesite has been a well-known flooring material for many years, usually known by a trade name or as 'composition flooring'. It is made from a mixture of magnesia, magnesium chloride solution, fillers and pigments. Less commonly used in housing than it was formerly, it still has many industrial uses. It is particularly suitable where freedom from friction-sparking and resistance to organic solvents is required, as in paint shops, and it is better than any other jointless material for laying over boarded sub-floors. It should always be laid by specialists. In the absence of a complete standard specification for the magnesia (B.S. 776 gives methods of test but no test limits), reliance must be placed on experience in selecting a suitable raw material. Pipes or other metalwork embedded in or passing through this flooring need to be protected, for example by a heavy coating of bitumen; in the presence of moisture, chlorides are highly corrosive.

Metal tiles

There are two types of metal tile. One is in the form of a shallow tray, $\frac{7}{8}$ in. deep, of 10-gauge steel. The wearing surface is punched to give twisted metal anchors which are then embedded in the filling. These tiles, 12 × 12 in. or 12 × 6 in., are beaten into high-quality concrete until the concrete extrudes through the punch holes. The finished floor is approximately $1\frac{1}{2}$ in. thick.

The other type of metal tile consists of a 12 in. equilateral triangle of cast iron 1 in. thick, with a projecting foot at each corner and with a chequered surface. The tiles are bedded in mortar so that the feet bear directly on the base floor. This transfers load evenly to the structure but requires a very even base to produce a level floor.

Metal grids

Metal grids are frequently used as a surface reinforcement to increase the impact resistance of an otherwise hard-wearing floor. The grids may be of cast iron or steel, and of hexagonal or rectangular mesh. They may be supplied as mats framed all round or on only two sides, or as a roll of inter-locking metal strips which are built into a grid on the site. The grid can be filled with concrete, asphalt, or latex-cement. The top edges of the grid are part of the wearing surface. The resulting floor can be very noisy with wheeled traffic.

Pitch mastic

Pitch-mastic flooring resembles mastic asphalt in many ways; it is similar in composition except that coal-tar pitch is used as the binder instead of bitumen. This confers on the finish a resistance to grease and oil rather greater than that of asphalt.

Polyvinyl acetate flooring

Floor finishes based on polyvinyl acetate emulsion with fillers have been developed in Germany. The hardening of this finish depends on the evapora-tion of water from the emulsion; it therefore has to be applied in thin layers, but a multi-layer finish may be built up.

Polyvinyl chloride sheet and tiles

Plasticized polyvinyl chloride, manufactured in various ways, is the most significant new material in flooring in recent years. Flooring is available in a wide diversity of types; development is very rapid and new forms are continually being introduced.

Rubber sheet and tiles

Rubber flooring is available in sheet or tile form and in varying degrees of hardness. There is also what is known as 'American tile', in which the laminae forming the tile become harder from bottom to top. Rubber can also be laminated to a resilient sponge-rubber backing.

Terrazzo

Terrazzo is a special form of concrete using coloured cement and a decorative aggregate such as marble. The surface is ground to expose the aggregate. Terrazzo laid *in situ* is liable to crack because of shrinkage, and to avoid this there has been much greater use of terrazzo tiles.

Thermoplastic tiles (asphalt tiles)
Since their introduction in about 1946, thermoplastic tiles have become the third flooring material, after linoleum and carpets, in volume of production. Although sometimes called 'asphalt tiles,' they have no resemblance to the compressed mastic-asphalt tiles previously discussed. From them have developed vinyl asbestos tiles which, although similar in appearance, are more resistant to abrasion and to oils and have cleaner colours.

Timber
Strip and board flooring. 'Strip flooring' is the term applied to tongued-and-grooved strips not more than 4 in. wide; above this width the term 'board' is used. The usual thicknesses are 1 in., 1¼ in. and 1½ in. nominal. 'Strip overlay', ½ in. thick, is for fixing to a board sub-floor.

Wood-block flooring. The usual sizes of blocks are: length 6 in. to 15 in., width up to 3½ in., and thickness 1 in. to 1½ in. nominal. Blocks may be tongued-and-grooved, metal-tongued, or dowelled, with at least ⅜-in. wearing surface above the joint. As the wood below the joint serves no useful purpose, wood blocks only ⅜ in. thick have been developed. These are usually 4–6 in. long by 1 in. wide, with butt joints; after cramping together they are mounted on a felt, hessian, foil or paper backing in panels about 18 in. square. These panels are then stuck to the concrete base. This development has continued until some blocks are now only 0·1 in. thick on a heavy felt back.

Parquet flooring. This term is often wrongly applied to wood-block flooring. Parquet is prepared from selected hardwoods, ¼–⅜ in. thick, glued and pinned to a board sub-floor in decorative patterns.

End-grain paving block. For heavy industrial use where the floor is subjected to impact, wood blocks presenting the end-grain as the wearing surface are sometimes used. The blocks may be 1 in. or more thick with the wearing face up to 9 × 3 in.

CONSTRUCTIONAL DETAILS

Nearly all of the materials listed above require some preparation of the base floor before they can be laid. Usually the requirement is only for a plane smooth finish on the base, but many troubles with floor finishes can be traced to inadequacies of the sub-floor.

When concrete floors are cast *in situ*, either on the ground or as an upper floor, it is possible to finish the concrete itself to a standard adequate for most floor finishes. However, this is seldom done, partly because of the difficulty in fixing services, but largely because of the risk (often overestimated) of damage to the surface by subsequent operations. It is much more common on these floors, and it is necessary on precast floors, to provide a screed on the structural floor. The problems that can arise with this screed are in general those that are common to heavy-duty concrete finishes laid on a hardened base.

The screed tends to shrink as it dries, and if it is not restrained by a good key to the base it will crack. As the screed dries from the surface it tends to curl. The sub-floor should therefore be clean and thoroughly roughened to achieve maximum bond, and the mix for the screed should be as lean and as 'dry' as possible to reduce shrinkage to a minimum. To avoid cracking the area of screed laid at one time should not exceed 150 sq. ft. The finish required on the screed depends on the flooring to be used; most flooring contractors are specific about their requirements. Sheet and tile materials laid with adhesive usually require the dense smooth finish obtained with a steel trowel. For *in situ* materials, and for tiles laid in mortar, the rougher open finish achieved with a wood float is more appropriate.

Lightweight screeds are often required for one reason or another. They may be formed either of lightweight-aggregate concrete or of aerated concrete. There is an important difference in behaviour between these two types. Lightweight aggregates absorb moisture in the mixing process, and very high water/cement ratios are required to obtain workable mixes. The water in the pores of the aggregate requires a long time to evaporate; with many floor finishes, the screeds therefore require long periods of drying before the finish can be laid. Aerated screeds dry much more quickly.

Neither type of lightweight screed lends itself to obtaining a surface smooth enough to receive thin floor finishes, and it is common to provide, at the time of laying, a thin surfacing of cement and sand; this also prevents damage to the more friable lightweight material. Both types shrink more than cement-sand screeds and are therefore more liable to crack if adhesion to the base is not adequate.

Some floor constructions involve the use of several layers of material laid at different stages of construction. Each layer usually has different shrinkage characteristics and there is a danger of their separating. It should therefore be the aim to reduce the number of layers to the minimum.

MAINTENANCE AND REPAIR

Maintenance

Floor finishes receive maintenance attention much more frequently than other parts of a building. 'Maintenance' is used here to refer to cleaning and to the application of protective layers to the finish.

The main need in maintenance of a floor is for cleaning, because the floor gradually collects all the dust from the room. Regular sweeping or vacuum-cleaning is therefore a necessity. Various 'sweeping compounds' are available to aid the loosening of dirt and also to reduce the amount of dust thrown into the air; basically these are moist sawdust, sometimes mixed with sand. The sawdust is kept moist with light mineral oil, wax emulsion, or deliquescent salts such as calcium chloride. Compounds containing oil may attack some flooring materials; salt-based materials should not be allowed to accumulate in cracks, otherwise damp streaks will appear.

In addition to cleaning, it is common to apply a surface dressing. Traditionally, this dressing was of wax and its primary purpose was presumably to protect the floor finish from wear; the gloss provided, however, has become an equally sought-after property, and glossy finishes are applied to materials irrespective of their need for protection. A great many dressings containing natural or synthetic waxes are available. Basically they are of two types—emulsion and paste. Emulsion types are the more widely usable because they do not soften any finish. Paste types are based on organic solvents, which soften some finishes, as indicated in Table 4.3.

Although the use of wax floor dressings is widely accepted in industry, it introduces a high labour cost into maintenance. Considerable effort is being made to develop finishes that retain their gloss for long periods with no other treatment than sweeping. These finishes are based on modified drying oils or synthetic resins. It is doubtful if any of these products endow a floor finish with all the properties sought, but development is rapid.

Mention should be made here of surface-hardening treatments for concrete floorings. Solutions of sodium silicate, or of magnesium or zinc silico-fluoride, applied to the surface of a good quality concrete floor, will often increase its resistance to abrasion and dust formation. Such a treatment is of little use if the surface is weak and friable, as when too wet a mix has been used and there is consequently a thin skin of laitance at the surface.

Industrially, many problems arise from the scale on which cleaning maintenance operations are required. Advances in mechanization have occurred in this field, and machines are available for dry cleaning, scrubbing and drying floors.

Repair

As mentioned earlier, the ease with which a worn finish can be repaired has an important bearing on costs. In a factory, the repair of a floor finish may involve shutting down a process, and there is considerable demand for finishes that can be repaired quickly so that the job can be done in the annual holiday.

Tiled floors have the advantage, when repairs become necessary, that the area to be repaired can be kept small. Indeed, some materials are used in certain situations, even though they have a low wear resistance, because they are easily replaced. At the other end of the scale, repairs are most difficult with jointless floors containing metal grids, because large areas must be cut out.

Patching repairs are possible on most floor finishes by the use of bitumen-cement or latex-cement mixes. These require only that the worn area shall be freed from loose material. The patching compound adheres firmly to the floor and can be brought to a feather-edge. Such patches can be completed over a week-end and be ready for traffic when the plant resumes work on Monday.

Chapter 5

FLOOR HEATING

THE Romans developed warmed floor construction to a remarkable extent not only in baths but also in houses. Their system of construction in masonry and concrete made possible the provision of an open space below the floor, the hypocaust, through which hot air and smoke from a furnace could be passed. Modern floor heating systems, in which hot-water pipes or electric warming cables are embedded in the floor, have not been in widespread use for very long, and there is still much scope for development. This chapter summarizes the main considerations that influence the design of a heated floor.

In hot-water pipe systems the hot water is circulated by pump through $\frac{3}{8}-\frac{5}{8}$ in. pipes, spaced 6–15 in. apart. The water temperature in most systems is between 100°F and 120°F, but in some it may be as high as 160°F. The pipes are completely encased in a concrete screed, 2–2½ in. thick. Steel or copper pipes are most usual but pipes of polyvinyl chloride have also been used. The heat input is controlled, at the boiler, by adjustment of the flow temperature.

There are two main types of electric cable system: the withdrawable system, in which conduits of metal or other material are provided in the concrete so that the heating cables can be withdrawn and renewed if necessary, and the embedded systems, in which the cables are buried and fixed in the concrete. The cables are either copper-sheathed or have p.v.c. insulation. Both systems need ducts with removable covers to house the supply cables, junction boxes, etc.

It is not at present economic to take a continuous supply of electrical energy throughout the day; normally power is supplied at a cheaper rate during 'off-peak' periods. The thermal storage capacity of the concrete screed enables advantage to be taken of this. A 2½-in. thickness of concrete will release stored heat for about eight hours after the electricity has been switched off, although the heat released towards the end of this period may not be enough to maintain full comfort conditions. The first control for an off-peak cable warming installation must be by time switch, to ensure that energy is supplied only during off-peak hours; further control is by thermostat.

For comfort, floor surface temperatures should not exceed 77°F continuously. In very cold weather a temperature of 80°F could be allowed with electric cable installations at the end of the 'off-peak' period. If persons have to stand on the floor for long periods, a lower temperature, perhaps 75°F, is desirable. The depth from the surface of the concrete to the bottom of the heating element depends to some extent on the type of floor finish, but is normally between 2 and 2½ in.

In a solid ground floor with no insulating layer below the heating plane, the heat losses to the ground are obviously greater than with conventional heating systems. The extra heat loss may be between 10 and 20 per cent of the total for large floor areas and up to 30 per cent for small areas (12 ft by 12 ft), and it may be advisable to provide insulation to reduce this. As most of the heat loss occurs round the margin of the heated area, edge insulation is generally sufficient, i.e. a layer about 3 ft wide having a thermal resistance of between 3 and 4 units (Fig. 5.1). With fully carpeted floors, a layer of insulation under the whole area is preferable. Insulation carried down vertically at the edge of the floor appears to be less effective, and is more difficult to place and to keep dry.

Where the intermediate floors of a multi-storey building are heated, some heat must pass downwards from each floor. If tenants pay separately for heating, and the temperature on each floor is under individual control, insulation below the heating elements is needed. This layer of insulation, if of appropriate material (p. 41), can also serve as a resilient layer for sound insulation; the construction then becomes a floating concrete raft with the heating elements incorporated in it.

CONSTRUCTIONAL REQUIREMENTS

Provision of floor heating will influence the design of a floor in several ways. A layer of thermal insulating material may be needed below the heating elements and, with electrical heating, the thickness of the concrete cover must be sufficient to provide thermal storage. The presence of the heating elements must be considered in relation to the design of the concrete screed in which they are embedded, to the choice of a floor finish and, in a solid ground floor, to the nature and position of the damp-proof membrane. Some types of electric cable may require protection from damage by movements of the sub-floor or screed, and metal pipes and ducts may require protection against corrosion.

Thermal insulation

Dense resin-bonded glass or mineral wool, expanded polystyrene or rubber, and cork, are suitable for both edge and base insulation. The minimum thicknesses should be of the order of $\frac{3}{4}$ in. or, for cork, 1 in. Two methods of placing edge insulation in a solid ground floor are shown in Fig. 5.1.

Damp-proof membrane

If the damp-proof membrane is laid below the base slab (Fig. 5.1*b*), it will be well separated from the heating elements; however, all drying out of the base of sub-floor must then take place upward, and ample time must be allowed for this before a floor finish susceptible to moisture can be laid. The membrane may be laid on top of the base (Fig. 5.1*a*) so that all excess construction water is sealed off from the screed; this will be essential if sufficient time for the concrete to dry out cannot be allowed. The heating cables should not be in direct contact with a bitumen or tar membrane, which would soften considerably at 120°F; moreover, if the cable were covered with p.v.c., the plasticizer in the p.v.c. might migrate into the bitumen, its loss impairing the insulation. A thin layer of concrete or mortar should therefore be provided above a bitumen or tar membrane. This precaution would not appear necessary with a synthetic-resin membrane (p. 59).

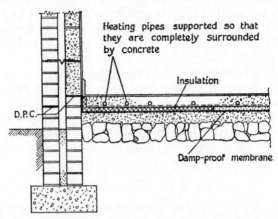

(a) Damp-proof membrane and insulation above base concrete, heating pipes in screed, with sheet or tile wearing surface

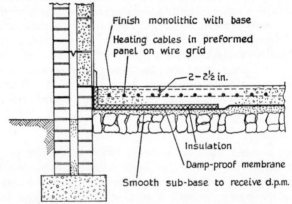

(b) Damp-proof membrane and insulation below base concrete, heating cables embedded in the concrete base, which is monolithic with the granolithic finish

FIG. 5.1

Placing of heating elements in solid ground floors, with edge insulation

Concrete screed

The tendency of thin layers of concrete to curl because of differential drying shrinkage has been discussed in Chapter 2. This tendency may be aggravated when the presence of heating elements also imposes thermal gradients across the section. Even when every precaution is taken to reduce potential shrinkage of the concrete, some movement may occur.

Curling at the edges will seriously weaken a heavy-duty concrete floor screed. It is always better for such a finish to be constructed monolithically with the base concrete, and this is particularly important if it contains heating elements (Fig. 5.1*b*). The laying of the heating elements will be greatly facilitated if they are first made up into panels of appropriate size; preformed pipe panels can readily be made and electric cables can be attached to a grid of steel wires. The heating elements may then be covered with the same mix as that for the lower part of the base, with a wearing surface not less than ½ in. thick of 1 cement : 1 fine aggregate : 2 coarse aggregate.

If it is not practicable to avoid the screed being laid on a hardened concrete base, preparation of the base will help to ensure good bond. If the screed is laid on an insulating layer or on a damp-proof membrane there can be no bond and every precaution is then needed to minimize shrinkage.

Floor finishes

As already mentioned, a heated floor with a granolithic finish should be laid monolithically. Other continuous *in situ* floor surfaces, such as terrazzo and magnesite, are not recommended for use with floor heating because of the risks of cracking. All types of tile finish—clay, concrete, terrazzo, linoleum, rubber, cork—behave satisfactorily, as do the adhesives normally used, provided that the concrete has had time to dry out properly. Residual moisture may be driven off by operating the floor-warming system for several days before the finish is laid, but this must on no account be done until the floor has had some time to dry out naturally.

Wood block and strip finishes will absorb moisture when the heating is turned off, and during a wet summer they may swell to such an extent that they are forced upwards. Only the more stable timbers should be used, and should be laid at the correct moisture content. Narrow-strip flooring is preferable to block flooring if moisture movements must be considered. A comprehensive list of the more stable timbers is given in Forest Products Research Laboratory Bulletin No. 40, 'Timber for flooring'.

Provision for movement

Precautions are needed lest heating pipes or cables are fractured by shrinkage of the screed or by displacements resulting from shrinkage or thermal movements of the structural floor or base; cables, particularly metal-sheathed cables, are much the more vulnerable in this respect. The individual circuits should be confined to the screed or floor bays. If it should be necessary to cross a joint, the cable should be looped in a layer of sand and covered with bitumen-impregnated sheet or board to prevent adhesion of the concrete. In a floor consisting of precast concrete units, the cables should run parallel to the beams if possible, and all end loops should be left free to move by laying in sand and covering as already described. If fully embedded cables must be at right-angles to the precast units, a cover to the cable that will permit some movement, e.g. p.v.c., will reduce the risk of trouble.

Corrosion

The best safeguard against corrosion of any steel components, such as tubes or ducts, is to ensure that they are completely surrounded by good, dense concrete. A steel tube in contact with, say, the insulating layer and merely covered over with concrete is liable to attack by pitting corrosion if there is dampness. Steel tubes should always rest on small concrete blocks or steel rods (*not* wooden blocks) so that they may be completely surrounded by the concrete mix. Clinker, or crushed brick containing plaster, must not be used around any metal.

Sound insulation

Where the heating elements are incorporated in a floating floor, all ducts and conduits must be above the resilient layer. If any such component touches the structural floor or the walls, the sound insulation properties of the construction will be largely nullified.

Chapter 6

ROOFS

GENERAL

THE need to provide horizontal floor and ceiling surfaces and to minimize
the effective thickness of floors, so as to avoid unnecessary and uneconomic
height in buildings (particularly in multi-storey structures), imposes on
floor construction restrictions that do not apply with roof construction, where
much greater freedom in structural form is possible. With roofs, however,
the need for weather-proofness, durability, the ability to resist the general
and local effects of wind, and the provision of adequate heat insulation,
lighting and ventilation, are considerations that may have a major influence
on the type of construction chosen.—

In a multi-storey building, the roof area is usually only a small part of
the total external surface. For such construction, and particularly for framed
structures, it is logical and economic to construct the roof in the same way as
the floors, thus using the same tradesmen, materials and equipment as are
employed in the rest of the structure. Only a minimum of specialized labour
and materials for weather-proofing, heat insulation and other treatments
is then necessary. In single-storey construction, however, the roof forms the
greater part of the total external surface of the building, and its structural
form may govern that of the rest of the structure. In some specialized forms
of construction, such as the shell, the roof may span from ground level and
so largely eliminate the need for vertical walls. The general form of the building as a whole and its function may thus be seen to have an important
bearing on the choice of type of roof structure.

FUNCTION

The roof, as a constituent and sometimes a major part of the external covering of a building, must provide an environment and facilities suited to the
intended occupancy. Its external appearance may be required to meet
certain requirements associated with surrounding structures or countryside,
either to conform with the general plan for the locality or to meet some
special requirements of the owner or occupier. The internal appearance of
the roof, where there is no suspended ceiling, may be required to give a
sense of spaciousness, or to contribute to congenial working conditions in a
factory.

The roof must have sufficient strength to carry its own weight, together
with loading resulting from accumulated snow or from the effects of wind,
without collapse or excessive distortion of the whole or any part of the
structure or cladding. Distortion is excessive if it is perceptible to occupants,
even though there may be no risk of collapse, as this may lead to lack of
confidence in the structure. Distortion is excessive also if it is sufficient to
cause damage to decorative finishes, to insulating or weather-proofing

81

layers, or to services or other installations fixed to the roof structure. Where a roof is constructed of prefabricated structural elements, these should be so designed that the individual units are sufficiently stable for handling and lifting into position, and that during assembly the partially completed structure is at no stage overloaded or likely to become permanently distorted. Allowance must also be made in design for loading resulting from the installation of services such as lighting and heating equipment and ventilation ducts, and, where appropriate, for the possible future extension of such services.

The general character of the building, and therefore of the roof structure, is much influenced by its purpose and by the degree of protection it will need to give against the weather. Where people or goods are in transit, as at railway termini or at coach stations, the building may cover a large area and be open on one or more sides; protection against rain and snow is needed and the lighting conditions must be considered, but heating, ventilating and acoustic conditions are of little or no consequence and, although the covered area may be large, the roof supports may be placed relatively close together provided that there is no interference with the flow of traffic.

Accommodation for living or for sedentary work must supply comfortable conditions of heating, lighting, ventilation and sound insulation. This, in terms of the roof construction, means the provision of adequate heat insulation in addition to protection from the weather, but usually does not pose any difficult structural problems.

Industrial and storage buildings may require heat insulation of the roof to maintain reasonably uniform temperatures, and often the planning of the use of the space and of the flow of goods or products will permit fairly close spacing of the roof supports. In some single-storey construction, as for garages and aircraft hangars or assembly shops, there is a need for roofs of large span clear of intermediate supports, and the form of the roof is then primarily dictated by structural considerations. In all single-storey industrial construction where large areas are covered, natural lighting through the roof is almost essential. For some industrial processes, such as those concerned with food production or the manufacture of inflammable or toxic products, it may be necessary to have a roof structure without horizontal ledges that could collect dust; such a requirement would influence the form of roof and ceiling chosen.

Buildings for leisure activities are of great variety and present a number of special problems affecting the form of the roof. In sports stadia and arenas, the roof must have a large span without intermediate supports, to provide an uninterrupted view of the central feature from all parts of the building. In auditoria, theatres and cinemas, consideration must also be given to the design of the roof for acoustic treatment.

The distance between points of support has a profound influence on the structural character of the roof. For economic reasons, the spans between supports should be the minimum consistent with achieving the building's main purpose. In considering the different types of roof construction, it is helpful to adopt the classification of short-span (up to 25 ft), medium-span (25-80 ft), and long-span (over 80 ft) roofs. Generally, for a particular form of construction, an increase in span leads to an increase in the cost of

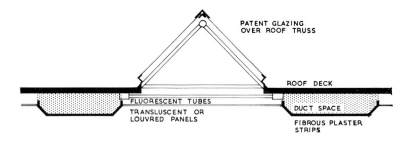

PATENT GLAZING
OVER ROOF TRUSS

ROOF DECK

FLUORESCENT TUBES

TRANSLUSCENT OR
LOUVRED PANELS

DUCT SPACE

FIBROUS PLASTER
STRIPS

MEAN LEVEL OF DRAWING BOARDS

(Photo: Architect and Building News)

*A well integrated roof-lighting arrangement for the drawing office at Northfleet
Paper Mills. The glazing is screened from view by corrugated opal plastic sheets
alternating with panels of metal louvres. Above each louvre is a fluorescent tube,
again screened from sight at low angles, the light from which reaches the working
plane directly through the louvres and also illuminates the plastic sheets. The
ceiling space between roof-lights is used for heating ducts, cased in white-painted
fibrous plaster. Architects: Farmer and Dark.*

PLATE 6.1

F★

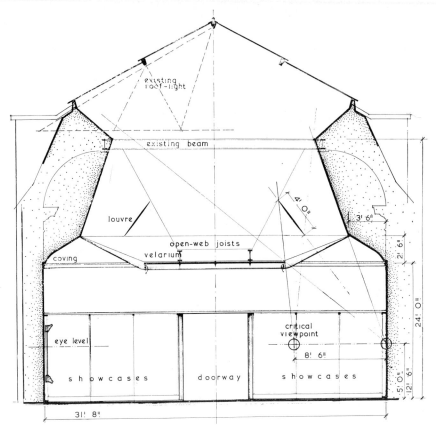

Section of reconstructions at Birmingham City Museum and Art Gallery as proposed by the Building Research Station. The existing roof-light is retained and preferential light on the pictures combined with sky-screening is achieved by the shaping of the side walls above cornice level, the translucent velarium, and the single suspended louvre above each edge of the velarium.

View of the completed gallery. Screened artificial lighting is incorporated in the edge of the velarium.

PLATE 6.2

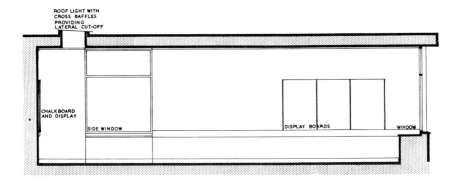

A classroom at Woodside County Junior School, Amersham. In addition to general daylighting from side-windows, a small roof-light is included with deep screening to give extra local light to the teaching and chalkboard area. The lining of the roof-light is painted light grey to prevent its appearing too bright in comparison with the white but partially shadowed ceiling. Architects: Ministry of Education, Architects and Building Branch.

PLATE 6.3

*An example of continuous horizontal roof-lighting in a small factory, as seen from
mezzanine level.   In terms of area of glazing required for a given level of light and
working plane, this arrangement is highly efficient, but the addition of some form of
cross-louvres is desirable to prevent glare.*

PLATE 6.4

the roof structure per unit area; reduction in cost on greater spans can only be achieved by changing to more complex forms of construction. As, however, the cost of the roof usually represents only a small fraction of the total cost of the building, considerable freedom in choice or type is often economically possible.

CHOICE OF ROOF STRUCTURE

For short spans, the roof in its simplest form can consist of a slab, which, besides providing for weather-proofness and other protective functions, possesses sufficient strength to fulfil its structural function. With increasing span of slab, the provision of adequate strength in design becomes increasingly important, and eventually the thickness of slab required structurally becomes uneconomic. Ribs may then be introduced to support the slab over the main span, so spaced that the depth of slab needed for adequate strength and stiffness in spanning between the ribs is also sufficient to provide the necessary protection. Over greater spans, secondary ribs can be used to span between ribs and provide support to the slab at the most economic spacing. With this form of construction, the strength of the ribs defines the spans possible; for larger spans, therefore, the depth of the rib must be increased. This leads to the use of lattice type girders, in which weight is saved by eliminating material in those regions making little contribution to strength.

Since, for the roof, there is more space available for the construction than there is for the floor, the shape of a lattice frame need not be confined to that of the parallel girder; it may take the form of the triangular truss. The structural slab is then replaced by cladding, usually of sheeting materials supported on purlins spanning between the trusses. In slab construction with solid ribs, the loading is carried through the bending resistance of the material, but in lattices and trusses the individual members are stressed directly in compression or in tension.

For larger spans, the general form of the structure must contribute to its capacity for supporting load. The arch provides an illustration of the value of form; its shape under a particular system of loading can be so chosen that it is subjected only to compressive stress throughout. It is often convenient to depart from this shape, however, and to cater for the bending moments so caused. Even greater economy in weight can be achieved by changing, from a form of construction that can be considered as acting in a single plane, to a three-dimensional form—for example by changing from an arch to a dome.

As the design of a roof is considerably influenced by its weight, the particular form chosen in any instance will be governed largely by the weight of the materials necessary to provide the required degree of protection against the weather. As already emphasized, the effect on the structure of the dead weight of cladding materials increases with span, and for long spans it may govern the type of structure selected.

SHORT-SPAN ROOFS

Most of the requirements for domestic roofing come within the category of spans of less than 25 feet. For houses the roof structure is usually of timber, which has the merits of being easily worked with simple tools and freely adaptable to meet modifications necessary for the installation of services or other individual requirements.

The common form of pitched timber roof has been developed from experience. It consists of rafters, which carry the battens and tiles or slates, supported by purlins strutted from an internal transverse loadbearing wall. This interaction of battens, rafters and struts is not amenable to calculation, and the dimensions of the various members are decided empirically with the main object of avoiding unsightly deflections under the relatively heavy cladding material. With smaller types of semi-detached or terraced houses, the rafters may be supported by purlins spanning between gable and party walls; by this means, the need for a loadbearing internal wall is dispensed with, so giving greater flexibility in planning the layout of the house. Similar freedom of layout can be obtained by using timber trusses to replace the purlins.

The pitch for roofs clad with tiles or slates is determined primarily by the requirements of weather-proofness. The weight of these cladding materials is sufficient to ensure that damage from wind due to internal pressure on the leeward side of the roof is unlikely under normal conditions of exposure.

With the development of cladding materials that may be used with a much lower pitch and are generally much lighter in weight, it is possible to avoid the large, almost unused, roof space of the traditional house. With such lightweight roofs, however, consideration of uplift due to wind loading is important, not only in the design of the method of fixing the cladding but also in the anchoring of the roof structure to the walls. For houses, this structure often consists of a series of main ribs bearing on the walls and supporting transverse secondary ribs, which in turn support a timber sub-roof with a skin-cladding. If the pitch for the roof can be small, it may be convenient to adopt a mono-pitch form for simplicity of construction.

With impermeable cladding materials there arise problems of avoiding condensation in the roof structure, unless deliberate provision is made for the ventilation that occurs fortuitously with tiles and slates.

So far mention has been made only of timber as a structural material for roofs. Others are steel, aluminium and concrete. None of these is common in house construction, although during periods of timber shortage they have all been used for roof trusses of small span. The economic spans for trusses of these materials are greater, however, than those common in house construction. Moreover, they are not as adaptable on site as timber is, and so are less welcome to most house builders. The characteristics of roof trusses are therefore more conveniently considered in dealing with roofs of medium or large span.

For multi-storey blocks of offices or flats, or for other multi-storey buildings in which each floor level has a similar occupancy, the individual spans between supports for the roof will be the same as those for the floors, and will often fall within the short-span category. The construction of roofs for these buildings is likely, for economic reasons, to be of the same form as that of the floors, so that the same labour, equipment and materials can be employed as in the rest of the structure. From aesthetic considerations, and in the interest of the occupier, this may not be the most satisfactory form of roof, and a more imaginative design might not be unduly costly. Where different storeys have different occupancies, as in some industrial buildings, the form of roof structure may need to be different from that of the floor to fulfil its main function. Daylighting requirements might, for example, favour some form of trussed steel roof in a building with reinforced concrete floors. It might also be desirable to introduce greater spans for the roof than for the floors, to accommodate, on the top floor, processes that require uninterrupted space.

Where the construction of the roof is of the same general character as that of the floor, the considerations governing its design closely follow those governing the design of floors, though the protective role of the roof must be taken into account. Most other types of roof suitable for short spans which might be used for multi-storey buildings are of more general application within the category of medium-span roofs and are discussed below. A few single-storey industrial buildings also have roofs of shorter span than 25 ft., but these also are best examined within their more normal range of use in the medium-span category.

MEDIUM-SPAN ROOFS

Roofs with spans between supports of 25–80 ft cover a large variety of single- and multi-storey structures, and include those for many industrial buildings, warehouses, transit buildings and small assembly halls such as school class-rooms. For smaller spans in the range, concrete beam-and-slab construction may still be economically feasible, particularly if prestressing is used. It is trusses, lattice girders and portal frames, however, that have particular application within this range of span. With these, the cladding (including insulating materials) may be supported directly, or indirectly with purlins; the decision whether a roof is to be pitched or flat may be influenced by the type of cladding, the daylighting requirements, the need for accessibility, and aesthetic values, rather than by structural considerations.

For beam-and-slab construction in concrete, the roof may be cast *in situ* or it may consist of beams cast *in situ* with some form of partially precast deck construction of proprietary manufacture. Within this range of span, the economy in weight offered by prestressing as compared with ordinary reinforced concrete may be particularly advantageous. If the roof consists of a large number of similar bays, it may be economical and practicable to precast the beams and slabs; where there is no precasting factory in the vicinity, site production of the units can be considered or alternatively the larger units may be made in short elements for ease of transport and assembled on the site by prestressing. The use of such prestressed concrete units, which are relatively robust, can lead to very rapid rates of construction, and structural continuity (permitting reduction in the weight and size of the main beams) may be achieved by prestressing after erection.

Materials

In the fabrication of trusses, lattice girders and portal frames, structural steel sections have been used for so long, and have proved so reliable, that their use has become almost traditional. Concrete and other materials, however, are now strong competitors.

Structural steel in the form of hot-rolled standard sections has been widely used for over 70 years. The sections (joist, channel or angle) are formed, on the site, into structural units, which are then assembled in the complete structure by bolting. More recently, welding has been introduced for making the connections; this produces a cleaner and lighter form of construction, but the saving in material may be largely offset by the higher cost of fabrication. For light roofs such as those on open sheds, the hot-rolled joist section may be cut longitudinally through the web to a castellated pattern and rejoined by welding to form a deeper section with a perforated web (Fig. 6.1). These castellated beams have greater strength and stiffness than the original beams, and are therefore more suited to longer spans.

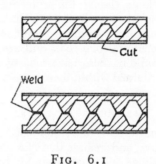

FIG. 6.1

Castellated beam, made by cutting
web of rolled joist and rewelding

The use of welding as a means of structural fabrication has led to the use of steel tube for roof construction. Generally the quality of the steel is the same as that for hot-rolled sections, and the tubular form has several advantages; with the ends sealed against corrosion, the external area that requires painting is smaller than for rolled sections of similar strength, and the tubular form provides greater resistance to buckling. Tubular frames are neat in appearance and have no ledges to collect dirt (with the further advantage that corrosion is less likely to be initiated). Savings in weight of up to 40 per cent, by comparison with the use of hot-rolled steel sections, are possible, and, although the cost of connections is high, there is generally also some net saving in cost. With the likely future development of tubes of approximately square section, connections may be simplified, with a further saving in cost.

In recent years, cold-formed sections fabricated from steel strip or sheet have been used increasingly in a wide range of structures, particularly in the automobile and railway industries. For building frameworks, the sections, which are usually angles, plain channels or inwardly lipped channels, are cold-rolled from strip. This is usually between 16 swg ($\frac{1}{16}$ in.) and 8 swg ($\frac{5}{32}$ in.) in thickness and can have a width of up to 18 in. or more. Being of thinner material than hot-rolled sections, the cold-formed sections have a greater stiffness for the same weight of steel, but their surface area is much greater and protection against corrosion is a major problem. Although high-tensile corrosion-resistant steels are being used in other industries, these have not yet been adopted for building construction, where either coating with non-ferrous metal and protective paint, or phosphate treatment followed by a rust-inhibitive primer and painting, is needed, according to the corrosion risk (*see* p. 12). For roof structures of cold-formed sections, fabrication is usually carried out by welding, and either welded or bolted joints are used for site assembly. For these sections to be competitive with other materials in roof construction, standardization of design is essential.

As a result of developments in the aircraft industry, a range of aluminium alloys is available in various forms of extruded section. For heat-treated alloys, fabrication by welding leads to a reduction in strength at connections and therefore riveting and bolting are more usual. However, it is possible to extrude more complex forms of section than can be produced by rolling, so that fewer connections are needed. Aluminium alloys are generally regarded as being corrosion-resistant, but they show some deterioration in appearance under normal conditions of exposure and some care is necessary in their use with other building materials. Protection with paint at points of contact with other metals and with packing compounds in crevices at joints is needed, as otherwise corrosion products can build up sufficiently to cause structural distortion.

Concrete is commonly employed as a structural framing material for roofs. In its earlier uses, it was normally reinforced with mild steel, but more recently cold-worked steels with higher tensile strength have been used; these do not reduce the weight of construction appreciably, but they offer a saving in weight of steel up to 30 per cent. Assembly of structures made up of precast reinforced concrete members presents some difficulty, as the usual forms of connection cannot be relied upon to transmit moment. Joints are therefore made near points of contraflexure where moments are small. The advent of prestressing has provided a solution of the problem for structures of medium and long span, where assembly is carried out by post-tensioning longitudinal cables which cross the joint and subject it to compression; the joint is then capable of carrying almost as high a moment as it would if the member were continuous. This development makes possible the use of slender trusses and girders, giving an appearance that at one time was associated only with structural steelwork. It enables small structural elements to be cast in concrete under factory conditions and assembled on site as easily as steelwork.

Structural concrete has one major characteristic distinguishing it from all other materials used in roof structures; it is the only material that can be made in position. It therefore confers on the designer a freedom in choice of shape which is governed only by limitations of formwork and of design procedures. The shell roof consisting mainly of a thin concrete membrane with single or double curvature exemplifies one logical and imaginative use of concrete, which usually has applications for spans greater than 80 feet.

Recent developments of adhesives in the plywood industry have increased the range of application of timber as a structural material in roofs. The strength of timber is variable and structural members made from single pieces may contain faults and local weaknesses. These local weaknesses can be overcome by building structural members up of laminated pieces glued together, thus reducing the risk of a fault occurring throughout the full thickness of the member. Used in this way, very light frameworks can be built which, if suitably treated, have adequate durability with little need for maintenance.

Structure

Roofs can be generally classified as either pitched or flat. Roofs with a slope greater than 10° are conventionally described as pitched, and those with a slope of 10° or less as flat (*see* p. 94). The symmetrically pitched roof is the most common form and, when trusses are used, is generally regarded as the cheapest method for covering a working area (except perhaps in multi-storey construction, as noted on p. 81). Requirements for adequate daylighting, heating and ventilation may have an important influence on the shape. Consideration of daylighting has led to the use of the asymmetrically pitched or 'saw-tooth' roof with one slope nearly vertical and glazed. The asymmetrical form is structurally inefficient and consequently is more costly than the symmetrical form. The flat roof, which may be supported by lattice girders or portal frames, avoids the enclosure of the triangular space in the pitched roof; from one point of view, it may be considered more efficient, as this space must be heated and, having a larger surface area, tends to lose more heat. To provide adequate daylighting and ventilation, portions of a flat roof may be raised to form monitors, the vertical or near-vertical sides of which are glazed. As a result, the monitor has become a recognized form of roof outline.

The symmetrically pitched roof (including the symmetrically curved roof), the asymmetrically pitched roof, the flat and the monitor roof can all have a structural framework consisting of triangulated trusses or lattice girders, or of portal frames which may have a solid or lattice web (Fig. 6.2). The trusses

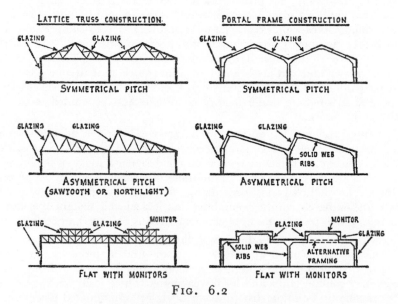

FIG. 6.2

Roof outlines and framing methods

and lattice girders are built up of a number of structural elements, stressed either in direct tension or compression; these present obstacles to natural lighting and give a spidery appearance which may be aesthetically undesirable and suggests a wastage of space, and for some occupancies a suspended ceiling may be used to hide the structure. Portal framing gives cleaner lines, and, for pitched roofs, provides storage space and freedom of movement above eaves level. Although portal frames are more costly initially than trusses and lattice girders, painting is simpler and maintenance cost may be smaller. The design of the portal frame, unlike that of the simplest forms of truss and lattice girder, is affected by the column height, as the columns and roof structures are integrally connected. This gives scope for the introduction of 'plastic' methods of design, which, by comparison with elastic methods, can reduce the weight of steel in a portal frame by amounts of up to 25 per cent. By plastic design methods, the cost of portal frames can be reduced and brought closer to that for trusses and lattice girders.

The pitched truss consists, basically, of interconnected rafters with a horizontal tie at the eaves and some internal bracing. Over the larger spans, its height may become excessive and the roof may then be broken up into what is in effect a series of trusses supported by transverse lattice girders, which are accommodated within the truss to give an 'umbrella' form of construction. Lattice girders may also be used for flat roofs, with additional sraming for monitors if required; they are generally more economical than folid-web girders, and services may be housed within their depth. Usually the structures are of steel; within the medium-span range, aluminium alloys are not likely to save sufficient weight to be economic, and are not used unless greater corrosion-resistance is particularly required. Concrete is not normally economic for small trusses or lattice girders, but slender pre-stressed concrete beams have been used instead of steel lattice girders to support steel roof trusses; for longer spans, concrete lattice girders assembled by prestressing together a series of precast elements may offer an economic form for roof construction provided that standarization can be adopted extensively. For steel construction with hot-rolled sections, welding can give an overall saving in materials as compared with riveting, by eliminating gussets and cleats (which also gives a neater appearance); there may be no saving in cost, however, and indeed cost may be increased. Tubular steel members are more efficient structurally and collect less dirt than hot-rolled sections, and their use for this type of construction can lead to economies in materials and in cost. Cold-formed sections may have some advantages where standardization is possible, and when structures are particularly light and the smallest available size of hot-rolled section is greater than is required structurally.

The portal frame consists essentially of a continuous member conforming to the outline of the roof and connected to vertical columns. Series of individual portal frames or of inter-connected portal frames may be used to roof large areas. Portal frames of steel are usually built up by welding to form a continuous member of I-section, which may have a solid or lattice web. For heavy loading, the frame is usually fabricated from hot-rolled sections and plate; for lighter loading, the frame may be of hot-rolled angle or channel, of tubular sections, or of cold-rolled sections with lattice webs. Most of the frame connections are welded before reaching the site, and, while further assembly by welding is possible on the ground, it is often considered that the final connections after erection should be bolted. Aluminium alloys may be used but, as for trusses and lattice girders, their advantages may be most apparent when the environment is corrosive. Concrete frames, either reinforced or prestressed, have wide application and, where fire resistance is a requirement, have economic advantages over all other materials. Where large numbers of similar frames are needed and standardization is possible, precasting can lead to very rapid construction on the site. If precasting is not feasible, then casting the concrete *in situ* will reduce the rate of construction much below that for steelwork. Laminated timber portal frames have been built successfully, but as yet their design and construction is a highly specialized procedure, outside the experience of those normally concerned with structural design.

Concrete shell structures are sometimes used for spans within the medium range, but their most economic application would seem to be in the range of long spans.

LONG-SPAN ROOFS

As the spans for roofs increase beyond 80 feet, there is increasing scope for the use of highly specialized forms of construction, showing major departures from those used for medium spans.

Lattice girders and trusses with curved top booms are common forms of triangulated structure with spans of up to 200 feet or more. Portal frames of these spans, whether of pitched or rectangular form, are also normally of lattice construction. While steel in the form of hot-rolled sections or tubes is the most commonly used material, light alloys or timber may be structurally and economically advantageous, particularly for spans greater than 200 ft. By means of prestressing, concrete can also be used for long-span roofs, even though, by comparison with other materials, the weight of construction is high.

An important characteristic of prestressing, which enables concrete lattice girders, hollow box sections and slender flanged beams to be used for long spans, is that the stresses in the structure can be modified during construction, by prestressing cables at different stages. As the dead load increases with the progress of construction, the precompression in the concrete, imposed by stressing some of the cables, is reduced; by stressing further cables, the precompression can be reimposed, so off-setting very largely the dead-load stresses in the structure. In effect, therefore, the structure itself with the aid of some of the cables carries the live load, while the remainder of the cables support the dead load.

This use of prestressing for counteracting dead-load stresses need not be confined to concrete construction. Practical proposals, supported by the results of laboratory trials, have been made for prestressing long-span steel structures. High-tensile steel is employed for prestressing, and its use in this way represents a logical modification of the principles of carrying load over large spans, as in the suspension bridge, by suspended cables or chains of high-tensile material. Prestressing of materials other than concrete provides some difficulties in protecting the cables from corrosion; in concrete, protection is relatively easily provided by grouting and a similar approach might be adopted for other forms of construction, by enclosing the cables in tubes suitable for the dual role of allowing grout injection and providing structural strength.

The use of suspended cables or chains for carrying roofing over large spans, which is referred to above, is a form of construction in which the main structural member is in tension. Even when the cables or chains are used to support a stiffening girder carrying the cladding, this form of construction often lacks rigidity, and the towers required to support the cables tend to give a cumbersome appearance and call for frequent inspection and maintenance. Apart from exhibition structures, therefore, this form of construction would seem to have few applications that could not better be fulfilled by prestressing.

Arches, on the other hand, in which the main structural member is primarily in compression, have important applications for roofs of long span. Such structures consist essentially of a series of arch ribs, with cladding which may be of the same material as the arch. Having a relatively high compression strength, concrete reinforced with mild or cold-worked steels is commonly used, with thin concrete slabs spanning between the arches. It is not usually advantageous to prestress the arch ribs, unless the loading and the form of the arch result in high bending moments, or unless the ribs are precast and subjected to high erection stresses. Slabs between the ribs may however be prestressed with advantage, to reduce weight; they may also be designed with openings to admit daylight.

So far, only those structural forms have been considered in which the roof loads are transmitted to its supports by members acting in a single plane (i.e. in two dimensions). For some of the largest spans, loads must be carried by structures acting in three dimensions. These structures may consist of lattice frameworks spanning between supports in both longitudinal and lateral directions, or of shaped structures such as concrete shell roofs, folded-plate roofs or other roofs of similar outline but consisting of lattice-work with a skin cladding. The constructional depth for the former type of roof can usually be sufficient to provide an economic form of construction using hot-rolled sections or tubes of steel, light alloys, concrete or timber, while the latter types, which may use the same materials, give the cleaner appearance and greater freedom from internal obstruction.

FACILITY OF CONSTRUCTION

Constructional procedure and its requirements may have some bearing on the choice of structure. In the progress of the different materials from their natural sources to their final positions in the roof, they are transported, processed and erected, bringing into use a wide variety of mechanical plant and tradesmen's skills. The raw materials may be available in only a limited number of localities, and much of the plant and labour for the preliminary treatment of the materials may also be located in these areas. Further treatment may need further movement to specialized industries. Finally, the materials arrive at the construction site: for some roofs, such as those of structural steelwork, the framework reaches the site with only a few bolted connections to be made before fixing the cladding; for others such as concrete cast *in situ*, the aggregates come direct from their natural sources, with a minimum of processing, for mixing with cement at the site. Often there may be little choice of where various processes should be carried out, but, where there is some choice possible in the location of treatments or in the order in which they can take place, some thought may lead to economy in the construction.

Of all materials used in construction, concrete probably offers the greatest variety of procedures for roof construction. Concrete may be cast in its final position. This involves the erection of formwork at a level appreciably above the ground or the nearest working platform, provided possibly by the floor below; the concrete must then be mixed, transported and placed in the moulds, and a further period must elapse before all the formwork can be finally removed. As an alternative, the concrete can be cast at ground level, so avoiding staging and excessive lifting of materials until the concrete is sufficiently hard for the whole roof to be lifted simultaneously. This is achieved in the 'lift-slab' method of construction, where the roof and floor slabs are cast in layers on the ground and later are jacked up the columns for fixing in their final position. For complex forms of concrete roof, the erection of formwork at ground level may simplify construction very considerably; it may also permit the installation of heating, lighting and other services, and interior decorations before the roof is lifted to its final position, so that subsequently scaffolding and the inconvenience of working from staging can be avoided. A further alternative is the extensive employment of precasting techniques in the factory, where workmanship can be well supervised, work is not stopped by bad weather and ample space is available for storage; this may increase the rate of construction possible, particularly for restricted sites. With the increasing use of mechanical plant on building sites, it should be possible to increase the size of individual precast concrete elements, and, by prestressing, many of the problems of jointing during erection may be overcome.

While the flexibility in methods of construction using concrete may not hold for other materials, the possibilities of further prefabrication and pre-assembly of services fixed to the roof structure may be worthy of consideration generally.

STRENGTH AND STABILITY

Design roof loads

In considering the strength and stability of roof structures, the loadings to be used in design are the dead loads, the imposed loads, and loads arising from the effects of wind.

Dead loads. These comprise the self-weight of the roof structure, the roof covering, and any insulating lining or ceiling that may be provided. It is usual also to include as dead loads the weights, where they are known at the design stage, of all permanent construction associated with the provision of such services as storage tanks and their contents, lighting, ventilating and heating, together with gangways accommodated in certain types of roof to afford access to these services. A comparison of the weight per unit area of some different forms of roof covering is given in Table 6.1.

TABLE 6.1

Weight per unit area of roof coverings

Type of roof	Cladding material and construction	Approximate centres of supports for covering (ft)	Weight per sq. ft (lb)
Pitched roofs	Asbestos slates	(on battens)	3–4
	Shingles		1·5
	Slating		7–14
	Tiling		10–18
	Glazing (¼-in. wired glass on bars) . . .	8–11	6·0
	Corrugated (protected) steel sheet, 22 swg . .	6½	2·8
	with ½-in. insulating board. . . .	6½	3·8
	Asbestos-cement corrugated sheeting . . .	3–4½	3·1–3·5
	with underlining sheet	4½	5·8
	with underlining sheet and 1-in. glass fibre . .	4½	6·2
	Corrugated aluminium, 18 swg	9	1·0
	22 swg	5½	0·7
	Corrugated plastic sheeting	6	1·2
Pitched or flat roofs	Steel decking (20 swg), depth 1¾ in. . . .	10	4·4
	with insulating board and felts	10	8·0
	Asbestos-cement troughing, depth 3½ in. . . .	6½	4·6
	with a-c lining sheet	6½	6·9
	with a-c lining sheet and 1-in. glass fibre . .	6½	7·2
	Insulated and weathered aluminium decking, 20 swg		
	depth 1 in.	4½	3·0
	depth 2½ in.	7	3·2
	Woodwool (reinforced), depth 2 in., with ¾-in. screed and felting	7	12.0
Flat or near-flat roofs	Aluminium ridged sheeting with insulating quilt .	2	1·0
	Resin-bonded plywood and joist panels with bituminous felt	12	7
	Concrete (including reinforced and prestressed precast units)	12–30	30–60

Imposed loads. The imposed loads in relation to roofs include an allowance for the weight of snow, for possible concentrations of load in the roof structure, and for foot traffic in the roof and on roof coverings.

The British Standard Code of Practice CP3 (Chapter V) distinguishes, for the purpose of snow loading, between flat roofs, including roofs with a slope not greater than 10°, and roofs with a slope greater than 10°. The former must be designed to take an imposed load of 30 lb/sq. ft where access to the roof has been provided in addition to that necessary for maintenance, i.e., where the roof is open for resort; with the provisos that the design imposed load on roof slabs or coverings per foot width, uniformly distributed, is not less than 240 lb, and the design imposed load on roof beams, uniformly distributed, is not less than 1920 lb. If there is no access to these roofs other than that necessary for maintenance, an imposed load of 15 lb/sq. ft must be used in design. These loadings are intended to include an allowance for loose snow up to two feet in depth.

The loading of 15 lb/sq. ft (measured on plan) also applies to pitched roofs of slope between 10° and 30°. For a slope of 75° or more, no allowance for snow is necessary, a proportional allowance being made for intermediate slopes.

For most localities in Britain, the weight of any likely accumulation of snow is amply covered by the arbitrary imposed loads quoted above. On a flat roof of considerable area in a severely exposed situation, however, snow may drift and lodge against a parapet, or it may accumulate in a long valley between two roof slopes. In both cases it is important that gutters should be covered by snow boards so that water from rain or melted snow shall not be prevented by the accumulated snow from reaching the down-pipes.

As regards roof coverings, Code CP 3 (Ch. V) specifies an imposed load for the covering to allow for loads incidental to maintenance. Thus all coverings (other than glass) at a slope of less than 45° must be capable of carrying a load of 200 lb concentrated on any area 5 in. square at normal stresses (these stresses being those commonly adopted for other design loads for the covering material in question).

The imposed roof loads described above can be regarded as reasonable for most conditions and types of roof, but the designer may often have to consider cases where provision for special loads may be necessary. For example, roofs of spectator stands in sports grounds, if accessible, may be used as vantage points, and special values of imposed load greater than 30 lb/sq. ft should be used.

Special imposed loads (hung loads). A special type of load imposed on roofs of buildings other than domestic dwellings is that of plant or other equipment hung from the roof structure. Clearly, where such loading was never envisaged at the design stage, as for a light economical roof designed just to take specified loads, the builder, specialist contractors, or the occupier must not be allowed to hang weighty objects on it without first investigating their possible effects. On the other hand, it would be extravagant with many buildings to provide a roof structure so strong as to leave no doubt that it could carry any internal load at any position. However, it is becoming more and more apparent in the wide field of factory construction that lack of foresight in this respect at the design stage can seriously limit the usefulness and adaptability of single-storey factories; in multi-storey factory design, short comings of this sort can be even more embarrassing.

There is not at present any standard classification to help designers to make an allowance for the kind of service loads that may be hung from factory roofs, but some guidance is offered in Factory Building Study No. 4, 'Structural loading in factories' (H.M.S.O., 1960). Suspended tools, such as welders and power drills, with their counterweights, are now common in some types of industry, and there is a general trend to increase the amount and variety of overhead plant. Often tools are scattered; as distributed loads they might average only 1–2 lb/sq. ft, but as individual point loads they may be more significant. If they are likely to be clustered, the loadings obviously can become much larger, and in addition a special sub-frame system is usually needed which may be quite heavy in itself. Overhead conveyors, whether of chain or runway type, carry loads in suspended trolleys. The weights, if taken as distributed loads, range from about 3 to 30 lb/sq. ft, the higher value being for very heavy equipment in fairly closely spaced lines.

If there is much disparity in the weight of plant, and if freedom is wanted for future alterations, the management must describe to the designer the likely order of weights of exceptionally heavy items. The designer can then arrange for roof trusses to carry loads hung from panel points; loads of $\frac{1}{2}$ to 1 ton at panel points are not uncommon, but it may be necessary when coping with heavy equipment to provide for loads considerably greater than this.

Wind loads. In addition to resisting the dead load, the roof must be designed to counter the effects of wind, whether considered separately or in conjunction with the imposed loads described above. Some general information on wind loading on buildings has been given in Volume 1, Chapter 1, where it was explained that Code CP 3 (Ch. V) tabulates the basic wind pressure p to be used in design. These basic pressures are related to the height of the roof (taken to be half-way between eaves and ridge levels of pitched roofs) above general ground level, and are coupled with four degrees of exposure relevant to different localities in Britain. For the purpose of deciding the exposure grading, the maximum value of the mean wind velocity over a period of 1 minute (at a height of 40 ft) is taken to be the normal wind velocity for the particular locality.

It might be mentioned here that meteorological records are usually in terms of the one-hour mean velocity or of maximum gusts. It is usually sufficient to assume that the Code one-minute mean velocity is 10 mph more than the one-hour mean velocity.

On most coasts the wind velocity decreases markedly with distance from the sea. All the coasts of the British Isles are strongly exposed to winds, although the winds experienced on the east coast are on the whole less than on the west. The highest mean hourly wind velocity, likely to be exceeded only once in 50 years, is around 50 mph in southern England, about 60 mph on eastern coasts, and 70 mph or more over much of the western coasts. The corresponding highest gust velocities (Fig. 6.3) give a rather similar picture. The maximum gust to be expected is around 90 mph in southern England, 100 mph or more along most coasts, and up to 120 mph in the Western Isles. All these values apply to well exposed sites, with recorders 33 ft above ground.

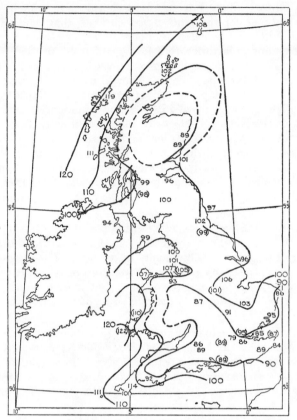

Fig. 6.3

*Highest gust speed (m.p.h.) at 33 ft likely to be exceeded
only once in 50 years (values based on less than 15 years of
record bracketed)*

The wind at any place depends also on the type of country. In hilly country the wind may vary greatly over short distances. There is a tendency for the air flow to be channelled along valleys, irrespective of the direction of the wind in the free air. Locally, these valley winds may be exceptionally severe with particular wind directions. When wind encounters a hill it is forced to rise and the stream-lines of the air flow are brought together; there is in consequence a region of high wind velocity near the brow of the hill. This effect is most prominent over steep-sided hills facing into the wind, but may be important even with quite gentle hills in relatively flat country.

It will be clear that, owing to the importance of local topographical features, the four exposure gradings of Code CP 3 (Ch. V), based on geographical location, should be used only as a rough guide, and designers must obtain more information about the particular site before deciding on the wind velocity to be assumed. The local authority concerned with the control of building will usually decide the appropriate value on the basis of experience and records of previous high winds. They in turn may obtain advice from meteorological authorities.

It might be noted here that buildings themselves affect the flow of the wind. Under some conditions a sheltering effect may be noticed for a distance down-wind of several times the height of the building. In the immediate vicinity of a building, however, especially around the edge of the roof, the wind velocity may be appreciably greater than in the free air, just as it is over a hill. In general, the wind will be greatly slowed down in a town, although in places there may be appreciable channelling of the wind, as in a valley. It is uncertain whether these channelling effects can give rise to wind velocities high enough to cause damage during an otherwise normal wind, but it has been found that the distribution of damage during gales may be markedly affected by the layout of roads and buildings.

The main effect of wind on a roof takes the form of an external pressure normal to the surface of the roof. In Code CP 3 (Ch. V) the term 'pressure' is used in a general sense, a negative sign being used to indicate suction. Thus Fig. 6.4 indicates the external wind effects on various shapes of roof, expressed as fractions of the basic pressure p (lb per sq.ft). But, in addition, air flow through the cladding of the building and through openings in the cladding can build up an internal pressure acting perpendicularly to the underside of the roof surface.

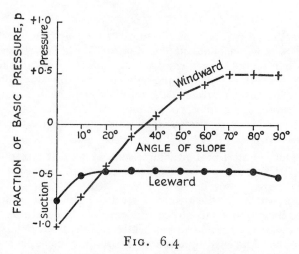

F I G . 6.4

Wind pressures for various roof slopes, as a fraction of basic pressure, p

Generally, the designer is concerned with buildings where the cladding permits the flow of air into, or out of, the building, but where there are no large openings. Such buildings may be described as being of 'normal permeability', and the internal pressure recommended in the B.S. Code for them is $0.2p$, acting perpendicularly to the roof surface. This value will be positive or negative depending on the direction of the wind and on the disposition of the openings. If the openings are mainly on the windward side the wind will blow in through them, creating a positive internal *pressure*. If the openings are mainly on sides other than the windward side, the wind will tend to draw air out of the house, creating an internal *suction* (negative pressure). Hence, for normal conditions of permeability, the internal pressure may be expressed as $\pm 0 \cdot 2p$.

Where the openings on one side of a building are large compared with those elsewhere (as, for example, in hangars), the internal pressures may be as much as $\pm 0 \cdot 5p$, depending on the direction of the wind. If one side of a building is completely open, these same pressures are applicable, but Code CP 3 (Ch. V) gives no guidance as to the pressures on roofs of buildings with no walls at all.

The wind pressures discussed so far are the average pressures acting over large areas of the roof. Pressures much higher than these often occur locally; also, high pressures can occur near the edges of the roof owing to local eddies set up where the wind first strikes the roof. These local wind effects are important as regards the roof covering and its fastenings, and the allowance made for them in the Code is, in effect, an increase of $0 \cdot 1p$ on the *total* design pressure for the main roof structure. Also, to allow for the more serious effects of wind near the edges of the roof, it is recommended that fastenings for the roof sheeting be designed to resist a suction of $2p$ when they are within a distance of 15 per cent of the span from the eaves, and 15 per cent of the length from the gables (*see also* p. 124).

Strength

The strength of a roof is its ability to carry the worst combination of the design loads with an adequate margin of safety against failure by over-stress. The design of a roof of normal construction on a stress basis, using working loads given in codes or byelaws, presents no great difficulty, although the designer has to consider carefully the effect of wind, which may lead to a reversal of stress in the members of the roof structure. It is common practice to allow increased working stresses when wind effects are considered, so long as the increase is wholly due to wind.

Certain types of steel roof structure, such as welded horizontal portals and ridge-type portals, can be considered as being 'fully rigid' structures and can be designed according to the plastic theory. With this method, a not inconsiderable saving in the weight of steel is possible as compared with older elastic design methods, but the designer has to ensure that adequate support is provided to prevent lateral bending of relatively slender members of a roof structure designed by this new theory. Roof covering connected to the structure either directly or through purlins is usually considered adequate in this respect.

Stability

The stability of the roof is its ability, by virtue of its self-weight alone or with anchorages or fastenings, to counter the uplift effects of wind. With roofs of traditional design and material, stability rarely calls for special anchorages. But the considerable wind suction that may occur on some forms of roof makes it incumbent upon the designer to investigate the possible need for anchorages to give a margin of safety against the roof as a whole being detached from the rest of the building.

The margin of safety to be used in designing roofs to resist uplift or over-turning is not stated in any British code or byelaw. British Standard 449, for the design of steel-framed buildings, specifies that the stability moment of any structure be at least $1 \cdot 5$ times the overturning moment due to wind and other forces. It is usually assumed that gusts of wind, lasting only a few seconds, will be of little importance in their overall effect on whole buildings, since a gust affects only part of a large building and the increased local pressure may be out-balanced by a momentary reduction in pressures elsewhere, and, furthermore, the inertia of the building will reduce the effect of short-period gusts. However, since roofs are more responsive to the effect of wind than the building as a whole, a higher margin would seem desirable. For small house roofs, for example, it would be reasonable to ask for a stability factor of at least 3. This is twice the value called for in respect of a steel building as a whole; these factors are related to the wind effects deduced from the maximum value of the mean velocity used in Code CP 3 (Ch. V), and the factor of 3 for roofs corresponds roughly to a factor of $1 \cdot 5$ in relation to the effect of the maximum likely wind velocity of a 10-second gust.

DIMENSIONAL STABILITY

It is necessary to limit the deformations of various types of roof made with different materials and under different conditions, mainly because large deformations may be the cause of serious damage in the roof itself or in the supporting structure, as well as in adjacent buildings. However, in this respect, the comfort of the users or the occupancy of the building need not be regarded as such an important factor as with floor structures, since roofs generally serve as a mere protective lid to buildings; the occupants are seldom, if ever, in physical contact with the roof.

Roof structures must obviously fulfil two main functions—protective and structural. To fulfil these primary functions, the weight of the protective cover and other outside forces must be resisted by a supporting structure with an adequate margin of safety against excessive deformation or collapse.

With some methods of construction the supporting structure itself is in the form of a continuous slab or shell; this alone will give a measure of protection and insulation, but additional weather-proofing and thermal insulation are commonly needed.

With other methods of construction the supporting structure is discon-tinuous—a framework of beams or trusses—and the protective roof cover is a separate membrane which does not contribute materially, if at all, to the loadbearing capacity or to the stiffness of the structure. In such roof systems the loadbearing structure must support and anchor the protective sheeting and insulating layers. The continuous cover may be rigid, for example where precast lightweight concrete slabs or timber boarding are used as a deck (*see* p. 122); it may be fairly flexible (for example, corrugated metal or asbestos-cement sheeting); or it may consist of a large number of relatively small separate elements, such as tiles. Neither tiles nor flexible sheeting can be expected to contribute to the strength or to the stiffness of the roof structure.

The effect of large deformations or discontinuities that may occur in a roof structure will depend to a considerable extent on the type of construction and on the materials of which it is made. These factors must be considered in designing buildings, since excessive deformation may lead to costly failures, for instance cracking of the plaster of ceilings or walls, and more serious structural deterioration may occur where the movements of the roof are restrained by its own supporting structure or by adjacent buildings.

The most important factors that may cause deformation are:

thermal movements;

the reversible and irreversible movements due to drying shrinkage, moisture movement, or creep, in roof systems containing concrete or reinforced concrete members;

elastic deflection, due to the self-weight of the roof system and applied loading;

ageing, which may lead to brittleness in certain types of material and cause fracture under even relatively small loads or deformations.

Thermal expansion and contraction

Sudden and extreme changes in temperature and humidity are unlikely to occur in the interior of most buildings; thermal and moisture changes affecting the floors in buildings are therefore unlikely to cause excessive deformations or stresses. For roofs, conditions tend to be much more severe. The interior parts of the roof are normally in a condition of long-term thermal and moisture equilibrium, but the outside is exposed to a combination of natural agencies—solar radiation, rain, snow and wind—each of which has important and immediate thermal effects. The exterior surfaces of a roof are therefore continuously subjected to thermal changes, which tend to be both rapid and of considerable magnitude.

In a rigid roof system, thermal movements are apt to be particularly destructive because—through its very rigidity—such a roof will deform the building it serves as well as adjacent buildings with which it may be in contact. Some examples were described in Volume 1, pp. 22–27.

In such roof systems, the effect of thermal changes depends largely on the rate at which they occur. Where the component parts of a building are heated or cooled at a uniform and slow rate, the structure can generally accommodate itself through gradual movements at the joints or through creep; such changes of temperature (for instance, those brought about by seasonal variations) rarely, if ever, cause trouble. With a more rapid rise or fall of temperature, however, there will be relatively sudden movement, which may cause damage; and differential movements, which do more harm than those of the building as a whole, are also more likely: there may be a time-lag in the response of different parts of a building to a change of weather because they are differently exposed, and they will respond at different rates to the same change of temperature, in accordance with their different heat capacities. A rapid change in temperature also allows less time for the structure to accommodate differential movement due to differences between the coefficients of thermal expansion of different building materials.

An even more complex and potentially dangerous situation will arise where different component parts of a building are heated at a different rate and to different temperatures; these differential temperature variations will lead to stresses which may become very high, particularly when changes take place rapidly. During a run of hot summer days, a rigid roof slab will be subjected to a rapid swing in temperature, between a maximum temperature at noon and a minimum at night, leading to daily repetitions of high differential deformations in the roof and the walls, as well as to stresses within the roof itself due to uneven temperature distribution within it. It is easy to see that structural damage is more liable to occur where a rigid roof covering is exposed to the sun's rays than where a roof covering is relatively flexible; the latter cannot exert an appreciable force on its own supporting structure or on the walls, since it can deform by buckling or bending.

The damaging consequences of thermal movements in rigid roof structures are due mainly to the restraint imposed upon them by the surrounding walls or frame which support them. One obvious way in which damage can be avoided is to eliminate these restraints by providing sliding joints between walls and roof, or by dividing the structure into suitable lengths, with provision for relative movement between them (*see* p.130).

It may also be possible to reduce thermal movements by restricting the temperature changes in a roof. Heat gain from solar radiation can be reduced by giving a roof a white surface. This is particularly important where asphalt, bitumen felt, or other dark-coloured coverings have been used, and is discussed in more detail in Chapter 7.

The provision of thermal insulation can be advantageous, not only to limit the escape of heat from the interior of a building, but also to diminish the rate at which temperatures rise in the fabric of the building through solar heating (p. 136). Lightweight porous building materials for loadbearing roof structures or roof coverings are also being used increasingly with the same effect.

Drying shrinkage and moisture movement

Materials that contain Portland cement as an essential constituent are liable to shrink on first drying out, and if this shrinkage is restrained, the resulting stress may lead to cracking.

After the first shrinkage due to drying, cement products expand by a lesser amount on being wetted, and shrink again on being dried. The first irreversible drying shrinkage is about 50 per cent greater than the movements due to wetting or drying at a later stage, which are approximately constant (*see* Volume 1, p. 189). Complete drying out under conditions of moisture equilibrium is a very slow process and indeed may never be attained, particularly in members exposed to the weather.

With precast concrete products the irreversible initial drying shrinkage takes place before they are placed in a structure, and the subsequent reversible moisture movements are rarely sufficient to lead to serious trouble. In cast *in situ* concrete structures, however, the first drying shrinkage must be controlled and distributed by suitably designed reinforcement. Clearly, moisture movement and drying shrinkage are a far more important source of deformation in large flat reinforced concrete slabs than in other types of roof structure. Although movements can be controlled to some extent by proper design and good workmanship, it is often advisable to separate a large structure into units of suitable size by movement joints. Where this is not done, or where the joints are inadequate or become ineffective, shear failure can occur through shrinkage cracking in the absence of sufficient shear reinforcement.

Elastic deformation due to loading

In floors, the self-weight and imposed loads are the predominant causes of deformations. In roof systems, imposed loading is not generally an important cause of movement, and the design imposed loads are generally also much lower than the floor loads. Some types of roof, particularly where the weather covering and the loadbearing functions are separate, are mainly designed to resist only snow and wind loads, apart from their own weight; they are not designed to be walked on except with special precautions.

Self-weight is an important factor to bear in mind for the dimensional stability of some roofs. With heavy roofs such as concrete or clay tiles or reinforced concrete slabs, the self-weight of the structure is usually sufficient to resist the lifting force of the wind; excessive deformations due to wind suction are not common. Where the weatherproof cover is a light sheeting separate from the supporting structure, however, the deformations and movements due to wind suction can be considerable, as noted previously, and may even cause local fractures at the joints, followed by failure of the whole roof system.

Creep

A factor that must be taken into consideration by designers of concrete roofs is the irreversible deformation that occurs in structures subjected to long-duration loading. Creep in concrete may be the cause of considerable deflections (in addition to the elastic deflections), particularly in shallow beams. It seems to be generally innocuous, however, and in fact may have a beneficial effect in relieving thermal and shrinkage stresses.

In recent years, experience of the performance of various kinds of structure has encouraged the development of new and less conservative design theories, combining a reduced load factor against failure with higher permissible deformations. The design of roof structures was naturally influenced by this development, particularly for reinforced concrete. More scope has been gained also for the construction of flat roofs, including roofs using new materials such as reinforced lightweight concrete. Where such materials or methods of construction are used, it seems reasonable that the load factors against excessive deformation should be set higher than would be thought necessary with well-known and established materials or methods of construction.

EXCLUSION OF RAIN AND SNOW,
AND ROOF DRAINAGE

A roof must prevent the penetration of water and of fine snow, and must also provide for the drainage or shedding of water, clear of the building, through gutters and downpipes. Even slight penetration through a roof can lead to serious damage.

There are two ways of producing a satisfactory roof. One of these is to provide an impervious covering, which can be flat or nearly flat; the other is to provide on a slope a series of over-lapping units which need not necessarily be impervious.

Flat roofs are commonly covered with asphalt, several layers of bituminous felt, or metal sheet. All movement joints and discontinuities are made to stand above the general level of the roof, so as to minimize the risk of water penetration; a movement joint in asphalt or felt is formed as a double upstand with a capping, and the joints in metal sheets are made over rolls or as upstand welts. Apart from roofs that are designed to be kept permanently under water, all flat roofs should have sufficient falls to ensure complete drainage. It has in the past been considered that a fall of 1 in 80 is adequate where a covering provides no impediment to the flow of water. So slight a fall, however, is often insufficient to prevent ponding unless workmanship is of a very high standard, and a designed fall of 1 in 50 is advisable.

Pitched roofs can be covered with small units such as tiles, slates or shingles, or with large units such as corrugated asbestos-cement or metal sheets. Some of the materials used are impervious or very nearly so but others are porous. Clay tiles and asbestos-cement sheets keep out rain because the pores in them are very fine and water does not pass through them readily under the small pressures that are set up.

The amount of lap in pitched roofs and the size of upstand joints on flat roofs must be related to the wind pressure, because water can be driven uphill by the wind, into joints or over upstands. The pressure exerted by a 60 mph wind will support a column of water about 2 in. high and, if a roof has to withstand such a wind without leaking, the laps and upstand joints must be such that more than a 2-in. head of water will need to be moved upwards before leakage occurs. It should be remarked also that there are sudden variations in wind speed and pressure; a gust will commonly raise the pressure to $1\frac{1}{2}$ times the steady value. For safety, this larger value should be assumed. The relation between wind speed and the height of a water column that can be supported is as follows:

Wind speed (mph)	Head of water (in.)
10	0·05
20	0·2
30	0·5
40	0·8
50	1·3
60	1·9
70	2·6

If the space behind a pitched roof covering such as tiles is unsealed, there is a risk that fine snow may be blown in through the interstices between the tiles; this can be prevented by providing a lining (sarking) beneath the tiles, as described on p. 156. In designing a roof, another possible source of moisture that must be considered is condensation. This will be dealt with in relation to thermal insulation, p. 109.

as described on p. 156.

ROOF DRAINAGE—EAVES GUTTERS

Like many other design features in building, that of eaves guttering has evolved largely through trial and error, and there are rules-of-thumb on which designs are commonly based. Existing provisions for roof drainage, often based on these rules, give satisfactory results, but in fact they are often over-generous in comparison with real requirements. An experimental study has been made of the behaviour of gutters and downpipes, and this section presents data that provide a basis for rational design of eaves gutters and downpipes. The design calls for knowledge, first, of the flow load, and then of the capacity of gutters and downpipes of various sizes.

The flow load

The flow load with which a given gutter may have to cope depends on the area of roofing discharging to the gutter, its pitch, the peak rate of rainfall (usually expressed in inches per hour) and the angle at which the rain falls when it is at a peak. To some extent, also, the duration of rainfall peaks is important: if the gutter is almost empty to start with, a sharp peak lasting only a minute or two might be accommodated, although its continuance until after the gutter was full would cause overflow.

Fortunately, for present purposes, it is permissible to adopt a simplified approach to the vast mass of available rainfall statistics. Regional differences may be ignored. They are significant in relation to total rainfall, but there is no evidence that they are significant in relation to peak intensities. It is worth noting, however, that in Britain peak intensities tend to occur in summer months; wind speeds then tend to be lower than in winter, and the rain falls more nearly vertically, and this mitigates the flow with pitched roofs.

The important features in the rainfall pattern are: average intensity of a fall, its duration and frequency of occurrence, and angle of incidence.

The average intensity recommended as a basis for general design purposes for eaves guttering is 3 in. per hour. This intensity is found to occur, in any given locality, over a period of five minutes about every other year, and over a period of ten minutes only once in about eight years. (To give an idea of the margin of safety overflow offered by this basis, it is worth mentioning that an intensity of 4 in. per hour lasting for five minutes occurs only once in five years, for ten minutes only once in about nineteen years). With regard to the angle of incidence of the rain, meteorological data indicate that an angle of 25° to the vertical provides a reasonable basis for design.

As a simple approximation which takes this angle of incidence into account, for roof pitches up to 50°, the actual area of the roof surface may be taken as the basis for calculation, ignoring the pitch and the angle at which the rain comes down; this gives the flow load (gallons per minute) as

$\dfrac{2 \cdot 6}{100}$ × actual roof surface area in square feet.

Flow capacity of gutters

The flow capacity of a simple straight gutter, i.e. the amount of water in gallons per minute that it can carry, depends on its area of cross-section, its shape, length and slope. Experimental work has shown that for level half-round and ogee gutters, only cross-section area affects capacity. Quite a slight slope markedly increases the capacity, though there is a limit to the advantage that can be achieved. An indication of the effect of slope is given by the following figures for a 36 ft length of 4½-in. half-round gutter laid to various falls:

Level	15 gallons per minute
1 inch in 54 feet	22 gallons per minute
1 inch in 27 feet	25 gallons per minute
1 inch in 18 feet	26 gallons per minute

Too big a fall is to be avoided; apart from appearance, too wide a vertical gap between roof edge and gutter may cause some water to miss the gutter altogether.

Length has no influence on the flow capacity of level gutters. With sloping gutters, the capacity tends to increase with length until the total fall of the gutter is of the order of the depth of the gutter. Some idea of the order of magnitude of this effect may be gathered from the fact that in the case of a gutter of total length of 50 ft with a fall of 2 in., the capacity for a length of 50 ft is about 8 per cent greater than for a length of 20 ft with the same slope.

Effect of bends. A right-angle bend reduces flow capacity if it is near an outlet. As a general rule for level gutters, if the bend is within 6 ft of an outlet, a 20 per cent reduction in capacity should be assumed for a sharp-cornered bend, but only a 10 per cent reduction if the bend has a corner rounded to a 1-in. radius; for sloping gutters the reduction should be taken as 25 per cent for both rounded and sharp corners. If the bend is within 6–12 ft of the outlet, half these reductions may be assumed.

Effect of outlets and downpipes. The shape, size and position of the outlet and downpipe all affect the flow capacity of a gutter.

Round-cornered outlets give a smoother flow (Fig. 6.5) than sharp-cornered ones and this has a marked effect on gutter capacity with the smaller outlet sizes.

The area of cross-section of outlets and downpipes can usually be smaller than that of the gutter because a gutter rarely flows full at the outlet and the speed of flow increases markedly at this point. A survey showed that the downpipe sizes commonly used are unnecessarily large, and smaller sizes may be used without affecting the capacity of the gutter. If smaller downpipes are used they will tend to run full under conditions of heaviest rainfall, and joints should be sealed to avoid leakage. Swan-necked offsets and bends and shoes at the bottom of the downpipe do not significantly affect the performance of downpipes.

The position of the outlet will markedly affect the flow capacity of a gutter but, in deciding at what point in the length of a gutter the outlet should be placed, the ease of connection to the underground drainage system and the appearance have also to be considered.

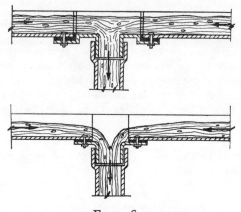

Fig. 6.5

Flow with (top) sharp-cornered and (bottom)
round-cornered outlet

Assuming it is of adequate size, when an outlet is placed centrally in the length of a gutter, the gutter capacity required will be one-half of that needed for an end outlet. Generally, if the outlet is not at the end, the gutter capacity required will be a fraction L_1/L of the total flow load, where L_1 is the length of the longer arm of a gutter of total length L.

Design data

Table 6.2 gives the flow capacities of various sizes and shapes of straight level gutters with an outlet at one end. The figures are calculated from the formula

$$\text{Flow capacity} = 1 \cdot 15 \ A^{5/4}$$

where A is the area of cross-section in sq. in. This formula is based on the results of experiment. The figures apply strictly only to the gutters specified, but the flow capacity may also be calculated from it for other shapes of gutters approximating to the half-round or ogee type.

After allowing for the position of the outlet as above, allowances for other factors that affect the flow should be made as follows:

   (*a*) Slope: for slopes of 1 in. in 50 ft or greater, the capacities may be increased by 40 per cent.

   (*b*) Right-angled bends:

    (i) Within 6 ft of outlet:

        Level gutters, sharp-cornered bend, 20 per cent reduction, round-cornered bend, 10 per cent reduction.

        Sloping gutters, 25 per cent reduction for both sharp and round-cornered bends.

    (ii) Within 6-12 ft of outlet, half the above reductions.

   (*c*) Length: for sloping gutters up to 20 ft long, 10 per cent reduction.

TABLE 6.2

*Flow capacities (in gallons per minute) for level gutters
with outlet at one end*

Half-round gutters			Ogee gutters			
Gutter size (in.)	True half-round gutters [1]	Nominal half-round gutters [2]	Gutter size (in.)	Asbestos-cement[1]	Metal gutters[1,2]	
					Aluminium, cast-iron	Pressed steel
3	5·6	4·2	4	14	6·5	12
4	11	8·8	4½	20	8·8	18
4½	15	11	5	24	11	23
5	20	14	6	38	Not standard	35
6	31	24				

[1] Pressed steel to B.S. 1091: 1946
  Asbestos cement to B.S. 569: 1956.
[2] Aluminium to B.S. 1430: 1947
  Cast iron to B.S. 1205: 1948.

TABLE 6.3

*Recommended minimum downpipe sizes (diameter in inches)
for level and sloping gutters*

Half-round gutter size (in.)	Outlet*	Outlet at one end of gutter	Outlet not at one end of gutter
3	S.C.	2	2
	R.C.	2	2
4	S.C.	2½	2½
	R.C.	2	2
4½	S.C.	2½	3
	R.C.	2	2½
5	S.C.	3	3½
	R.C.	2½	3
6†	S.C.	3½	4
	R.C.	3	4

* S.C.= sharp, R.C. = round-cornered.
† Values for 6-in. gutters are provisional.

Details of appropriate downpipe sizes which do not restrict flow are given in Table 6.3. Where there is a liability to blockage, e.g. from leaves, it may be advisable to increase the downpipe size by ½ in.

Example

To calculate size of gutters and down-pipes required to drain a roof 160 ft long by 36 ft broad (distance from ridge to eaves) with 30° pitch.

Area of roof=36 × 160=5760 sq. ft.

Since pitch of roof is less than 50°,

$$\text{Rainfall load} = \frac{2\cdot6}{100} \times 5760 = 150 \text{ gal/minute.}$$

From Table 6.2, a level 6-in. true half-round gutter with outlet at one end can accommodate a flow of 31 gal/minute or, if gutter has a slope not less than 1 in. in 50 ft to the outlet, the flow capacity is

$$31 + 31 \times \frac{40}{100} = 43\cdot4 \text{ gal/min.}$$

By providing an outlet at the centre the flow capacity is increased to 86·8 gal/minute. This would cater for half the roof, hence if this system were duplicated then adequate drainage of the whole roof would be attained, i.e. 6-in. true half-round gutters sloping to outlets 40 ft from each end.

Table 6.3 shows that 4-in. downpipes are required; preferably they should have round-cornered outlets.

The roof edge

The manner in which the water leaves the edge of a roof varies with the kind of roof covering used, and this bears on the fixing of gutters. For some roofs, e.g. a slate roof, the water leaves the edge with very little spread to front or rear. The obvious position of the gutter is then centrally under the edge and it is possible for the gutter to collect all the water even when it is fixed some distance below the roof edge; this is useful for a long sloping gutter, but in any case the distance should not be more than 2 in. On the other hand, for some roofs, e.g. clay pantiles (with sharp upper corner to the edge), the water leaves the edge with a wide spread, and the gutter must be close to the edge with its centre slightly forward of the under edge of the roof. When the lower corner of the roof edge is rounded, the water may be deflected more to the rear, and the centre of the gutter should then also be placed slightly to the rear. The most satisfactory roof edge is one with the upper corner round and the lower corner sharp.

Installation and maintenance

Continued good performance depends on good installation and regular maintenance. Needs will depend on locality. Below trees, gutters should be cleared at least once a year after the leaves have fallen; wire balloons can assist in preventing downpipe blockage. Near some power stations, monthly inspection may be desirable owing to fuel-ash deposits.

Sagging, because of careless installation or subsequent disturbance by ladders, causes back-falls, which affect drainage performance, and ponding, which can affect durability. Unsuitable choice or fixing of gutter clips can lead to sideways tilt and thereby reduce gutter capacity. The use of sloping gutters not only increases the capacity but also helps to prevent back-falls and ponding.

Metal gutters may be corroded by water dripping from roofs. The main corrosive influences were described in Volume 1 (p. 89), but two others need to be mentioned here. Rainwater can take a very small amount of copper into solution; if it runs off a copper roof into a steel or galvanized-iron gutter, the traces of copper may be sufficient to cause electrolytic corrosion (*see* p.12). With cedar shingles, organic acids leached out by rain may cause corrosion of lead gutters.

Wherever there is a risk of corrosion by run-off (and *all* the surfaces over which the rainwater may flow should be taken into consideration—not only those adjacent to the gutter), gutters should be protected internally by a coating of bitumen of heavy painting consistence.

Valley gutters

Much of what has been said about eaves gutters is applicable also to valley gutters.

Thus, the method of calculating the quantity of water falling on the roof remains the same except that the plan area of the double roof should be used in place of actual sloping roof area. The formula relating quantity of water to area of gutter has not been verified experimentally for gutters larger than 5-in. half-round, but failing further experimental work it should give guidance on the appropriate cross-sectional area of larger half-round gutters.

THERMAL INSULATION

Of the structural elements of a building the roof is the most exposed, and if its area is large compared with that of the enclosing walls, the heat flow through it may be the most important factor in determining the heat loss from the building.

Thermal insulation results in a saving in heating costs. This is of major importance to the occupier of the building; such economy is also in the national interest. Both the Thermal Insulation (Industrial Buildings) Act of 1957, and the revisions in 1953 and 1959 of the Model Byelaws applicable to housing, aim to secure worthwhile reductions of heat loss from basic roof constructions at a cost to the user which, if not negligible, is likely to be more than offset by the saving in heating costs. Further, much of the discomfort caused by cold or heat, in winter or summer, can be avoided, often at little cost, by improved insulation. The risks of condensation, also, will be reduced.

Any deficiencies in the thermal insulation of the roof will be most apparent in single-storey buildings; here they have a pronounced effect on the overall rate of heat loss (or heat gain in summer) and also on the occupants' comfort. In buildings of two or more storeys the influence of the roof on overall heat loss is much less pronounced, but the effects on the topmost storey remain substantially the same.

Condensation

On a clear night, a roof radiates heat to the sky and its temperature may fall even below that of the surrounding air. If the relative humidity of the air inside the building is greater than about 60 per cent, there may then be a risk of condensation, particularly within a lightweight roof structure.

There are three means of countering trouble from condensation in roofs: thermal insulation will reduce heat loss; a vapour barrier (on the 'warm' side of any insulation) will prevent moisture vapour diffusing through the insulation to condense against the cold outer layer of the roof covering; and ventilation of a cavity between the insulation and the outer covering will help in drying out, during the day, any moisture that may have condensed there during a cold night.

According to the type of roof construction, the vapour barrier may consist of a continuous membrane of pitch or bitumen, polyethylene sheet, metal foil, sprayed p.v.c. film, or high gloss paint. It is important to ensure that all joints are sealed and that there are not other breaks. Splits in a paint film can be minimized by using as a base for the paint a plastic spray (such as 'Cocoon'), which can bridge small gaps without breaking.

It is worth noting here the experience of designers in colder climates, where condensation problems are more severe, on the avoidance of roof condensation. In Canada, the general trend has been towards providing a vapour barrier, either at the inner surface of the roof structure, or at the inner boundary of the thermal insulation. In Scandinavia, designers tend to distrust vapour barriers and prefer to provide ventilation of roofs as well. (The ventilation system for flat roofs is described on p. 139).

Pattern staining

All surfaces tend to collect dirt from the air, and the rate of precipitation increases with the difference in temperature between a cool surface and warm air. This gives rise to 'pattern staining', which it is appropriate to discuss here as it most commonly occurs on roof linings and top-floor ceilings.

If there is a fairly high rate of heat flow through a construction whose thermal resistance varies from point to point, there will be a corresponding variation in surface temperature. This variation in the inside surface temperature of a wall or ceiling may be sufficient to cause noticeable differential staining. With a ceiling of plaster on wood laths, for instance, resistance to heat flow is greater through the wood laths than through the plaster keys between them; the surface of the plaster between the laths will therefore be cooler than that below the laths. In a cement filler-joist roof, the steel joists provide paths of relatively low resistance to heat flow; in cold weather the ceiling below them will therefore tend to be cooler than it is between them.

The prevention of pattern staining depends either on reducing the overall heat flow or on providing extra insulation between the inner surface and any 'cold bridges' that lie behind it. Both measures are desirable in any event, to reduce heat losses, as has been discussed in general terms in this section and in Volume I.

Solar heat gain

In summer, a roof will gain heat from solar radiation. Thermal insulation in the roof structure will reduce the transfer of this heat to the interior of the building, but it will also result in the roof covering itself being raised to a higher temperature, which may accelerate deterioration. Provision of a reflective external surface to the roof, however, will reduce the amount of heat actually absorbed. More commonly employed on flat roofs, this treatment is described on p. 134.

FIRE PROTECTION

The roof of a building may be subjected to attack by fire from both inside and outside the building; as with the external wall, these are two quite separate hazards and the design of the roof must be considered from both aspects.

For fire within the building to be contained by the roof, the complete roof structure and covering must achieve fire resistance comparable with a floor. This would generally call for the use of a concrete slab or a deck of comparable fire resistance. With many forms of roof construction, particularly pitched roofs, it is difficult to achieve a specified grade of fire resistance; in respect of the roof covering, this is generally unimportant but it is always desirable to have sufficient fire resistance in the structure to delay its collapse. Methods of protecting structural steel trusses are available. Other factors that affect fire spread are the provision of openings specifically designed for venting the fire through the roof, and the presence of fire curtains in the roof space.

The development of a fire within a building will be influenced by the nature of the roof lining. Preference should be given when choosing roof linings to those materials which do not contribute significantly to the fire load of the building nor to the spread of flame across their surfaces (*see* Vol. 1, pp. 141–2).

A roof exposed externally, to fire in a neighbouring building, may be subjected to radiant heat, flame and hot gases, and frequently burning brands may lodge on it. To withstand these conditions, the covering must be not easily ignited and must not spread fire rapidly over its surface, and the roof as a whole must prevent penetration of fire into the interior for a sufficient period. It is to measure the ability of roofs to meet these requirements that Part 3 of B.S. 476: 1958 'External fire exposure roof tests' has been issued. By subjecting roof constructions to the tests described in this Standard they may be graded in respect of all these factors. Provided they pass the preliminary ignition test, the time for which the specimen resists penetration and the degree of flame spread across the outer surface are indicated by pairs of letters (*A* to *D*); a covering with a resistance to penetration of more than 1 hour and no surface flame spread receives the highest designation, *AA*. A suffix *X* may be added if burning material drips from the underside of the specimen or if holes or any other sign of mechanical failure are evident; a prefix shows whether the roof sample was tested sloping or flat.

Most of the non-combustible coverings, including slates, clay or concrete tiles and metal or asbestos cement tiles and sheets will achieve a designation *AA* whether laid sloping or flat. The nature of the supporting structure or the presence of thermal insulation layers below the covering will not generally affect the performance.

TABLE 6.4. *Minimum expected designations* of bitumen-felt roof constructions (B.S. 476, Part 3: External fire exposure roof tests)*

	Details of felt		Combustible deck				Non-combustible deck		
					Steel or timber beams		Asbestos cement cavity deck	Steel or aluminium deck, single skin or cavity	Concrete or clay-pot slab, cast in situ or precast
Roof	Upper layer	Under layer(s)	Timber joists with P.E. or T. & G. boarding	Stressed skin plywood cavity deck	Supporting compressed straw slabs	Supporting wood-wool slabs with cement screed finish	Overlaid fibre insulation board	Overlaid fibre insulation board	
Sloping roof with single-layer felt	Type 1E, 80-lb, organic-base, mineral surface	—	CC	CC	AC	AC	AC	—	AC
Sloping roof with two-or-three-layer felt, 30 lb/100 sq. ft. bitumen bonding compound between layers and between under layer and deck unless fibre insulation board is used	Type 1E, 80-lb, organic-base, mineral surface	Type 1C, 40-lb, organic base, self-finished and lightly sanded	CC	CC	AC	AC	AC	AC	AC
	Type 2C, 80-lb, asbestos base, mineral surface	Type 1C, 40-lb, organic base, self-finished and lightly sanded	BB	BB	AB	AA	AB	AB	AA
	Type 2C, 80-lb, asbestos base, mineral surface	Type 2B, 40-lb, asbestos base, self-finished and lightly sanded	AB	AB	AB	AA	AB	AB	AA
	Type 5B, 60-lb, glass-fibre base, mineral surface	Type 5A, 30-lb, glass-fibre base, self-finished and lightly sanded	BC	BC	AC	AB	AB	AB	AB
Flat roof with three layer felt covering, layers bonded as above	Type 1C, 40-lb, organic base, self-finished and lightly sanded	As upper layer	With no *in situ* finish, designations will be the same as for corresponding multi-layer sloping roofs listed above.				With no *in situ* finish, designations will be the same as for corresponding multi-layer sloping roofs listed above.		
	Type 2B, 40-lb, asbestos base, self-finished and lightly sanded	Type 1C, 40-lb, organic base, self-finished and lightly sanded	With bitumen-bedded tiles, of asbestos cement or other non-combustible material, all these constructions will achieve : AA				With bitumen-bedded mineral chippings, or bitumen-bedded tiles of asbestos cement or other non-combustible material, all these constructions will achieve : AA		
	Type 2B, 40-lb, asbestos base, self-finished and lightly sanded	As upper layer	With bitumen - bedded chippings spread evenly shoulder to shoulder, asbestos-base three-layer finishes will achieve : AA						
	Type 5A, 30-lb, glass-fibre base, self-finished and lightly sanded	Type 5A, 30-lb, glass-fibre base, self-finished and lightly sanded	AA						

*This table, based on data from the Joint Fire Research Organization, is intended *as a guide only*. Particular constructions when subjected to the B.S. test may give a superior performance.

Of the externally combustible coverings, some bitumen-protected metal sheets and asphalt may be expected to be designated *AA* even when a combustible thermal insulation layer is incorporated below the covering. Wood shingles on battens are designated *CC*.

The results for bitumen-felt roofs vary according to the base material of the felt, the nature of the supporting deck, and the presence of any applied *in situ* finish. In general, without an applied finish, the highest designation, *AA*, will be achieved by multi-layer asbestos-base felts laid on non-combustible decks or on decks finished with a cement screed. Under similar conditions glass-fibre-base felts are likely to be designated *AB* and organic-base felts *AC*. With timber decks the highest designation can only be achieved by applying an *in situ* finish.

TABLE 6.5

Use of roof coverings

Designation B.S. 476, Pt. 3	Recommended restrictions in use			
	Minimum distance from another building or from boundary of site (ft)	Type of building	Size of building	Miscellaneous
AA, AB	No restriction	No restriction	No restriction	Combustible coverings should not be carried across separating walls or division walls unless laid on a non-combustible deck of concrete or hollow clay pots extending at least 10 ft. on each side of the wall
AC	No restriction	No restriction	No restriction	Should not be carried across separating walls or division walls
BA, BB, BC, CA	20	No restriction	No restriction	Ditto
AD, BD, CB, CC, CD	40, or twice the height of the building, whichever is greater, up to a maximum of 100 ft.	Domestic buildings only	Building not more than 40,000 cu. ft. in capacity	Should not be carried across more than one separating wall in a terrace of houses. Alternate separating walls should be extended not less than 18 in. above roof surface
DA, DB, DC, DD	75	No restriction	No restriction	Should not exceed 20 sq. ft in area, and any two such areas should be spaced apart by a distance at least as great as the largest dimension of either area

Table 6.4 shows the designations of currently recommended felt roof constructions.

Coverings achieving the highest designation may be used without restriction. Decisions on using coverings of the lower designations should be related to the separation of the roof from possible fire hazards, which may be represented by another building or a stack of combustible materials. The roof should also be separated by the same distance from the site boundary. In addition, where the designation shows that a particular covering will spread fire readily, it should not be used on large buildings or buildings with high fire load or high fire hazard contents. This is necessary to limit fire spread if a fire, originating inside the building, breaks through the roof from below. For the same reason the continuity of combustible coverings should be broken at all separating and fire-division walls. Table 6.5 indicates how these principles can be applied in practice.

The roof of a factory building is now required by the Thermal Insulation (Industrial Buildings) Act to have an adequate resistance to loss of heat. In many cases this is provided by an insulating lining exposed internally. The nature of this lining has a marked influence on the rate at which fire will spread within the building. Non-combustible materials afford the highest standard of safety and should be used when the occupancy hazard is high. Where combustible linings are used their surfaces should have very low flame-spread characteristics. Materials complying with this requirement are defined as Class 1 in B.S. 476, Part 1, and this Standard is specified under the Thermal Insulation Act.

DAYLIGHTING

Generally, daylighting through the roof is provided for only in buildings that are too large in plan for sufficient daylight to penetrate to all parts from windows in the external walls.

The principles of good lighting have been discussed in Vol. 1 (p. 57). These entail two functional requirements that must be met in the design of roof-lighting: the amount of daylight provided should be adequate in quantity and distribution, and there should be freedom from sky-glare. In addition, penetration of sunlight may have to be partly or even completely prevented, and heat gains or losses through the glazing have also to be considered.

In practice, the particular form of a roof-lighting system will depend not only on lighting requirements, but also on the structural design and the arrangements for any overhead services. A good system of lighting cannot be designed in isolation but must result from integration with other associated elements of the design, For example, if a novel type of roof-structure were imposed arbitrarily, regardless of the limiting effect it might have on the position and extent of glazing, the possibility of good roof lighting would obviously be lessened if not ruled out. Similarly, a roof-lighting system adopted for a factory without foreknowledge and study of possible obstructions such as gantries, ducting or heating units, is liable to be very much reduced in efficiency.

The following notes briefly enlarge on the more important functional aspects of roof-lighting design, and Plates 6.1–6.4 illustrate particular examples.

Amount and distribution of light

The first function of roof-lighting is that it should provide a sufficient amount of light at the required positions in an interior. The main contribution of light will be received direct from the sky through the glazing, but quite often this can be supplemented to some extent by reflected light from the illuminated surfaces of the interior, provided these have colour of suitably high reflection factor. In most work places the roof-lighting should be designed to give an even distribution of light over the whole working plane, the amount at any point being sufficient for people to see the detail involved in their work clearly and quickly (*see* Volume 1, p. 64). More occasionally the need will be for preferential lighting on certain parts of an interior, as in art galleries where the best illumination is required on the walls or screens carrying the pictures, or where limited use is made of roof-lighting to allow greater flexibility in the planning of single-storey buildings otherwise dependent on side-lighting.

At this stage it is appropriate to consider the relative merits of different roof-lighting arrangements in terms of the Daylight Factors resulting from them. This is done in Figs. 6.6 *a–j*; these relate to factory lighting, and they also serve to demonstrate points of general significance. In each example the distribution of light is plotted graphically; the approximate relative efficiency of the systems is indicated by expressing the total glazing area as a percentage of the floor area. For convenience they are divided into three groups, giving minimum Daylight Factors at the working plane respectively of 5 per cent, 10 per cent and 20 per cent (assuming that light colours have been used for the major internal surfaces). It is important to note that a non-uniformly bright sky (the C.I.E. standard overcast sky) is assumed, having a ratio of brightness of 3 to 1 between zenith and horizon. In each case it has been assumed that there are typical losses of light due to absorption by the glass and the dirt that accumulates between regular cleanings. Allowance is also made for loss due to glazing bars, but none for obstructions, either external or internal.

It will be clear from these examples that the level of illumination depends on the arrangement of glazing as well as on the area of glazing. Horizontal or low-pitched glazing tends to be more efficient for illumination on horizontal surfaces than vertical or steeply-pitched glazing. It should be noted that the levels of illumination shown in the examples are for the precise sections drawn. Marked differences may occur if only slight adjustments are made to the designs, particularly to the detailing around the windows. If projecting eaves were introduced above the monitor lights, for example, the reduction of light at the working plane could be considerable.

In addition to the arrangement, area and detailing of the glazing, and allowances for dirt and absorption by the glass, the following factors condition the efficiency of any roof-lighting system:

Obstructions. Efficiency will be reduced if there are obstructions to the entry or penetration of light, these being mainly of three types:

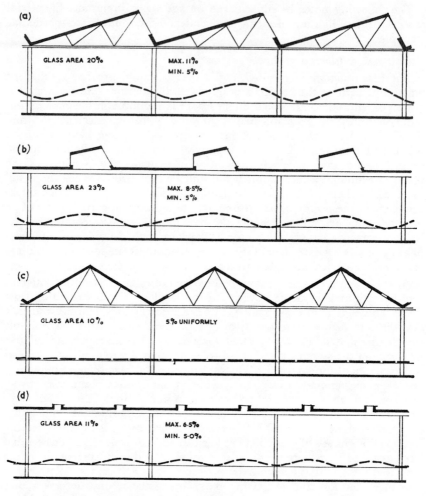

(a) North light roof giving unilateral lighting
(b) Monitor roof with north face at 60° slope, and smaller south face vertical, designed to lessen sun penetration
(c) Shed type roof with continuous strips of glazing
(d) Continuous horizontal roof lights
(e) North-light roof giving unilateral lighting
(f) Monitor roof with 60° glazing both sides
(g) Shed type roof with continuous strips of glazing
(h) Continuous horizontal roof lights
(i) Shed type roof with continuous strips of glazing
(j) Continuous horizontal roof lights

FIG. 6.6

Daylight factors for various roof types. Glass area is expressed as a percentage of floor area

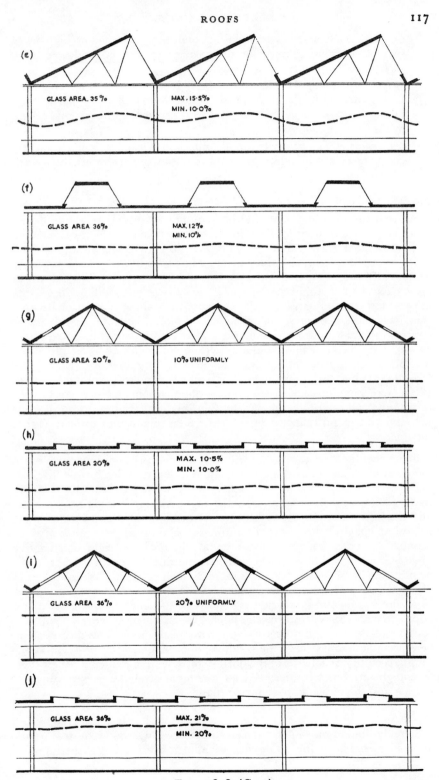

FIG. 6.6 (*Cont.*)

external, such as trees or adjacent buildings; internal at high level, such as ventilating ducts or other services; internal at lower level, such as tall machines or equipment.

Internal colouring. Efficiency will be reduced if the internal colouring is predominantly dark. A fairly light-coloured floor is particularly desirable, to act as a reflector and to assist in the integration of light in the interior as a whole.

Cleaning. Efficiency will rapidly diminish if glazing is not regularly cleaned. Access should be provided for cleaning glass internally as well as externally.

Freedom from glare

As well as providing light in the required quantity, roof-light design should be aimed at limiting sky glare so that the available light can be used to best advantage. The more obvious form of glare is that resulting from views of bright sky through the glazing. The sky itself may be too bright to be tolerated with comfort, but even when it is relatively dull, glare of a less obvious kind is still likely to occur if the surfaces surrounding the glazing appear dark by comparison, either because they are shadowed or because they have dark colouring. For avoidance of glare, therefore, it is desirable to screen the glazing from normal view, that is from angles less than about 40°–45° with the horizontal, and also to raise the brightness of the surrounding surfaces. It is sometimes possible for the structure itself to give adequate screening; failing this, some method of baffling or louvring will be required. If the screening surfaces receive good illumination and are given light colour, they will not only appear suitably bright in relation to the sky but will also add useful reflected light to the direct light onto surfaces within the interior.

Some roof-light arrangements will lend themselves to reduction of glare more readily than others. Figures 6.6d and a illustrate this. In the first, the 5 per cent Daylight Factor is given by narrow strips of glazing at fairly frequent intervals, the up-stands to the roof-openings forming cross-screens and the beams forming lateral screens. Depending on the spacing of these beams, it may be necessary to introduce additional vertical baffles at suitable intervals between; these could be of lightweight inexpensive material and should have light colour. In contrast, the north-light arrangement in Fig. 6.6a presents a much more difficult problem. It has the initial disadvantage that light enters from one direction and must therefore result in shadowing on the south side of objects in the interior and make them appear dark in views towards the light. In particular, however, there is a considerable area of glass exposed to full view and no obvious means, short of a special louvre system at the windows, of overcoming this problem. It can thus be seen that the merits of the north-light system in reducing penetration of sunlight are offset by the need for a comparatively large percentage of glazing and the difficulty of reducing glare.

Sunlight

Some limitation on sunlight penetration is nearly always required, partly to avoid glare but mainly to prevent occasional overheating of the interior.

Systems of roof-lighting that allow some penetration are usually acceptable, provided the glazing material used has a diffusing effect and prevents concentrated shafts of sunlight. Large areas of glass facing other than northwards, however, will require protective devices in the form either of permanent louvres or adjustable blinds. In certain cases it may be necessary for sunlight to be totally excluded because of possible damage by radiation; instances of this occur in the manufacture of pharmaceutical and food products. Total exclusion of sunlight is difficult but not impossible. It cannot be assumed that glazing facing northwards will be completely satisfactory without some such extra protection as louvres to exclude low-angle sunlight in mornings and evenings during summer. In general it can be said that the more efficient lighting arrangements employing horizontal or near-horizontal glazing of a type which diffuses sunlight will normally be satisfactory. Also, where there is a special requirement to exclude sunlight, this will involve special screening or louvring together with relatively larger areas of glazing, and will result in a considerably less efficient form of lighting than is otherwise possible.

NOISE AND SOUND INSULATION

As regards sound insulation, roofs are similar to external walls, in that they constitute part of the external envelope of the building and may be called upon to exclude outdoor noise or to prevent the escape of indoor noise. The proportion of roof to wall, and consequently the importance of the roof for sound insulation, varies from the relatively small roof area of a tower block of flats or offices to the very large proportion of roof to wall area of some single-storey factories. Many halls and theatres lie in the middle of this range, with walls and roofs about equal in area and importance. The sound insulation may vary from about 50 dB for a concrete slab roof to no more than 15 dB for a sheeted roof. In deciding upon the degree of sound insulation to be provided by a roof, the exposure of the roof to outdoor noise (including, perhaps, noise from aircraft) or the exposure of other buildings to roofs that enclose noisy activities (relative to the exposure and insulating value of the walls in each case) must be taken into account. Thus the roof of a high building on a city street will be less exposed to road traffic noise than the walls, and lower insulation than that of the walls may suffice; but the roof of a low and noisy factory building adjoining a tall block of offices may need as much insulation as the walls or more, in order to avoid disturbance of the offices.

Types of roof structure in common use are listed below, with the range of sound insulation to be expected from each type.

Flat concrete roofs. The airborne sound insulation is similar to that of concrete floors and ranges from 45 dB to 50 dB, mainly depending on the weight, in accordance with Fig. 2.6. As with a floor, a roof giving 45 dB insulation from its weight (about 50 lb/sq. ft) can be raised to about 50 dB insulation without much increase of weight by adding a lightweight screed 2 in. thick or a suspended ceiling. The details of these items of construction are precisely as described for floors on pp. 43–44.

Shell concrete roofs. The sound insulation is similar to that of flat concrete roofs, except in so far as shell roofs are usually thinner, and therefore lighter, than flat slab roofs. The range of insulation is therefore 40–45 dB.

Pitched roofs with flat ceilings. This type includes the traditional pitched roof, with slates or tiles on rafters and a flat plaster ceiling at the base of the triangle, which gives insulation in the range 30–40 dB. A modern variation of this type is often used over halls and theatres; this usually has steel trusses but is not necessarily triangular in form, and has an outer layer of wood-wool or other slabs (spanning the rafters, purlins or beams) covered with a cement screed $\frac{1}{2}$–2 in. thick and finished with a waterproof covering, the ceiling below the trusses being of board or plaster. The outer layer of this roof is more airtight than most tiled roofs and therefore gives better sound insulation; 40–45 dB can be expected.

Thin sheet roofs, without ceilings but sometimes with a thermal insulating board separated from the outer sheet by a small air-space. The weight of the single or double membrane is usually less than 5 lb per sq. ft, and the joints between the sheets and between the boards are seldom airtight. Because of the low weight and the air gaps, the sound insulation is not likely to exceed 25 dB and may be as low as 15 dB.

Flat decked roofs. These are usually constructed either like ordinary wood-joist floors or with prefabricated hollow beams or slabs of sheet metal or asbestos-cement spanning between beams, and covered with a waterproof layer. The weight is probably between 5 and 10 lb per sq. ft and the sound insulation is of the order of 30–35 dB.

Any of these roof types, but especially the thin sheet type, may incorporate areas of glazing. This is unlikely to affect the insulation of thin sheet roofs, because the glazing itself (unless openable) has an insulation of about 25 dB, but the other roof types may well have reduced insulation if they contain roof lights. In the case of flat roofs with lantern roof lights, the provision of laylights would help, since laylight and lantern together (if airtight) give about 40 dB insulation.

The problem of impact sounds is not usually associated with roofs, but there is a special problem of drumming caused by rain or hail beating on thin membranes such as metal or asbestos-cement sheeting, especially the former. It is not possible at present to say what is the simplest method of overcoming this drumming, but probably the best approach is to 'damp' the vibrating membrane. This might be done by providing a layer of soft insulating fibre wallboard or other suitable material in close contact with the membrane; or possibly, in the case of metal sheeting, by coating it with sufficient thickness of 'anti-vibration' compound such as is used for under-sealing cars.

A similar problem is the rattle of metal roof sheeting caused by thermal movement. Again it is not yet possible to make any firm recommendation for remedying the trouble, but damping may be one solution.

DURABILITY AND MAINTENANCE

The durability required of roofs ranges from that of temporary buildings, such as the prefabricated bungalows erected after the last war and intended to have only a limited life, to that of monumental buildings intended to endure for hundreds of years. Old and well-tried materials, such as slates and tiles or sheet lead and copper, are commonly selected for very long life. They will give the required performance provided that they are of good quality and not used in unfavourable conditions. The more modern materials, such as asbestos-cement and preformed metal sheets, are more suitable for industrial buildings, for which it is more important to provide a weatherproof cover at low cost than a roof of very long life. Industrial requirements change rapidly, and a building that is admirably fitted for its purpose at the time of erection may be inadequate or obsolete 25 years later.

It is important that nails or other fixings should have a life comparable with that of the covering which they support, as otherwise premature failure of the roofing will occur.

The life of many coverings to pitched roofs is influenced greatly by the slope of the roof. Flatter slopes allow the materials less chance of drying out between showers and thereby tend to shorten the life of materials that are vulnerable to frost action and to corrosion.

ROOF DECKS

In this section, the decks that support the roof coverings will be considered. Decks are required in all flat roofs and sometimes in pitched roofs. They are supported on beams or on frameworks of steel, reinforced concrete or timber and these main structural parts are considered elsewhere.

The principal function served by a roof deck is to support the covering. The longer the span and the lighter the weight of the deck, the more economical will it be. It should be dimensionally stable, that is to say, it should suffer only small movements with changes in temperature and moisture content. This is particularly important where the roof covering is to be asphalt or built-up bitumen felt.

Beneath a discontinuous roof covering the deck may also serve as a wind break, and prevent the ingress of wind-borne fine snow.

The deck can, further, provide thermal insulation and so reduce heat loss in winter and heat gain in summer. As the deck is above the structural framework of the building its insulation is of value in reducing structural movement. Heavy decks, with a big heat capacity, prevent rapid temperature fluctuations in the structure, but this advantage may be offset by the extra cost of supporting them. The thermal insulation can also be of value in reducing the incidence of condensation in cold weather. A vapour barrier is required at the underside (*see* p. 110), to prevent moist air penetrating the deck and condensing at the underside of the cold roof covering.

The deck also increases the sound insulation of the roof, and reduces the drumming noise caused by heavy rain. Resistance to airborne sound will depend largely on the mass of the deck and on the absence of free air paths through it.

The roof deck may reduce the fire hazard, particularly that from flying brands. Fire resistance and incombustibility of the deck are especially important where the roof covering is combustible, for instance, built-up bitumen felt roofing with organic-based felts.

In addition to these functions, the deck must be durable under the conditions of use.

The common roof decks may be considered in the light of these requirements.

Timber boards have long been used for decks, and have some value in all the ways mentioned. Although their movement with change of moisture content is considerable, it occurs mostly across the grain and so is taken up by the many joints between the boards. Man-made timber boards, such as plywood and resin-bonded chipboards, are used in large sheets, and movement between the edges of adjacent sheets can be much bigger than the movement between narrow timber boards; moreover, if the upper and the lower surface of a large sheet are at different moisture contents, the sheet will curl, giving the deck section a saucer shape.

Wood-wool is a durable material with good insulating properties but can span only a short distance between supports. It is usually screeded or blinded with cement-sand mortar. The wood-wool is not sufficiently strong to restrain the drying shrinkage of this mortar which, in consequence, is liable to crack. If the mortar screed is to be covered with bitumen felt, it should be cut at intervals no greater than 10 ft, and the felt not stuck down around the cuts; in this way, stressing of the covering can be avoided.

Metal decks are light in weight and can bridge a larger span between supports. They have, however, no thermal insulation value and for this reason are usually topped with fibreboard. This combination has many attractive features, but it has been found that the metal deck does not, in itself, form a vapour barrier to prevent interstitial condensation in the fibreboard, and rotting of the fibreboard has been known to occur. Where this type of roofing is to be used over a building in which the humidity is likely to be high, the standard practice now is to lay bitumen felt in hot bitumen over the deck before placing the fibreboard in position.

Asbestos-cement decking is cheap, and again can be used with larger spans between supporting beams. It has little thermal insulation value in itself, but can be moulded into such a form that it can be filled with a lightweight insulator such as glass silk or mineral wool. Its movement with change of moisture content is less than that of timber, but the relative movement of units butted end-to-end can be appreciable. Changes of temperature can also produce significant movements; the deck has so little heat capacity that it readily warms up in sunshine.

Asbestos cement has a surface that encourages blistering of built-up bitumen-felt roofing laid directly on to it. For this reason, a layer of fibreboard should be included between the deck and the felt.

Strawboard is sensitive to dampness; a big increase in moisture content can cause it to swell or even to rot. However, the paper envelope on modern strawboard is, in itself, a good vapour barrier, and provided it is not punctured, the moisture content of the straw can change only very slowly. Given this precaution, the deck can be regarded as durable and dimensionally stable. There is still a need, however, to avoid long periods of dampness. Cases have been known where lightweight concrete screeds have been laid over strawboards and have been covered whilst still damp. Rotting of the strawboard has then occurred.

Concrete decks are used in a wide range of designs—some precast, some cast *in situ*. Reinforced slabs of lightweight aerated concrete may soon be available in this country, as they are now in many European countries. Dense concrete units suffer less movement than do the lightweight ones, but they have a low insulation value. This deficiency is usually made good with an added layer of thermal insulating material, often a lightweight concrete screed. Although the moisture movement of dense concrete is small, large gaps are often allowed at the joints. The extent of opening and closing of the joints can then be as large as at the joints between smaller areas of decks that are less stable dimensionally. Asphalt and bitumen felt roofing often reflect these lines of localized movement in ripples and splits.

Chapter 7

FLAT ROOFS

STRENGTH AND STABILITY

Wind effects

The general effects of wind described in Chapter 6 were derived primarily from wind-tunnel tests, and the experimental data so obtained were embodied in the simplified design rules of Code CP 3 (Ch. V). The information obtained in this way was limited mainly to tests in which the wind was usually directed at right-angles to one or other of the main faces of some basic shapes of model. The wind pressures and suctions given in Fig. 6.4 (p. 97) are for wind normal to the eaves of a building, and no reference is made to the effects of wind blowing in any other direction. The provisions for increased wind forces on fastenings near the ends of roofs allow partially for the effect of wind blowing on the ends, but for the general roof structure it can apparently be assumed that a consideration of the forces arising from wind normal to eaves will ensure reasonable safety against wind from any other direction.

Although, for general design purposes, it is necessary to avoid undue complication, it is worth noting that recent wind-tunnel tests on roofs have indicated that local pressures, particularly near the edges, may be greatest when the wind blows at an angle about mid-way between normal and parallel to the eaves. These tests, carried out at the National Physical Laboratory, were made on a rectangular model representing a relatively new shape of house roof, the 'mono-pitch', with a single slope of 6°. The wind direction was varied through 360°. The suctions determined with the wind normal to the eaves were not very different from those recommended in Code CP 3 (Ch. V). However, with the wind directed at a corner of the

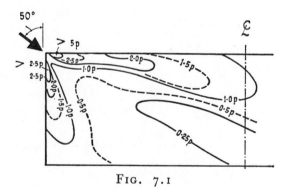

F IG. 7.1

Distribution of external suctions over mono-pitch roof of low slope (6°)

model, the suction over quite appreciable areas of the outer portions of the roof was greater than the basic pressure p; also, extremely high suctions, of the order of $5p$, were measured on very small areas of the roof near the corner at which the wind was directed. The actual distribution of wind suction for this worst condition of wind is shown in Fig. 7.1, in the form of contours on one half of the roof plan. This effect may be of particular importance for the roofs of small buildings such as houses, especially if the roofs are of low pitch and of lightweight construction.

The eaves projection is a common construction feature of the traditional roof. In many forms of roof, the effect of wind acting on the underside of a small roof overhang, as it may be called, would have no special significance, and this is probably the reason why the Code makes no specific mention of this feature in existing design rules. However, Code CP 3 (Ch. V) does deal with what might be termed the limiting case of a very large overhang—a building completely open on one side—and recommends an 'internal' wind pressure of $+0 \cdot 5p$ acting on the underside of the roof for wind blowing into the open side. A positive internal pressure is equivalent to a suction on the top of the roof. Where it is necessary to include the effect of wind on the underside of a roof overhang it is suggested that, until further experimental data are available, the value of $+0 \cdot 5p$ mentioned above be accepted for the pressure beneath the windward overhang. This corresponds to a suction load acting on the area of roof directly above the overhang, to be added to whatever external wind load has been calculated for the top surface of the particular roof. On the leeward side, it would seem, from a comparison of the actual wind pressures on windward and leeward walls recorded in Appendix 3 of CP 3 (Ch. V), that a value somewhat less, say $0 \cdot 3p$, might be assumed to act as a suction on the underside of the leeward overhang.

Lightweight roofs of low pitch. In view of the recent data on wind effects described above, it would seem that the present design rules may not be wholly satisfactory for lightweight roofs of low pitch ($0°–10°$). There has been considerable interest in this type of roof for domestic dwellings as a result of the present trend towards lightness in construction. Such roofs are more responsive to wind effects than heavier roofs of bigger buildings, and a more conservative basis for the design of these roofs is suggested.

Except for the end houses of a block of several houses, the external wind suctions should be deduced from Fig. 6.4, but the suction should be assumed to be increased to $1 \cdot 5p$ within a distance of 4 ft from the windward edge of the roof. The external wind suction on end houses should be taken as 50 per cent greater than that on the other houses, and it should be assumed to be increased to $2 \cdot 25p$ for a distance of 4 ft from the end of the roof for the whole depth of the house. For a flat roof these external suctions are shown in Fig. 7.2a.

The internal pressure, also tending to lift the roof, should be assumed to be $0 \cdot 2p$ as specified for a building with normal openings. Where a roof has overhangs, the upward pressure under the overhang on the windward side may be taken as $0 \cdot 5p$ and the suction under the overhang on the leeward side may be taken as $0 \cdot 3p$. The resulting total design suctions for an end house with a flat roof and overhangs are shown in Fig. 7·2b.

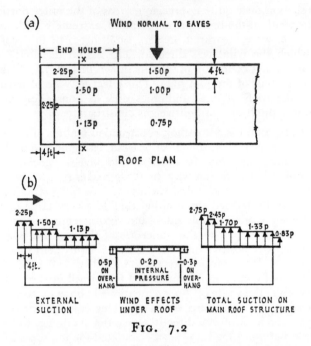

FIG. 7.2

(a) Design wind suctions for a block of houses with flat roofs of lightweight construction; (b) suctions on line X–X of end house

Mono-pitch roofs. External wind effects on roofs are given in the Code in the form of pressures (positive or negative) on the windward and the leeward slopes of the roof, and, while not specifically stated there, it can be inferred that the respective values apply not only to roofs with the windward and leeward slopes equal but to roofs with unequal slopes as well. This is probably reasonable enough if the difference in slopes is not more than 30° or so, but perhaps not where, as in a mono-pitch roof, one slope might be taken as 90°, on the assumption that the wall of the building may be considered as the second 'slope' of the roof.

However, suppose a mono-pitch roof with a slope of 6° downwards into the wind is considered in this way, i.e. as a dual-pitch roof with a windward slope of 6° and a leeward slope of 90°. The external suction on the windward slope according to Code CP 3 (Ch. V) would be $0.8p$. With the same roof sloping upwards into the wind, the windward slope is 90° and the leeward slope is 6°, so that the external suction on the leeward slope is $0.5p$. Comparing these suctions with a mean suction of $0.875p$ for a flat roof, the suction for the mono-pitch roof sloping up into the wind is seen to be under-estimated by assuming that the present design rules can be applied in this way. Until more experimental data are available, it would probably be reasonable to assume that the external suction on a mono-pitch roof is the same as that given in Fig. 6.4, for a windward slope of the same pitch.

Strength

The strength of the structure of a flat roof, whether of timber joists covered with boards, aluminium sheets, etc., of steel lattice trusses, or of reinforced concrete, raises no outstanding problem.

With light timber roofs for houses, however, it must not be overlooked that the roof must act as a whole against both downward loading due to self-weight and snow and upward loading due to wind suction. For instance, where a light timber roof is supported inside the house on a top-floor partition, joists are sometimes lapped and spiked over the supporting partition. The roof structure may be amply strong in resisting the downward loads but its ability to act as a whole under wind suction will depend largely on the efficiency of the nailed joints of the lapped joists.

Whatever the type of roof structure, the roof coverings and fastenings should in general be designed for the total suctions calculated on the basis adopted in Code CP 3 (Ch. V). With lightweight house roofs, however, it is considered that, for interior houses of a terrace, fastenings within a distance of 4 ft from the eaves should be capable of resisting a design suction of $2p$ on the area of covering that they support. With end houses, it is probably best to design the fastenings for a suction of $3p$ on the covering, over the full area of the house.

Stability

In general the stability of the roof structure of flat or near flat roofs requires little further discussion.

It has not been necessary in the past to provide special anchorages for house roofs of traditional construction, but what has been said above shows that special provision is necessary for lightweight roofs of low pitch. Particular attention should be drawn to this need in the contract documents, so that adequate supervision is arranged on the site to ensure that the anchorage is satisfactory.

In order to provide the stability factor of 3, mentioned earlier as desirable for houses, the weight of the roof alone, if no special anchorage is provided, should be at least sufficient to prevent uplift or overturning when the forces due to wind are increased to three times the normal values calculated in accordance with the recommendations outlined above for lightweight roofs. When the dead weight of the roof is insufficient to satisfy this requirement, special anchorages must be provided, so that the weight of the roof and the holding-down strength of the anchorage together provide the required stability.

It is important that the assumed strength of special anchorages should be realistic, in relation to the variability of this strength and the standard of workmanship likely to be attained on the site. Where permissible working loads are given in codes or byelaws (e.g. for bolting or nailing) it should be assumed that the strength is not more than twice the working values. It should be noted that, although a minimum margin of safety has been introduced into these recommendations, a much higher margin can usually be obtained with little increase in cost.

DIMENSIONAL STABILITY

Most flat roofs in the United Kingdom are of reinforced concrete; such roofs have become a common feature of multi-storey buildings. Flat roofs consisting of a system of rigid or flexible covering and insulating membranes, supported on a separate loadbearing frame, are less common. Flat concrete roofs are therefore the most important type to be considered, and it is the dimensional stability of these which is also likely to be the cause of most concern.

The reinforced concrete slab has both a structural and a protective function, although, often, its waterproofing and heat-insulating properties are considered insufficient and additional insulation and an external water barrier are provided.

Dimensional changes in reinforced concrete slabs may cause damage to the supporting structure and to internal arrangements, fittings and decoration, and may also result in serious cracking or buckling of the roof slab itself. The most important causes of excessive deformation are thermal expansion and contraction, drying shrinkage and moisture movement, elastic deformation due to self-weight and imposed loading, and creep due to prolonged loading.

Thermal expansion and contraction

If the connections between a roof slab and the supporting members do not allow for differential movement, the expansion of the slab may cause damage in the supporting structure and even in the slab itself.

A concrete roof, whether a solid slab or an assembly of precast units, expands and contracts as a whole when it warms and cools. The amount of the movement, with the range of temperatures found in Britain from winter to summer, is sufficient, if the roof is not properly protected, to cause very troublesome cracking; for example, a roof 50 ft long can undergo a movement of about $\frac{1}{8}$ inch.

In most cases the defects caused by thermal movements can be readily recognized. They are almost entirely restricted to top storeys, and plaster finishes show them up. As the temperature changes during a summer day, the cracks open and close with the roof movement.

The cracking takes slightly different forms in framed and in unframed buildings. In unframed buildings the whole roof slab tends to bow upward slightly in the centre, owing to the higher temperature of the upper surface, and at the same time the slab spreads outward. The two movements together tend to cause local cracking at the tops of walls and partitions, rather jagged when the walls are in line with the expansion movement but otherwise with a simple type of horizontal break.

In framed buildings the effects are generally more disfiguring. Beams tend to bow upwards and may take part of the walls with them. Walls and partitions may be distorted as a whole: walls that are parallel to the movement of the roof show a diagonal fracture running downward from the top corner where the pressure is applied, as in Fig. 7.3; those across the line

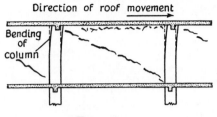

FIG. 7.3

Diagonal cracking, and local cracking along the top, of a panel fixed between columns, when the latter are bent by movement of the roof

of movement show a more simple horizontal break as in unframed buildings, but often farther down the wall, because the wall is bent by being connected to columns which themselves deflect.

The distribution of the cracking will depend on how the roof as a whole is restrained. In a simple symmetrical roof, movements will be outward from the centre. If the building abuts on another so that the roof can only move in one direction, cracking will be localized at the unrestrained end, and will accordingly be more severe there. Lift shafts and stair wells, and other projections above a roof, will tend to fix certain points, and areas that are shaded for long periods in the day will have the same effect. Expansion then takes place outward from these fixed points.

Expansion occurs when the slab is warmed by the sun, and contraction results from the loss of heat to a clear night sky. Protection against both effects is desirable, though the former is the more important in this country. Some forms of roof covering can serve both purposes reasonably well. The effectiveness of reflective treatments in countering solar heat gain is discussed on p. 134; in addition, insulating screeds of lightweight concrete have been used to reduce thermal movement. It is advisable to provide such a screed with its own expansion joints.

The protection of the roof slab by insulation treatments (p. 136) has many practical merits; it will tend to even out rapid temperature variations due to changes in the air temperature and solar radiation, and will reduce the temperature gradient in the roof slab. These are good reasons for putting thermal insulation generally above the slab, but there are occasions when part, at least, can usefully go below it: in buildings that are heated intermittently it will make for quick warming up and will also reduce the risk of temporary condensation. Sometimes, also, insulating materials such as wood-wool can be used for permanent shuttering, and sound-absorbing materials, which have some value for heat insulation, may be wanted beneath the slab. However, some insulation at least should generally be placed above the slab, to reduce thermal movements. The waterproof covering must then be given a reflective treatment, to prevent overheating and deterioration.

When all reasonable precautions have been taken, roof movements, and differential thermal movements between the roof and the walls and other connected parts, will be reduced but not entirely avoided. Some relative movement will always occur. In very long buildings, expansion joints should be provided to take up the movement without damage to the structure. Intervals of about 100 ft between joints are usually appropriate.

Expansion joints are sometimes put in the roof only. They should be inserted also in the external walls, and should extend inward at least part way through the buildings to enable the stresses of expansion to be distributed without causing obvious cracking. The best course may be to cut right through the building down to foundation level (*see* Volume I, Fig. 2.6).

The damage already described, at the junction of top-floor partitions with the ceiling due to thermal movements of a reinforced concrete roof slab, may be avoided by the design details described in Volume I (Fig. 2.5).

Precast concrete slabs are sometimes supported on a loadbearing roof system, with an intermediate waterproof layer, usually of bitumen. The concrete slabs provide a protective surface and can be walked on. The joints between adjacent slabs are usually filled in with a bituminous material which does not obstruct thermal expansion. Eventually, however, the gaps between the slabs become blocked with solid material such as sand, dirt and wind-blown debris, which cannot yield to pressure from the edges of the expanding slabs. As a result the concrete slabs tend to move gradually towards the edges of the roof, where they press against the parapets; these will finally give way or, where the parapets resist the pressure, the slabs may rise. Some initial clearance between the edge slabs and the parapet must therefore be allowed and any accumulation of solid material in the joints should be cleared out as part of the maintenance routine.

Drying shrinkage and moisture movement

The amounts of drying shrinkage to be reckoned with in large reinforced concrete roof slabs will vary considerably, but will probably not exceed about $\frac{1}{8}$—$\frac{3}{16}$ inch for a length of 50 feet, depending on the type of concrete used and the reinforcement in the slab. Excessive shrinkage accompanied by forcible restraint will lead to cracking of the slab and ocasionally to fracture in the supporting walls. The slab may also lift at the corners, leading to cracks in the supporting walls or damage to the supporting framework. It is, therefore, necessary for reinforced concrete slabs to be anchored adequately at the corners to the supporting structure.

With timber roof structures, the considerable expansion and contraction due to moisture changes may have to be taken into account in fixing the sheet covering. With sheet-metal coverings on flat roofs, the joints between the sheets (p. 147) will be able to take up the deck movement, and it is good practice to provide many joints; bitumen felt roofing should be fixed by a method of partial bonding (p. 146).

Elastic deformations due to loading

The self-weight of a reinforced concrete slab represents a considerable proportion of the total load it is designed to support, but in most flat roofs the deformations due to self-weight are unlikely to prove troublesome. In general, they are less important than thermal and moisture movements.

Excessive upward lift, however, may occur at the corners of slabs because of self-weight and imposed loading. The remedy is to provide an adequate anchorage to the supporting structure. To reduce the numbers of corners where lifting may occur, it is desirable that reinforced concrete roof slabs should be continuous, subject to the limit by the development of thermal and shrinkage cracking (the continuous length of a roof slab should not generally exceed 100 feet).

Among the more recent developments in reinforced concrete flat-roof construction are precast reinforced roof beams and slabs made of aerated concrete. Although the material has very low compressive strength and modulus of elasticity, these slabs are made to span up to 20 ft. Their resistance to cracking is greater than that of ordinary dense or lightweight aggregate concrete. They tend, however, to deflect excessively under loading and, owing to their high water absorption, their self-weight may vary considerably from time to time (for example, they may take up a large amount of condensed moisture). To keep deflections within reasonable limits it has been found necessary to combine these precast elements in such a way that they form a continuous slab, with additional reinforcement at the top over the supports, where the stresses are reversed compared with those at mid-span. This reinforcement is encased in dense concrete cast *in situ*.

There is no general ruling on the maximum deflection that may be tolerated for roofs subjected to loading. Some tentative recommendations were made by the Building Research Station in National Building Studies Special Report No. 1, 'Structural requirements for houses' (1948), for the permissible deflection in loading tests on houses. These recommendations include a limiting deflection equal to 1/300 of the span where the structure is subjected, in addition to its own weight, to a test load of 1½ times the specified imposed load, for a period of at least 12 hours. This recommendation applies to floor as well as to flat or pitched roofs.

Tentative recommendations are also contained in Bulletin No. 1, 'The structural sufficiency of buildings', issued by the Commonwealth Experimental Building Station of Australia, 1946, for the design and testing of 'domestic roofs'; 1/300 of the span is considered to be the maximum permissible deflection, including creep, for roofs subjected to dead and live loading. For live loading alone the deflection of any one part should not exceed 1/600 of the span. With industrial buildings much higher deflections would seem to be allowed for roofs.

Creep

Creep often has a beneficial effect since it tends to relieve shrinkage stresses and thermal stresses. If it is directly induced by dead load and imposed load, however, creep may lead to excessive deflections, particularly in shallow flexural members such as reinforced concrete roof slabs. Usually, increased deformation due to creep will cause downward deflection in roof slabs. With precast prestressed concrete roof systems, however, the combined effect of creep and thermal changes may cause the roof slab to bend upwards. The constituent beams are so designed that they have a slight upward bow and, since the aggregate compressive stress in the concrete is often higher at the bottom than at the top, creep in the concrete will tend to accentuate this upward bow. Thermal expansion might then lead to cracking of the slab and considerable damage to the waterproof layers. Accuracy in manufacture is important with these systems, and it is also particularly important to restrict solar heating, by a reflective surface treatment or by providing a layer of insulation above the slab.

EXCLUSION OF MOISTURE

Entrapped moisture

There is good reason to ensure that the structure and insulating layers of a flat roof are dry at the time of covering. The covering is impervious, and ventilation of the underside to the open air is rarely provided. There may be access to the air within a building but this is usually at a humidity higher than that of the air outside; in certain circumstances it can lead to condensation and increased dampness in the roof structure.

With some forms of construction, however, moisture is likely to be entrapped. For instance, a lightweight concrete screed contains a large amount of water when first laid. The screed is usually given two or more weeks to dry out, but it is not protected from rain during this period, and even with only a few showers it is likely to gain rather than to lose moisture, because of the slowness of drying. It is particularly important in such roofs to drain away the rain that falls on them. If the lightweight screed is laid on a dense concrete slab, rain can penetrate to form ponds on the surface of the slab, and these may still be present when the top of the screed is dry. If the roof covering is then laid on the assumption that the whole roof has dried out, the entrapped water may cause serious trouble; any such ponds must therefore be drained, as described on p.142, before finishing the roof with an impervious covering.

Water entrapped within the screed itself is at first distributed fairly uniformly throughout the material; in time, however, it tends to concentrate in certain parts, either flowing downwards or distilling towards the cooler parts. Flow under gravity will result in ponds on impervious parts of the structure or drainage into any openings, such as those provided by electrical conduits. Temperature gradients cause migration of moisture from the warmer to the cooler parts; in winter moisture will tend to concentrate in the upper parts of the roof, and in summer the movement will be in the opposite direction and moisture will be driven towards the underside. A day of hot sunshine in spring has been known to cause so much migration that water has dripped from the underside of a concrete roof. Moisture may also migrate from an area of roof that is in sunshine to an area that is shaded most of the time. The effects of this moisture migration are particularly unpleasant when a large quantity of water is entrapped in a concrete roof covered with bituminous felt or with asphalt laid on an underfelt. Water, containing alkali leached from the cement, may dissolve brown, tarry substances from the felt, and these may be transferred to the underside of the roof or to its junction with the walls and produce unsightly stains. Entrapped moisture may also encourage the corrosion of metals and the decay of organic materials. It is bad practice to combine a screed in which moisture may become entrapped with organic materials, such as timber, fibreboard or strawboard; moisture will, at some stage, migrate into the organic materials and cause rotting.

Recently, there have been attempts to get rid of unwanted moisture in some flat roofs by providing small vents through the impervious coverings. The vents cannot be regarded as providing true ventilation but they do release pressure when the roof warms up in sunshine and so should be of some assistance in the elimination of entrapped moisture. A system of ventilation ducts has been used in Scandinavia (*see* p. 139).

Rain exclusion

Flat roofs must be covered with an unbroken impervious membrane. Both the quality of the material and the workmanship must be good enough to exclude rainwater completely. Any discontinuities, such as the welted joints between metal sheets, have either to be in a well-drained area or to be raised above the general level of the roof. Where there is a discontinuity in an asphalt roof, for instance at a movement joint in the structure, the asphalt is usually taken up to a height of 6 in. at curbs alongside the joint, and a capping is provided to protect the curbs and upstands. The same type of joint is made at parapets or walls that project above the general roof level; an asphalt or felt covering is taken up 6 in. and tucked into the wall; the top is then covered by a metal flashing which joins up with a damp-proof course in the wall (Figs. 7.4, 7.5, p. 144). This arrangement permits some slight relative movement to occur without rain getting in, and the flashing protects the top of the skirting of felt or asphalt.

Extra care is needed where there are tank rooms or other projections above the general roof level. Often these rooms, because they do not require a dry interior, are constructed in materials that have only poor resistance to rain penetration; they might be built, for instance, in 4½-in. brickwork. The exposure to driving rain is rather more severe above roof level than it is below, and so a higher rather than a lower standard of weather resistance is required. Unless this is provided, the floor of the tank room should be waterproofed in the same way as the main roof covering, and this water-proofing should extend up the walls to join the damp-proof course in them. A similar upstand should be provided around pipes or any other projections through the structural roof.

Roof lights are often difficult to make waterproof and must be given a mastic seating wherever relative movement is likely to occur. Glass domes are usually seated over an upstand which prevents water flowing in from the roof. They are, however, vulnerable to fine, wind-blown snow, which can penetrate between the glass and the upstand; this can be minimized by providing an air-tight lay-light.

EXCLUSION OF SOLAR HEAT

Sunshine on a flat roof can, as we have seen, cause thermal movements which may lead to distortion and cracking of the structure or of the roof covering. It also has two other undesirable effects. It accelerates the deterioration of many roof coverings, particularly asphalt and bitumen felt

The ultra-violet radiation encourages chemical changes involving embrittlement. The heating leads to loss of the more volatile constituents and so to shrinkage, loss of flexibility and cracking; in some circumstances it can lead to blistering. In hot weather, it also makes for discomfort in buildings beneath poorly insulated roofs. Apart from the heating effect, a layer of warm air just below the hot ceiling reduces air circulation.

As noted earlier (p. 129) there are advantages in providing the thermal insulation *over* the structural roof. This cuts down the roof movement but, at the same time, it makes the roof covering reach an even higher temperature in hot sunshine and this can lead to rapid deterioration unless a reflective treatment is applied to the surface.

In many hot, dry countries it is customary to build massive flat roofs; often they are covered with a thick layer of earth. Such a roof has a heat capacity so large that fluctuations in the temperature of the upper surface barely reach the ceiling, and the underside of the roof and the rooms below remain at a more even temperature day and night. This advantage of a massive roof is not always appreciated, particularly with present trends towards lighter roof construction. Nevertheless, it may be worth considering the provision of sufficient thermal capacity to 'buffer', at least to some extent, the daily variations in external surface temperature; it makes for greater comfort and might on occasion lead to economies in running costs.

Reflective treatments

The simplest and, in many respects, the best way of excluding solar heat is to provide a surface that reflects most of the sunshine. Much of the sun's heat arrives in radiation of short wave-lengths corresponding to visible light. To reflect low-temperature radiation, for example from heating appliances, polished metal reflectors are the best; for solar radiation they are only moderately effective, and a white surface is very much better.

The reflection coefficients of various surfaces have been measured and the results give an indication of the relative merits of various surfacing materials. Some typical results are given below:

Material	*Reflection coefficient*
New asphalt	0·09
Weathered asphalt	0·17
Mortar	0·35–0·65
Asbestos cement, new	0·58
,, ,, after 1 year exposure in London	0·29
Granite (reddish)	0·45
Marble	0·56
Aluminium paint	0·46
Limewash	0.79–0.91

It can be seen that a matt white surface of limewash is much more effective than any other finish. Moreover, a lime-tallow wash is the only coating that has been found to cause no deterioration in asphalt and bitumen felt. A method of making a suitable wash is as follows.

A white high-calcium quicklime is broken into small lumps and 10 per cent by weight of tallow is shredded and placed on top of the lime. Enough cold water is then added so that the heat developed in slaking just melts the tallow, without charring, and disperses it within the mass. When slaking is complete, more water is added to enable the mass to be worked up into a stiff cream which can, if desired, be screened to remove coarse lumps. Only a thin film is needed to provide the white surface and the cream is therefore thinned considerably with water before use, so that the dark surface to

TABLE 7.1

Exclusion of solar heat—effectiveness of roof coverings

Maximum temperatures at the upper surface of a concrete roof slab on a
sunny day in England
(Max. shade temp. about 80°F)

Roof covering	*Maximum temperature (°F)*
1 in. medium-grey mortar screed	112
3 layers of bitumen felt, gritted	110
¾ in. asphalt—1 in. mortar screed	95
½ in. fibreboard—¾ in. asphalt sanded finish . . .	87
3 layers of felt—sanded with white grit . . .	85
3 layers of felt—gritted—1 in. mortar screed . . .	85
¾ in. asphalt—white spar chippings rolled-in . . .	80
¾ in. asphalt—2 in. loose gravel	79
1 in. cork—¾ in. asphalt—sanded finish	78
¾ in. asphalt—limewash	75
2 in. cork—¾ in. asphalt—sanded finish . . .	73

which it is applied is barely obscured while the limewash is wet, but becomes white on drying. Additions of materials such as glue or size are almost certain to have bad effects on the bituminous surface and should not be used.

The only safe alternative to tallow is wool grease, which should be used in the same proportions and by the same method. The wool grease is not so readily dispersed as tallow, nor is the product so durable. Higher proportions of wool grease should not be employed, however, for they may damage the bitumen surface.

The lime-tallow wash is itself not very durable; it may need renewing every year or, at least, every other year, preferably in late spring. Moreover, in urban atmospheres the surface soon becomes dirty and an annual renewal is needed to maintain a white surface.

A more durable, although slightly less efficient, coating can be obtained by sticking a layer of white stone chips to the surface. The stone can be limestone, marble or spar. Darker chips of calcined flint, granite or gravel may also be employed; these, although less effective than the white finishes, still reflect far more sunshine than would the untreated asphalt or bitumen-felt surfaces. If the chips are present as a substantial layer, say ¾ in. or more, the extra heat capacity will be significant.

A cement mortar covering is sometimes provided. Care is needed, however, to ensure that it does not cause deterioration of the underlying asphalt or bitumen felt. In particular, the mortar has to be cut up into small areas, not more than 2 ft square, so that the movement of the mortar slabs with change of temperature and moisture content does not over-stress the felt or asphalt on which they rest. Moreover, the accumulation of dust and grit in the joints between the slabs must be prevented by maintenance cleaning, otherwise these joints will tend to widen and the stresses set up may lead to arching of the slabs or distortion of parapets (*see* p. 130).

Asbestos-cement tiles have similar properties but provide rather better insulation.

In the tropics, flat roofs are sometimes given total protection from sunshine by means of a further covering of slabs or sheets supported above the roof proper. The slabs or sheets are not in any sense a water barrier; that function is performed by the roof covering below. The space between the sheets and the roof is ventilated to the open air, and so the effects of hot sunshine are minimized.

Table 7.1 affords some comparison of the merits of insulation and surface treatment in maintaining a low temperature in the roof.

THERMAL INSULATION

The Model Byelaws require the U-value of flat roofs to be not greater than 0·42 Btu/sq. ft h °F, and the Ministry of Housing and Local Government has recommended a value of $U = 0·3$ for dwellings. However, the U-value system of assessing the merits of flat roof constructions is necessarily only a rough guide. Very few types of flat roof have, so far, been tested for heat loss. The accepted U-values are based on approximate calculation, using recognized figures for the thermal conductivity of the various components of the roof system.

In addition to cutting down heat loss, thermal insulation leads to greater comfort in a building, not only in winter but also in summer, when there is a heat flow from the warm upper surface to the relatively cool surface below. On a sunny day conditions under a poorly insulated roof can be very uncomfortable, while under a well insulated roof the sudden rise in temperature of the upper surface will not be transmitted to the room below. As indicated in the last section, however, the provision of insulation is only one way of avoiding an undue temperature rise under the roof; a reflective treatment on the upper surface of the roof is at least equally effective.

Thermal insulation may be placed above or below the structural roof and, as already mentioned (p. 129), the decision on this may depend on a number of factors, not necessarily relevant to the thermal properties of the roof (for instance, the heat insulating material may also be required to provide sound absorption, or to act as permanent shuttering for concrete).

Generally, with a flat concrete roof, at least part of the insulation should be placed above the slab. Insulation above the structural roof will reduce the rate of temperature variation to which it is exposed and also reduce the temperature gradient within a concrete slab, and will therefore minimize thermal movements, cracking and distortion. However, it may lead to overheating and more rapid deterioration of the roof covering, unless this is given a reflective treatment.

Insulation below the structural roof can provide a ceiling surface that can warm up quickly when the building is heated, and this will reduce the risk of condensation; this is of particular value in an intermittently heated building with a heavy roof slab. With continuous heating, the position of the insulating layer is from this point of view of less importance, except that it is better *below* a roof slab that projects beyond the walls, forming a cooling 'fin'. If *all* the insulation is placed beneath the structure, however, the roof will be exposed to wider temperature variations, and distortion and cracking are more likely.

Sometimes the choice of insulation is governed by the economy that can be effected when the provision of thermal insulation can be combined with another function. For instance, lightweight concrete screeds can be so laid that they give the upper surface of the roof falls for drainage; however, this cannot be done without certain disadvantages, mentioned on p. 132 and discussed further in a later section (p. 140).

The use of insulating material as permanent shuttering to concrete or as the ceiling finish has already been mentioned. Thus, wood-wool is frequently used as permanent shuttering and is sometimes decorated directly on the underside. Fibreboard and insulating plasterboard are used as ceilings in lightweight roof constructions.

The role of insulation in avoiding condensation has already been discussed (p. 110). Of particular importance in flat roofs is the avoidance of

TABLE 7.2

Thermal transmittances of insulated roofs

Construction	Insulating material	Application	Thickness (in.)	U-value
Concrete slab insulated with lightweight concrete	Aerated concrete	About 40 lb/cu. ft, screeded on top	5 falling to 3	0·24
	Foamed-slag concrete	About 70 lb/cu. ft, screeded on top	4 „ „ 2 5 „ „ 3 6 „ „ 4	0·31 0·26 0·22
	Vermiculite concrete	About 30 lb/cu. ft, cement and sand slurry on top	4 „ „ 2	0·22
Concrete slab with fibrous insulation*	Corkboard	Laid in bitumen	1	0·19
	Insulating fibreboard	Laid in bitumen with lapped joints	Two ½-in. boards	0·22
	Wood wool	Laid in cement mortar and brushed over with cement and sand slurry	1 2 3	0·30 0·20 0·15
	—	Dense concrete, flat, uninsulated	6–4	0·60

* Screed: screeded cement and sand, or fine concrete laid to falls.

TABLE 7.2 (cont.)

Thermal transmittances of insulated roofs

Construction	Insulating material	Application	Thickness (in.)	U-valve
Timber joist roof, insulation above boards	Corkboard		1	0·15
	Fibreboard		½	0·22
			Two ½-in. boards	0·17
	Wood wool	Cement and sand slurry brushed over slabs	1	0·21
			2	0·16
	Compressed straw		2	0·16
Timber joist roof, insulation below boards	Aluminium foil (combined)	One corrugated, one plain	½	0·16
	Eel grass	Quilt	¾	0·15
	Glass wool or slag wool	Quilt	¾	0·14
Timber joist roof, insulation in place of boards	Wood wool or compressed straw		2	0·18
	As above, but with no ceiling		2	0·22
Timber joist roof, insulation above ceiling	Aluminium foil (combined)	On ⅜-in. plasterboard		0·16
		On ½-in. fibreboard		0·14
	Aluminium foil (single)	On back of plasterboard	⅜	0·26
		On back of fibreboard	½	0·19
Timber joist roof, insulation in place of ceiling	Corkboard	Wire-brushed below to form key, 2 coats plaster, ¾-in. mesh chicken wire between coats	1	0·15
	Insulating fibreboard	Single coat plaster	Two ½-in.	0·18
	Compressed straw or wood-wool	2 coats plaster	2	0·16
			1	0·21
Timber joist roof, no insulation	—	—	—	0·32

NOTE ON DIAGRAMS: Roof coverings may be roofing felt and chippings, or asphalt on sarking felt; ceilings of timber joist roofs may be plasterboard or lath and plaster.

interstitial condensation which may raise the moisture content of the structural materials or insulating materials to a dangerous level. It may encourage fungal attack of timber or fibreboard, and even if this deterioration does not occur there is sure to be a loss of insulation value as the moisture content increases. A vapour barrier on the underside of the roof or at least on the underside of the major insulating layer will prevent interstitial condensation; in a lightweight roof construction it could, for instance, take the form of a foil-backed plasterboard ceiling (as in the lowest diagram in Table 7.2). For a good vapour barrier the edges of the boards would have to be bedded in mastic. An alternative way of avoiding interstitial condensation is to provide an air flow within the roof. The ventilation must be to the open air and not to the air within the building, and the major part of the thermal insulation should be provided below the ventilated space rather than above it, otherwise there will be a big heat loss.

In Scandinavia, ducts are provided in lightweight concrete insulation above a dense concrete structural roof; chamfered blocks are abutted to form a groove, which is covered with a felt strip before the screed is laid. It has been found that, for flat concrete, a duct area of one-thousandth of the roof area is needed to remove the surplus water present initially and to prevent the accumulation of water from condensation in winter. In the milder climate of this country less ventilation would probably be needed, but no quantitative information is available at present.

Some typical forms of flat roof construction and their calculated thermal insulation values are shown in Table 7.2.

FIRE PROTECTION

In considering fire problems in relation to flat roofs, the general principles of protection to supporting members, spread of fire in internal linings and the hazard associated with external coverings must all be taken into account.

Flat roofs fall into three broad categories:

(1) non-combustible roof slabs of concrete or hollow tile
(2) combustible roof decks supported on combustible or non-combustible members
(3) non-combustible composite decking units supported on non-combustible supporting frames or members.

The coverings to such roofs are usually asphalt or bituminous felt, which were discussed in the last chapter (p. 113).

Types (1) and (2), the non-combustible roof and the combustible roof deck, may, as regards resistance to internal fire, be considered in the same way as floors. Fire resistance of the non-combustible roof is achieved by the nature and thickness of the material; with a combustible roof it is achieved by the use of a suitable fire-resisting ceiling.

Type (3), the non-combustible composite roof decks of metal overlaid with bituminous products, may present a fire hazard when subjected to a fire from within a building. Although the lining may be non-combustible and therefore have no flame spread, the deck may warp and permit burning bitumen to flow into the building.

SCREEDS AND COVERINGS

SCREEDS

A screed provides a smooth surface on which the roof covering can be laid, and it is commonly used, also, to provide falls for drainage. By breaking up a large roof into small areas, sufficient falls—1 in 60 or 1 in 80—can be obtained with only a few inches variation in thickness of the screed; this arrangement is generally considered more economical than providing falls for drainage in the structural roof.

A lean cement and sand mix can be used for the screed; in most circumstances a satisfactory finish can be obtained with a mix of 1 part cement to 4 parts of coarse washed sand. By keeping the mix lean, drying shrinkage and the associated cracking and curling can be reduced to a minimum. Even so, unless there is sufficient key to a strong and dimensionally stable base, the screed should be cut along lines 10–12 feet apart so as to localize shrinkage movement, and provision made to accommodate this movement in the design of the roof covering.

A lightweight concrete roof screed will also serve as thermal insulation. A wide range of lightweight concretes is used; nearly all use Portland cement as a binder, but the aggregates include exfoliated vermiculite, foamed slag, and specially prepared lightweight aggregates made from shale or pulverized-fuel ash. Aerated concrete also is widely employed.

No great strength is required of a lightweight concrete screed: probably the hardest treatment it receives is from the workmen carrying out the next operation on the roof. With lightweight aggregates, mixes in the proportion of 1:8 or 1:10 cement:aggregate have better insulation value and suffer less drying shrinkage than richer mixes. They are usually strong enough, although the 1:8 mix or richer may be needed with very weak aggregates such as exfoliated vermiculite. Table 7.3 summarizes the properties of some typical roof screed concretes.

As mentioned on p. 132, a major trouble with concrete screeds, and particularly with those based on lightweight aggregate, is that much water can be trapped beneath the roof covering. It is customary to leave the screed for a time after laying, during which it is supposed to dry out, but at most times of the year in Britain it is in fact more likely to increase in moisture content. Rain passes through the screed into the lower layers and, although the upper surface may dry out subsequently, the lower part of the screed remains saturated. It is better, therefore, to lay the impervious roof covering as soon as the screed is strong enough to be walked on.

Certain steps can be taken to keep the water content of the screed to a minimum. Thus the screed can be laid in the form of a moist mix, with no more water than is needed to bind it together. Better still, in some circumstances, is to lay the concrete as a dry mix and then to sprinkle just enough water on it to enable the cement to set. This technique is being put forward for vermiculite screeds and has much to commend it.

Reinforced concrete structural roofs are rarely so true that all rain falling on them is shed. On most roofs ponds will form; with average workmanship these may be an inch or more in depth. If a roof of this kind is covered with a lightweight concrete screed, and rain falls before the impervious covering is laid, the water will still collect in ponds at the bottom of the screed, through which they will dry out only very slowly. The top of the screed will dry and the roof surfacing may be completed, but the entrapped water will almost certainly cause subsequent trouble within the building, spoiling thermal insulation, staining ceilings and causing corrosion of electrical conduits. For this reason, the location of the ponds should be found before the screed is laid, either after a period of rain or by flooding the roof with a hose to show up the low areas. The structural roof can then be punctured at appropriate points, to drain all the ponds. The drainage holes should be left open until the screed and roof covering are completed. They will serve to remove any surplus water that is incorporated in the screeding concrete and most of the rain that falls on the roof prior to completion. Where this scheme is adopted it is advantageous to use no-fines concrete mixes, which enable the rain to penetrate quickly to the structural roof and drain away.

Aerated concrete screeds have an advantage in that they do not readily permit the passage of water through them and so shed most of the rain that falls on them. They are, however, laid with a fairly high initial content of water, which can dry out only slowly from the surface.

It is customary to provide a topping of cement and sand on most lightweight concrete screeds. This strengthens the surface for the operation of laying the roof covering; for bitumen felt roofing, it is also useful in providing a surface that is less porous and so less conducive to blistering. As with the cement-sand screed there is a danger of cracking and curling; for this reason the mix should be a lean one made with washed sand and not richer than $1 : 4$ cement : sand, and again, the topping can with advantage be cut into areas 10–12 ft square. There is no reason for the topping to be thick; provided rapid drying is avoided, a layer $\frac{1}{4}$–$\frac{1}{2}$ in. thick will serve the purpose, and in some cases the topping need be little more than a blinding.

COVERINGS

The success of flat roof coverings—asphalt, built-up bitumen felt or metal—depends as much on workmanship as on materials. It is wise, therefore, to have the work carried out by an experienced firm—even a specialist firm—which has trained craftsmen, and the proper tools and appliances.

Asphalt

There are two types of asphalt in common use. One is made from natural rock asphalt, which is a limestone impregnated naturally with bitumen. A small amount of soft bitumen to form a flux is added. The composition and properties are defined in B.S.1162. The other type is made from ground limestone and bitumen obtained as a residue from the distillation of petroleum. This material is covered by B.S.988.

The asphalt is so compounded that when hot it flows and can be moulded to the required shape, whilst there is very little flow when it is cold—it is then brittle and should not be subjected to impact. With the normal laying technique two layers of asphalt are put down. The joints between the sections are laid staggered, to minimize the risk of a leak through both layers. Details of laying procedure are given in B.S. Code of Practice 144:201.

Table 7.3

Roof screed concretes

Aggregate	Density of aggregate (lb/cu. ft)	Mix proportions	Concrete density (lb/cu. ft)	Compressive strength* (lb/sq. in.)	Modulus of rupture* (lb/sq. in.)	Drying shrinkage	Thermal conductivity (Btu in./h ft² °F)
Pumice . . .	30–35	1 : 6 or more	45–70	200–550	100–150	0·04–0·08	about 1·4
Clinker . . .	45–65	1 : 6 or more	65–95	300–2000	150–300	0·04–0·08	2·8–4·0
Foamed slag . .	30–50	1 : 6	80–95	300–2000	200–300	0·04–0·05	1·5–3·0
		1 : 12	60–95	200–800	100–250	0·03–0·05	
Expanded clay .	35–65	1 : 6	75	2000	350	0·055	2·3–3·2
		1 : 12	60	850	200	0·055	2·3–3·2
Exfoliated vermiculite .	4–12	1 : 3 to 1 : 9	28–50	130–500	40–75	0·28–0·35	1·0–1·9
Aerated concrete with fine sand .		1 : 1 to 1 : 3	40–85	300–1200	100–250	0·1–0·3	1·0–3·0

* Compressive strengths are determined on dry blocks, and the modulus of rupture on wet blocks.

Asphalt is resistant to most weathering agencies and to many chemicals, but it is softened by organic solvents. Sunshine causes hardening and slight shrinkage, which often leads to surface crazing. The crazing is shallow and does not readily develop into cracks; its presence is no cause for alarm. Surface cracking from other causes may be more serious; once started, a crack tends to deepen until it reaches the far surface. Even the shrinkage of a paint coating can start this process, as can the movement of tiles, slabs or cement-sand screeds on the surface of the asphalt. On paved roofs it is therefore advisable to introduce a slip layer. Sand, gravel and building paper have been used for this purpose; polythene sheet might be better as it affords little resistance to relative movement of bodies in contact with it. But sheet materials unbonded at the joints may themselves cause the trouble they are intended to avoid: movement at the joint may start a crack in the asphalt.

At one time, blistering troubles were widespread with asphalt roofing. Often the asphalt was laid directly on to the roof decking, to which it adhered except for small areas; any moisture or air entrapped in these areas of poor adhesion would expand when the roof became hot and would cause a blister, which would in time crack at the crown and need local repair. This may be avoided by using a coarse open-textured underlay, to prevent adhesion between the asphalt and the roof deck, so that pressure cannot build up locally. The normal underlay is an impregnated flax felt, Type 4A of B.S. 747; when hot bitumen is laid on this, the joints are bonded so that the felt provides a uniform, jointless mat over the whole roof surface. With an underlay that does not bond at the joints, such as building paper, the asphalt is liable to develop grooves along the joints.

Even with the correct underlay, the asphalt can still be affected by movements in the roof structure. Thus, if there is a line across a reinforced concrete roof at which movement is concentrated, the asphalt above will, in time, show signs of rippling and cracking. In such a case, the asphalt covering should be made discontinuous; on each side of the joint it should be taken up a curb, and the two curbs should be covered with a metal capping fixed to one side only (Fig. 7.4).

Similar considerations apply at parapets and at other walls projecting above the general roof level. Where there is likely to be little relative movement between wall and roof deck, the asphalt can be carried up 6 in., to form a skirting, and tucked into the wall. This gives two lines where the asphalt is formed to an angle, where precautions are needed to prevent cracking. At the lower angle it is usual to introduce a fillet so as to make a more gradual bend; at the upper angle a metal flashing is provided to protect the asphalt from sunlight and so prevent it from becoming brittle. Even so, the vertical skirting is liable to give trouble before the main roof covering. It has to be applied directly to the wall without a porous underfelt, so that blistering is more likely, particularly in skirtings facing south. It is helpful to use a deep flashing or to whiten the surface of the asphalt to keep it cool. Where relative movement between the roof deck and the wall is expected, it is customary to turn the asphalt up over a fillet fixed to the roof deck and free of the wall, protecting it by a cover flashing fixed into the wall (Fig. 7.5). This allows for some relative movement between the roof and wall.

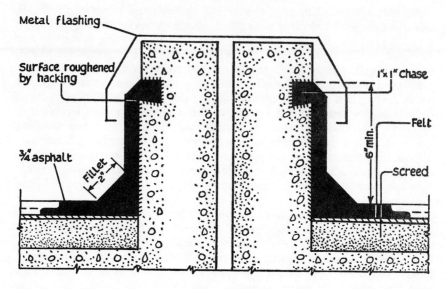

FIG. 7.4

Asphalt roof covering—expansion joint

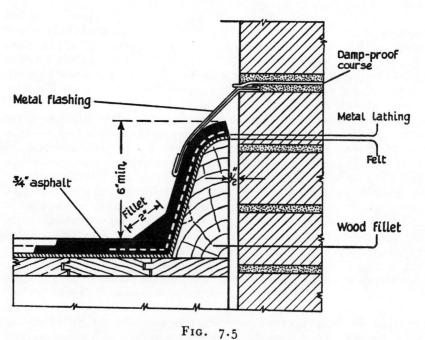

FIG. 7.5

Asphalt roof covering—skirting

Given a dimensionally stable decking, an asphalt roof covering can last as long as the rest of the building. Skirtings and upstands generally are more vulnerable; even with good design they are liable to break down before the rest of the roof covering. Many asphalt roofs appear to shrink slightly over a period of years, and this movement exerts a pull at the bottom of the skirtings. This stress, and the blistering already mentioned, may cause a breakdown of the asphalt either by splitting or by pulling out at the top of the skirting. However, on a good roof, the action is slow and little change is likely to be seen over a period of years.

Built-up bitumen felt

Built-up bitumen felt roofing consists of alternate layers of felt and bitumen. It can be considered as layers of felt with adhesive between them or as layers of bitumen with reinforcement. In this country the emphasis is on the felt; a typical roof consists of three layers of substantial felt bonded with a minimum of hot bitumen. In the U.S.A. and in some European countries the roofing is regarded as one of bitumen with layers of reinforcement; it is common to use five or more layers of felt, all of them thin, so that the bitumen between them forms the major part of the roof covering. This approach may be the wiser—it is the bitumen and not the fibrous felt that does the waterproofing.

Felts were originally made with organic (animal and vegetable) fibres; now, inorganic bases such as asbestos and glass-fibre are used as well. These have some advantage in reducing fire hazard; also they are rot-proof. With asbestos fibres it is usual to incorporate up to 20 per cent of organic fibres to increase the strength of the felt.

In all felts the fibres are impregnated with bitumen. The felt may also be coated on both sides, often with a bitumen of different quality from that used for impregnation, so that the fibres are better protected from dampness; these felts are therefore much safer when there is a risk of rain falling during the laying of the roof covering. The felt used in the upper layer is sometimes surfaced with fine mineral chippings. By providing the mineral coating in the factory good adhesion can be assured, but the underlying bitumen coating is thin, so that this type of felt is unsuitable for roofs where there may be standing water; unless the roof is well drained, a final application of soft oxidized bitumen followed by a blinding of stone chips is to be preferred. The first felt must be one that is not readily affected by moisture and, if the deck is of concrete, it must be resistant to alkalis. The various types of felt are defined in B.S. 747.

The technique of laying built-up bitumen felt roofing is still developing. It has been the practice to stick down the first layer of felt on to those types of roof decking to which it could not be nailed, but this has led to two common defects—tearing of the felt along movement joints in the roof deck, and blistering of the felt away from the decking. (Blistering between layers of felt is usually due to air or water being trapped during laying; it can also result from rain penetration through the top felt.)

Blistering of the felt away from the deck is most severe where the deck is of porous material that can absorb water, or solvent from a priming coat. When the roof warms up a pressure is set up which forces the felt away from the deck. Materials that are porous but do not readily release pressure, for instance asbestos cement and lightweight concrete, are particularly liable to cause blistering; and a powdery surface will give rise to areas of poor adhesion where blisters can readily form. On the other hand, porous materials that readily release any pressure minimize blistering; fibreboard appears to be the best material in this respect. One way of preventing blistering is to lay the first felt without sticking it to the roof, and to provide a loading coat of stone chips, gravel, tiles, or cement-sand screed cut up into small sections, to prevent lifting of the roofing by wind suction. The loading coat cannot normally be applied at the edges and these have to be stuck down; here, blistering may occur. To avoid the need for a loading coat, it has been suggested that the first felt, gritted to prevent adhesion to the roof, should be patterned with perforations, so that the second felt will in fact be stuck down to the roof in patches, between which the granule coating forms a continuous airspace that will prevent the build-up of pressure.

Splitting of bitumen felt stuck down to the roof decking is liable to occur along any lines where local movement is concentrated. All felts will stretch a little under load without splitting (usually between one and five per cent, depending on the felt and on the temperature), but not enough to cope with repeated movement across a crack or joint in the deck; the felt must therefore be left free of the deck for a short distance on each side of the line of movement. A strip of felt or paper about one foot wide may be put down initially along the lines of movement and stuck down only at the edges; the main felt covering can then be stuck down across the roof deck and the felt strips in the normal way. An alternative is to provide a roll in the felt along the line of movement. A simple way of doing this is to carry the felt over a piece of tubing, which is left in place to support the felt. Where movement is very large a joint consisting of two upstands and a capping, as shown in Fig. 7.4 for mastic asphalt roofing, should be provided.

When the roof deck is capable of holding nails the normal practice is to fix the first layer of felt at intervals with large-headed galvanized nails. This fixing is sufficient to prevent lifting of the roofing by wind, and it also avoids local pockets in which moisture can be trapped. The advantages are obvious, but the felt must be one that is unaffected by moisture, otherwise ridging of the roof covering is liable to occur. At edges of the roof deck where there is a parapet, the felt should be carried up a fillet attached to the deck and the top edge covered with a flashing tucked into the parapet. This design is similar to that shown for mastic asphalt roofing in Fig. 7.5.

A similar type of fixing can be used with concrete roofing if timber strips are let into the concrete. The timber should be pressure-impregnated with a preservative. Recently a technique has been evolved for nailing directly into gypsum plaster roof decking, and in the near future this type of fixing is likely to be extended to cement-bonded vermiculite screeds.

The laying of built-up bitumen felt roofing is covered by CP 144 : 201 (1952). This Code is still considered satisfactory for edge details and for nail fixing, but needs revision in other sections.

Sheet metal roof coverings

Metal coverings cannot be laid jointless to form a continuous membrane; they suffer appreciable thermal movement and, if this movement is re-

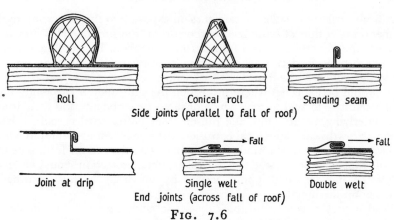

Roll   Conical roll   Standing seam

Side joints (parallel to fall of roof)

Joint at drip   Single welt   Double welt

End joints (across fall of roof)

FIG. 7.6

Metal roof coverings: jointing of sheets

strained, some parts of the metal become highly stressed during each cycle of temperature change and may in time suffer fatigue failure. All the non-ferrous metals used for covering roofs have an appreciably larger thermal movement than steel. The commonly accepted figures for expansion per °F are:

Aluminium	14×10^{-6}
Copper	$9 \cdot 6 \times 10^{-6}$
Lead	16×10^{-6}
Zinc	17×10^{-6}

It is necessary, therefore, to lay metal roof coverings in small sheets, with joints that permit a slight relative movement. Only in this way can a durable covering be provided.

Lead. Lead is believed to have been in use 7000 years ago. There are no lead-covered roofs of great antiquity but buildings are known where the lead covering has served its purpose for 400 years. At those times the lead was cast into heavy sheets; the area of each sheet was small and the metal thick, both of which helped to make the roof durable.

Most lead sheet is now rolled, but it is still used in a substantial thickness—in sheets weighing 6–7 lb /sq. ft for a very long life, or where traffic is expected, and 4 lb /sq. ft for small roofs where there is no traffic. Some constructional details are shown in Fig. 7.6. In a typical roof, 8 ft ×2 ft 9 in. sheets are laid with the length of the sheet at a fall of at least 1½ in. in 10 ft. Joints at the sides of the sheets are laid over wooden rolls about 2 ft 3 in. apart. The lower end of each sheet is formed into a drip, with a vertical section 2½ in. high between the bottom of the upper sheet and the top of the lower one. In this way one section of the roof covering is only about 7 ft long; the joints will permit sufficient movement to prevent fatigue failure.

An advantage that lead has over most other metals is its malleability. It can be hammered into any desired shape, and its full thickness can be maintained in the shaped parts. In this way the shaped portions can be made as durable as the plain sheeting.

A fresh surface of lead soon tarnishes on exposure to the air, owing to the formation of a film of basic lead carbonate on the surface. This film then protects the underlying metal from further corrosion. In a polluted atmosphere the basic lead carbonate is often associated with sulphate, but the protective action of the film is not lessened.

As would be expected where protection depends upon a carbonate film, lead is sensitive to acid waters, which dissolve the carbonate and then attack the underlying metal. Thus, the run-off from slated or tiled roofs bearing organic growths can cause local corrosion, the attack being most rapid where the water drips on to the lead. In a similar way, the run-off from a cedar-shingle roof can affect a lead roof covering; some protection should be given along the line where dripping occurs, by providing a thick coating of bitumen on the metal.

Lead is very sensitive to attack by acetic acid, and so is unsuitable for roofs in breweries, pickle factories or saw-mills. It may be attacked by acids present in oak and in unseasoned softwood. Attack has commonly occurred where lead has been laid on a deck of unseasoned timber boards. Such trouble can be avoided by providing a building-paper or felt underlay, but this must have no free bitumen on its surface which might stick to the lead and so prevent free movement.

Lead is attacked by alkalis. At all points where it is in contact with or embedded in concrete or mortar, a thick coating of bitumen should be provided.

Unlike most other non-ferrous metals, lead is little affected by sulphur gases. It can, therefore, be safely used in the vicinity of flue terminals or furnaces.

Copper. Copper roofing has been used in Europe since the 13th century. Like lead, it forms a protective coating, or patina, on exposure to the air, though the action is very much slower. A patina formed in clean air is often of an attractive green colour; in polluted air, it may be brown or black but a subsequent change to green often occurs.

Copper is a soft, tough metal but hardens rapidly when worked. For this reason, any shaping that has to be done must be completed with a few well-directed blows. Apart from this, the technique of laying a roof covering (CP 143:104) is similar to that used for lead. The copper should be laid on a felt underlay on either a concrete or a timber decking, to a fall of 2 in. in 10 ft. The underlay is similar to that used for asphalt-impregnated flax felt, type 4A in B.S. 747. The copper, to B.S. 1569, should be in a soft state and no thinner than 26 swg. With metal of the minimum thickness, sheets 2 ft wide and 6 ft long are used; for thicker metal the sheets can be slightly larger. The side joints can be made as standing seams unless the roof is likely to carry traffic, in which case rolls are preferable. Joints at right-angles to the seams or rolls can be formed by double welting, but on flat roofs it is desirable to have a drip with a vertical section 2-2½ in. high every 10 to 15 ft down the slope.

Copper is unaffected by alkalis and only very slowly attacked by acids. As with lead, the action is accelerated if there is dripping of water on to the metal surface. Salts, such as sea salt, can also accelerate the corrosion in these circumstances.

Because of the durability of copper roofing, attempts have been made in recent years to use very thin metal, down to 33 swg. It is too soon for a critical appraisal of such roofs; there is some concern lest 'fluttering' of the thin metal in a strong wind should cause fatigue failure. The most recent development on these lines is to use very thin copper foil stuck on to the surface of bitumen felt.

The run-off from copper roofs is liable to be corrosive to other metals, except perhaps lead. Zinc or galvanized iron are very badly affected and cast iron may suffer to some extent. The run-off can also cause staining; if water drips from a copper roof on to stonework, a green or brown stain soon develops and is very difficult to remove.

Zinc. This was used extensively as a roof covering in the early 19th century. In this country, its popularity has waned, particularly in the past 50 years. The greater pollution of the atmosphere may have had some influence.

As with lead, the bright metal soon tarnishes with the formation of a basic carbonate, but this affords little protection to zinc and corrosion continues until all the metal is converted to basic carbonate. Using 14-gauge zinc (0·032 in. thick) for a roof covering, a life of about 40 years can be expected.

The technique of laying is for the most part similar to that adopted for lead, although zinc is much less malleable. The standard sheets are 8 ft × 3 ft in size. They are usually laid on a deck that provides falls of 1½ in. in 8 ft to ensure drainage. Side joints are made over square rolls, and end joints by the formation of drips at a vertical face 2–2½ in. high. The metal can be laid on a paper or felt underlay.

Zinc is attacked by both acids and alkalis, and where it is likely to come into contact with water containing these, or is to be embedded in mortar, a protective coating of bitumen should be provided. Once again, dripping of water on to the metal surface calls for special precautions.

Aluminium. The commercial development of aluminium has taken place in the past 60 years. For roofing, it can be used either in a pure form or as a corrosion-resistant alloy. Super-purity aluminium (99·99 per cent pure) is very soft and easily stretched; it has some of the properties of lead but cannot readily be formed into the more complicated shapes. Other forms of aluminium used in roofing (specified in B.S. 1470) include commercially pure aluminium in grades designated S1A, S1B, S1C, and also alloys NS 3 containing 1¼ per cent manganese and NS 4 containing 2 per cent magnesium. They are all durable and are progressively harder in the order given.

The technique of laying aluminium roofing is similar to that employed for copper. The metal should have a minimum thickness of 22 swg. It is normally provided in rolls 2 ft 6 in. wide and up to 100 ft long, but for the purpose of flat roofing should normally be used in panels not more than 8 ft long. Side joints can be made as standing seams or flat rolls; the rolls used for aluminium are often triangular in section. End joints can be made as welted seams, but drips should be provided at 10–15 ft intervals. Between drips the decks should be arranged to provide a fall of 2 in. in 10 ft. An underfelt is normally employed between the metal and the deck.

The surface of aluminium exposed to the air gradually dulls through the formation of a corrosion product which is white in clean air and usually grey in a polluted atmosphere. With the pure metal or the alloys mentioned above the corrosion soon 'stifles' itself and so the underlying metal is protected. Thus, the main areas of roofing are likely to have a very long life, but the metal may suffer rather more rapid corrosion at crevices where water can be retained for long periods.

Aluminium is attacked only slowly by most acids, but it does not last very long in the vicinity of flue terminals. It is sensitive to alkalis and must be protected with a heavy coating of bitumen paint at any point where there is likely to be contact with mortar or cement. Embedment of unprotected aluminium in mortar or concrete can lead to bursting similar to that caused by rusting iron—the corrosion products occupy a bigger volume than the original metal. Aluminium is also likely to suffer corrosion if there is contact with other metals (except zinc) or if there is run-off of water from a copper surface.

A great advantage of aluminium is the saving of weight that can be effected by its use. Its specific gravity is only $2 \cdot 7$, whereas those of the other roofing metals are: zinc, $6 \cdot 7$; copper, $8 \cdot 8$; lead, $11 \cdot 4$.

MAINTENANCE

Just as the laying of covering to flat roofs is work for specialist craftsmen, so is their maintenance and repair. For the best results it is desirable to have repairs made by the firm that laid the roof covering. Roof leaks do call for emergency measures, which may have to be undertaken by a handyman, but it is far better to carry out regular inspections so that a breakdown can be anticipated and a proper repair made before rain penetration occurs.

Asphalt

A good asphalt roof should not require regular maintenance other than the clearing of dirt and debris which may interfere with drainage. There is, however, a case for making a regular inspection, taking particular note of the more vulnerable parts of the roof, guided by knowledge of the ways in which breakdown is liable to occur. Asphalt is brittle when cold and so might be damaged by impact. It might be softened by leakage of organic liquids on to the surface. Blistering might occur where there is no underfelt, for instance, at steep slopes and upstands. Rippling and splitting of the asphalt might occur as a result of movement of the supporting structure; when this happens, the defects in the asphalt usually follow closely the line at which the structural movement is concentrated. Lastly, the skirtings might have split; there is a tendency for asphalt roofs to shrink slightly after weathering a number of years, and to pull away at the edges, particularly at skirtings.

Temporary repairs to cracks can be made by the handyman with the aid of a filled bitumen mastic, but for a permanent repair it is advisable to call in an asphalter. The normal practice is then to replace the defective asphalt with new material. The old asphalt is warmed by application of poultices of new asphalt until it is soft enough for the defective portions to be cut out. These are replaced, taking care to bond the new asphalt into the old.

It is of course inadequate to repair simply by replacement of defective asphalt where there is an obvious and continuing cause of the breakdown. If, for instance, a flat portion of the roof has blistered, underfelt should be incorporated when the new asphalt is laid. Similarly, if cracking has occurred as a result of thermal movement, steps should be taken to avoid a recurrence of the trouble. If the movement is only slight, whitening the surface of the asphalt with a lime-tallow wash or with a coating of white stone chippings held in oxidized bitumen might be sufficient. Where the movement is large, it would be better to make a proper movement joint in the asphalt by means of a double upstand and capping, as shown in Fig. 7.4. Where skirtings have broken down, consideration should be given to the provision of extra deep flashings to protect the asphalt from sunshine.

Built-up bitumen felt

Up to a few years ago it was considered that regular maintenance treatment, consisting of the application of hot oxidized bitumen followed by blinding with sand or stone chippings, should be given to built-up bitumen felt roofing. Experience indicates that no such general recommendations of this kind can now be made. Regular treatment is still advisable where the upper surface of the roof has exposed bitumen or is only lightly sanded. There are, however, many roof finishes such as heavy mineral chippings, tiles or cement-sand screed, where a surface dressing is inappropriate. In these, the bitumen felt is protected from the main weathering agencies and is expected to have a longer life than an exposed felt. If small defects occur, local repairs can be made, but if there is much trouble with the roof, total replacement of the covering must be undertaken.

Once again, the main causes of breakdown should be considered and the repair made in a way that will minimize the risk of a repetition. A frequent cause of trouble is structural movement which is liable to split the felt along the line at which the movement had concentrated. A common practice is to patch such areas with felt that is reinforced with hessian. Though better than an ordinary felt patch, this will still not tolerate a big movement, and it is better to patch in such a way that the felt is not highly stressed. Two suitable methods are those recommended on p. 146 for new roofing: the line of the split can be covered with a strip of felt stuck down only at the edges, or, preferably perhaps, the repair felt can be carried over a tube so as to form a roll. Again, movement of the structure can be cut down by whitening the roof surface. If there is a very big movement, a double upstand and capping joint should be incorporated.

Where a roof has blistered it may be difficult to decide what measures should be taken. Blistering does not always lead to leakage and, unless it impedes drainage of the roof, may not be accompanied by a marked loss of durability. Where there is no obvious breakdown of the felt and no opening of the laps, a blistered roof is probably best left untreated. If, however, there is sign of impending breakdown or if there is to be traffic on the roof, the blisters should be cut, deflated and covered with a patch of new felt. A surface dressing of hot oxidized bitumen, blinded with sand or chippings, should be provided over the whole area as soon as all patching is completed.

If the roof covering is to be relaid, and the causes of breakdown are known, it should be possible to prevent further trouble. The precautions will be similar to those described for new roofs, p. 146.

The treatment of bitumen felt roofing where water is standing in ponds really requires a way of filling in the ponds so that all water drains off the roof, but no successful and economical method of filling in the hollows has so far been devised. The best existing treatment is to give the felt a heavy coating of soft bitumen to protect it from the standing water. The soft bitumen surface should be blinded with stone chippings so that it can be walked on without pulling up.

Metal coverings

Metal roof coverings require no regular treatment other than the clearing of debris. During this operation care should be taken to avoid damage; most of the metals are soft and are easily scratched by steel tools. Periodic inspection of the roofs is desirable, particular attention being paid to the regions where the metal is most highly stressed. These will be, generally, where the more complicated shaping has been done.

With lead, local repairs are often made by soldering. This is not entirely satisfactory as the solder has different properties, including thermal movement, from the lead. The repair, therefore, leads to local stressing of the metal and possibly to an earlier breakdown. Sometimes a temporary repair is made with bitumen. In an emergency this may be necessary but where possible it should be avoided as the presence of the bitumen makes the subsequent proper repair more difficult. Much the best treatment for small cracks or holes in the lead is to repair by lead 'burning'—a welding technique well known to many craftsmen. When lead burning, care must be taken to avoid charring of any timber immediately beneath the roof covering.

If any of the lead sheets are badly cracked or corroded they should be replaced. The value of the salvaged lead will offset much of the cost of the new material.

With copper, local repair by soldering in a copper patch is considered sound practice. Where there is much damage, replacement of the sheet is advised. When effecting a replacement it should be remembered that the old copper will have hardened. The welts should therefore be annealed before re-dressing.

Local repairs to zinc roofs also can be made by soldering. The solder used should be free from antimony to avoid embrittlement of the surrounding zinc.

So far, no similar treatment has been developed for local defects in aluminium roofs. A temporary repair can be made by sticking down a patch of bitumen felt. In the near future, a cold soldering technique may be developed; until then replacement of the defective sheet is the only permanent repair.

Chapter 8

PITCHED ROOFS

STRENGTH AND STABILITY

THE great majority of the roofs in the United Kingdom are pitched. Usually, a loadbearing structure supports a rigid or flexible weather-excluding membrane in addition to its own weight. This membrane usually consists of slating or tiling (concrete or burnt clay), of a flexible metal or bitumen-felt sheeting, or of a rigid sheeting such as asbestos cement.

Timber boarding under the membrane, or additional insulating layers over the ceiling, provide any additional thermal insulation that may be needed.

Wind effects

The effect of the pitch of the roof on the distribution of wind pressure on its surface has been established from wind-tunnel tests, and it has been found that this distribution is by no means uniform; however, for simplicity in design, Code CP 3 (Ch. V) specifies wind pressures considered as uniformly distributed over each of the main surfaces of dual-pitch roofs. It will be seen from Fig. 6.4 that, for any roof surface with a slope less than about 35°, wind forces take the form of suction; the effect of this suction can be increased if an internal pressure also due to wind is simultaneously acting.

The total pressures due to wind for which a roof structure must usually be designed, for a building with normal openings, are given in Table 8.1,

TABLE 8.1

Total design wind pressures on dual-pitch roofs

	Total pressure		
Component of roof	*Equal slopes of* $23\frac{1}{2}°$	*Equal slopes of* 45°	*Saw-tooth roof with slopes of* 30° and 60°
Main structure: windward slope	$-0\cdot50p$	$+0\cdot40p$ } or { 0	$-0\cdot30p$ } or { $+0\cdot60p$
leeward slope	$-0\cdot65p$	$-0\cdot25p$ } { $-0\cdot65p$	$-0\cdot65p$ } { $-0\cdot25p$
Roof covering: inward load	0	$+0\cdot50p$	$+0\cdot70p$
outward load	$-0\cdot75p$	$-0\cdot75p$	$-0\cdot75p$
Fastenings for sheetings away from edges	As for roof covering		
near edges*	$-2p$	$-2p$	$-2p$

* Within 15 per cent of span from eaves and of length from gables

for three types of dual-pitched roof, two with equal slopes and the third a saw-tooth roof. It will be noted that for a slope of 45°, two combinations of external and internal load due to wind must be considered, corresponding to the alternative internal conditions. It is not specifically stated in the Code that the recommended external wind pressures apply only when the two slopes of a dual-pitch roof are equal; in fact, the Code refers to roof shape in terms of 'slope of roof on windward side'. This can be taken to imply that the values in the Code apply to dual-pitch roofs with either equal or unequal slope; the values given in Table 8.1 for the main roof structure of the saw-tooth roof were based on this assumption and represent the worst combinations of external and internal pressures.

As mentioned on p. 95, the design wind loads for the roof covering and for fastenings for sheeting are greater than that for the roof structure alone. These loads are also given in the table.

Strength

In domestic building, wood is still the predominant structural material for pitched roofs. No comment on the strength of traditional timber roof construction is needed; experience has shown this to be ample. Scantlings were considerably reduced during the second world war when imported softwood was scarce; the Ministry of Works issued a Timber Economy Memorandum in which the permissible sizes of rafters, purlins etc. were tabulated, and the limited quantity of timber issued to builders under licence was based on these reduced sizes. These sizes were recommended by the Forest Products Research Laboratory after tests had shown roofs built with them to be safe.

All light roof structures may be subjected to considerable buffeting during high winds. If the pitched roof is fixed to the front and back walls, and to slender chimney stacks that are otherwise unsupported above first-floor level, the resultant jarring transmitted to a somewhat brittle structure such as a stack or a wall or light blockwork may lead to cracking at horizontal joints. If the roof is not fixed in this way, relative movement between roof and stack, or between ceiling and wall lining, could lead to unsightly cracking. On balance, it is probably preferable to connect light blockwork walls and stacks to the roof, but as flexibly as possible. The roof structure itself should be stiffened against horizontal racking by means of boards nailed to the ceiling joists, inclined to the direction of these joists to form a 'wind girder' as shown in Fig. 8.1. Details of fastenings will vary with the construction of the roof and the walls.

For steel roof structures, the designer should note that the forces calculated for the various members of, say, a pitched roof truss intended for one locality will not necessarily be the same, or even of the same sign, if that truss is used elsewhere. For instance, if a steel truss with a covering of asbestos-cement sheets and glazing is designed for a wind velocity of 54 mph (exposure *B* of Code CP 3, Ch. V), the wind may not cause reversal of stress in any member; however, if the same truss is intended for a locality on the West coast, with exposure grade *D* and a wind velocity of 72 mph, it is quite likely that revised calculations will show that the stronger wind would cause reversals of stress in many members of the truss.

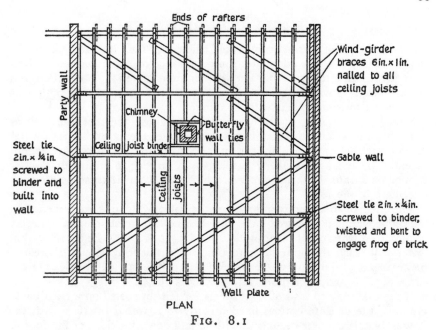

FIG. 8.1

Bracing of ceiling structure to stabilize pitched wooden roof and connected walls

Stability

The normal pitched roof of domestic buildings usually has an ample margin of safety against the wind uplift effects; with pitched roofs of sheds and factories, the wind uplift affects only part of the large roof areas—the leeward slopes—and this effect is relatively small compared with the total weight of the roof and the strength of standard anchorage devices.

DIMENSIONAL STABILITY

Pitched roofs are subject to thermal movements and to large moisture movements—particularly in timber structures—and also to deformations due to self-weight and live loading; however, these changes of shape or volume are rarely important structurally. Pitched roofs traditionally, and almost necessarily, function as a three-point arch whose stability is usually maintained with ties at eaves level or sometimes slightly above eaves level. It is not difficult to ensure that the deformations due to self-weight and superimposed loading are kept within reasonable limits, except where faults occur in the material. There is nothing here that cannot be dealt with by reasonable quality of workmanship and conventional engineering design.

Differential thermal or moisture movements cause trouble only where they are not free to take place without restraint. In most pitched roofs deformations can take place freely in the upward direction without disturbing any existing structure or causing any anxiety. It must be borne in mind, however, that such movements may affect flashings, valley gutters, ridge cappings and other weatherings. Large movements may strain materials at the hip and at the eaves, and may contribute to their deterioration with age.

EXCLUSION OF WATER

For a pitched roof to shed rain water efficiently, the pitch and lap of the roof coverings must be adequate; some guidance on these matters is given later in this chapter (p. 160). For the common materials, both pitch and lap are largely governed by tradition, but there is evidence that both may be reduced to some extent without danger.

Stretches of glazing, or features projecting above the roof line such as dormer windows and chimney stacks, may hinder the natural flow of water down a roof slope; particular care must be taken to treat these intersections carefully by means of soakers, flashings and gutters, to ensure that water cannot penetrate. Leakages are more likely to occur at these points than elsewhere in the roof.

The effect of an underlay in reducing the risk of water or snow penetrating the roof covering is discussed on p. 160. It is not the function of an underlay to provide a waterproof covering to a building, but it must be accepted that water will reach the underlay sometimes. The underlay should, therefore, be arranged so that any water which falls on it is carried out clear of the external walls and, preferably, into the eaves gutter.

If the underlay consists of rigid sheets (or felt supported on a rigid background), tile or slate battens fixed directly to it would interfere with the flow of water; counter-battens should be laid down the slope of the roof to pack the battens up clear of the underlay.

In mansard and similar constructions, where accommodation is provided in the roof space by closing in the underside of the rafters with plaster or wallboards, a small leak may go undetected for a long time. In the absence of ventilation, conditions favourable to dry rot may develop. It is wise, therefore, in such structures, to provide a clear air space, freely ventilated, or to use fully impregnated timber.

THERMAL INSULATION

The simple pitched roofs commonly used in domestic and industrial buildings are often inadequate to conserve heat unless some insulation is provided. The thermal transmittance value for a pitched roof covered with tiles, battens and felt is about 0·42, and this does not meet modern standards of comfort; fortunately, it is neither difficult nor expensive to improve these by any of the methods suggested in Table 8.2. Even for a modest level of house heating, such treatment would soon be repaid by savings of fuel, and it would add appreciably to the comfort of the occupants of top-storey flats and apartments. Where, as is most convenient, all the insulation is applied at ceiling level, the moderate amount of natural ventilation above it will usually avoid the risk of condensation without serious loss of heat. In roofs with felt underlays, ventilation is reduced and there is rather more risk of condensation; to counter this, the roof slopes themselves should be insulated, but it is as well to have some insulation at ceiling level as well.

The light industrial roof of corrugated sheeting, with no ceiling, has a thermal transmittance of about 1·40, and the capital and running cost of maintaining a reasonably comfortable temperature in buildings roofed in such a way is now considered to be unwarrantably high (*see* Volume 1, p. 40). Insulation can be added either above the purlins or, as a ceiling, below them, as shown in Table 8.2, or it may be sandwiched between the roof cladding and an integral lining, as in some proprietary forms of roof covering. If the atmosphere in the building is humidified or contains steam from industrial processes, condensation is likely to occur at the underside of the roof cladding. To avoid this risk, some circulation of air from outside should be encouraged between the cladding and the insulation, and, wherever possible, the resistance of the internal lining to vapour transfer should be increased by painting or sealing treatments. With roofs of metal decking, it is most convenient to include all the necessary insulation above the metal and to protect it by a covering of bitumen felt. Such roofs have the advantage that the decking can be sealed so as to provide a vapour barrier on the warmer side of the roof construction (see p. 122); provided there is sufficient insulation above to keep the internal surface at close to room temperature, the risk of condensation even in very humid conditions is slight.

Heat losses are greatly increased if roof glazing is provided. The heating costs in a building with a monitor roof may be more than twice those with a flat, unglazed roof, since the glazing has a high thermal transmittance and with the monitor type of construction there is also a larger roof space to heat. Where roof glazing has been decided on, considerations other than heating costs will have been decisive; these have been discussed in Chapter 6.

Roof glazing and thermal insulation are both important in relation to solar heat gain in summer, as discussed in Chapter 7.

FIRE PROTECTION

Whilst fire resistance, where required, may be achieved comparatively simply in many types of flat roof, the problem becomes complex and expensive in the normal types of pitched roof. It is primarily the structural members that have to be protected. Metal trusses are difficult to deal with, but methods of protection by sprayed coatings are available. Timber trusses may have a higher fire resistance than unprotected metal, but their combustibility has to be balanced against this advantage.

Apart from the roof structure and its fire resistance, consideration should be given to:

  (i) the type of covering and its background,
 (ii) the type of internal lining — whether combustible or non-combustible, its method of fixing, and its position in relation to the external covering,
(iii) the type of thermal insulation treatment, if any, not integral with the roof covering,
 (iv) the method of reducing the spread of fire between adjacent occupancies.

The types of external covering, whether combustible or non-combustible, have already been considered (p. 111). Internal linings in pitched roofs, especially those exposed within the building, may if combustible present a fire hazard. Care is particularly necessary where they are fixed in such a

TABLE 8.2

Thermal transmittance of roof and ceiling

Construction	Insulating material	Application	Thickness (in.)	U-value
Roof covered with concrete plain tiles on battens and felt, slope 40°				
Insulation laid on plasterboard ceiling	Glass wool or glass silk	Mat laid between joists over plasterboard	4	0·08
	Glass, slag or mineral wool	1 in. thick mat (bitumen-bonded) or quilt	1	0·16
	Gypsum granules	Loose, poured and spread	2	0·14
Insulation forming ceiling, without plasterboard	Cork board	Forming ceiling, with wire mesh and plaster	1	0·17
	Insulating fibreboard	Two boards, ½ in. thick, stuck together	1	0·20
	Wood-wool or compressed straw	With plaster in 2 coats, ¼ in. and ⅜ in.	2	0·18
Insulation above ceiling joists, plasterboard below	Aluminium foil	Combined corrugated and plain draped over joists		0·21
	Glass wool, glass silk, eel grass, mineral wool	Quilt draped over joists	1	0·14
			½	0·21
	Insulating fibreboard	Nailed on top of joists	1	0·16
	Cork board	„ „ „ „	1	0·15
	Wood-wool or compressed straw	„ „ „ „	2	0·15
Insulation under felt on slope	Insulating fibreboard		½	0·30
	Softwood boarding		⅞	0·31
No insulation	—	—	—	0.42
Roof covered with corrugated asbestos-cement sheets				
Insulation between sheeting and purlins	Insulating fibreboard	With aluminium foil on upper face	½	0·38
	„ „		½	0·26
	Straw-board or wood-wool		2	0·22

sheeting
T-section purlins
insulation

			Thickness (in.)	U
Insulation below purlins	Insulating fibreboard	On fibreboard	$\tfrac{1}{2}$	0·38
	Straw board or wood-wool	On plasterboard	2	0·22
	$\tfrac{1}{4}$-in. aluminium foil (combined corr. and plain)		$\tfrac{1}{2}$, $\tfrac{3}{8}$	0·18 / 0·22
	$\tfrac{3}{4}$-in. bitumen-bonded glass or slag wool	On fibreboard	$\tfrac{1}{2}$, $\tfrac{3}{8}$	0·27
	$\tfrac{1}{2}$-in. eel-grass quilt	On plasterboard	$\tfrac{1}{2}$, $\tfrac{3}{8}$	0·37
	Aluminium foil (single-sided)	—	1	1·40
No insulation	—	—	—	—
Roof covered with felt laid on boards or slabs over metal decking **Insulation above decking**	Insulating fibreboard	Laid in bitumen on decking	$\tfrac{1}{2}$	0·38
	" " two sheets		$1\tfrac{1}{2}+1\tfrac{1}{2}$	0·25
	Cork board	Laid in bitumen on decking	1	0·21
	Compressed straw-board or wood-wool		2	0·22
Insulating material in slabs in place of decking	Compressed straw-board or wood-wool	On T's at 2-ft or 4-ft centres	2	0·24
Insulating material on, or forming, ceiling	Insulating fibreboard	T's at 2-ft centres	$\tfrac{1}{2}$, $\tfrac{3}{8}$	0·21
	Plasterboard	" " " "		0·27
	Wood-wool	" " " "	2	0·15
	Compressed straw-board	" " 4-ft "		
	$\tfrac{1}{4}$-in. aluminium foil (combined corr. and plain)	On fibreboard	$\tfrac{1}{2}$, $\tfrac{3}{8}$, $\tfrac{1}{4}$	0·13
	or $\tfrac{3}{4}$-in. eel grass quilt	On plasterboard		0·15
	or $\tfrac{3}{4}$-in. bitumen-bonded glass or slag wool	On fibreboard		0·17
	Aluminium foil (single-sided)	On plasterboard	$\tfrac{3}{8}$	0·20

way that a cavity is formed between the external covering and the lining. To reduce the possibility of fire spread within the cavity, fire-stopping should be adopted wherever possible.

Thermal insulating materials in the form of quilts at ceiling level may, if enclosed within combustible coverings, constitute a fire risk. To reduce this hazard, coverings should be non-combustible or of very low flame spread.

Where a pitched roof spans one or more occupancies or divisions of a building, byelaws lay down requirements for the complete fire separation of the roof space. No combustible material may be built in or carried over the wall, other than battens, which must be properly bedded in mortar. Care should also be taken at the eaves; in traditional type roofs this is a point of weakness in relation to fire spread.

In domestic buildings with combustible external walls, domestic buildings over five storeys in height, and in certain other classes of building, byelaws require that the wall separating the buildings or divisions of the buildings shall be carried up as a parapet, if the roof is of a construction other than a slab of non-combustible material.

ROOF COVERINGS

Small units—slates, tiles and shingles

The materials of small roofing units may themselves be porous; and they are normally laid without any jointing material or bedding. Their effectiveness depends therefore on the adoption of suitable pitch and lap to shed water and snow from the surface of the roof. These two factors are interdependent and, in general, the flatter the pitch the greater the lap that should be allowed. Pitch may also have some effect on durability, as with a flatter pitch the materials may take longer to dry out, with an increased chance of freezing when saturated with water. Pitches of 30° to 45° are commonly adopted for coverings of this type.

Closely spaced supports are required, and are usually provided in the form of battens on rafters.

The high cost of timber, and the prohibition of its use as roof boarding for a period during and after the war, has almost brought to an end the full treatment of roofs with boarding, sarking felt, counter-battens and battens laid over the rafters. Bitumen felt is now available reinforced by a layer of jute hessian embedded in the coating on one side, and this is sufficiently strong to span between rafters as a sarking without a boarded support. The natural sag of the felt between rafters eliminates the need for counter-battens. Thermal insulation can be provided either at ceiling level or immediately below the rafters. An efficient roofing system can thus be devised at a cost lower than that of boarding, counter-battening, etc.

The functions of sarking felt should be clearly understood. No roof covering should rely on this to exclude moisture from the building. However, in the absence of bedding or jointing material, a free flow of air is possible through the roof covering, so that, under certain wind conditions, water or fine powdery snow may be blown through. A layer of felt below the roof covering hinders the flow of air and makes occasional penetration in this manner less likely. It cannot of course be guaranteed that such penetration will never occur, and for this reason the felt should be laid so that any water falling on it is discharged harmlessly, clear of the external walls of the building and, preferably, into an eaves gutter.

Bedding, pointing and torching of tiled and slated roofs have been the subject of a great deal of controversy. The practice is generally undesirable because it tends to retain moisture and to restrict thermal movements, but torching is sometimes of value in slated roofs. For example, a slated roof over a warehouse for the storage of combustible goods must not be felted because of the increased fire risk, but a reduction in air flow through the roofing may be safely achieved by torching. Haired lime mortar should be used for torching, but precise recommendations or specifications are not available, and the work should be entrusted only to craftsmen experienced in this operation; they will generally be found in districts where torching is customary.

The choice of nails for fixing slates and tiles depends on conditions of exposure, for instance to sea air or to industrial pollution; also, industrial processes carried on in the building below may have harmful effects. The cost of roofing nails is such a small percentage of the cost of the roof that it is foolish economy to use nails of inadequate quality, which may make early repairs necessary. Galvanized-iron or steel nails are not considered adequate, as the protective zinc coating is likely to be damaged during driving or by subsequent movements of the roofing in high winds and corrosion of the nails will follow rapidly. (Nails for fixing battens, however, may with advantage be given the added protection of a galvanized coating, particularly near the coast where the life of unprotected nails is likely to be short.)

Cast yellow metal ('composition') nails are the most durable of the types commonly used and are suitable for all but the most severe conditions. They are harder than copper nails, though these are also very durable. Zinc nails should not be used where atmospheric pollution is high or near the coast. Aluminium alloy nails are now available but have not been used long enough for their behaviour to be predicted confidently.

Slates. The durability of slates, even from different veins of rock in the same quarry, varies considerably. The best slates may endure, for hundreds of years, exposure to a city atmosphere in which poor slates would become unserviceable in ten to fifteen years.

Durability depends on the resistance to acid attack, particularly of the layers along the cleavage planes. Resistance is likely to be weak if the slate contains appreciable amounts of calcium carbonate: salts, particularly calcium sulphate, are formed which, as the moisture evaporates, are deposited as crystals and force the layers apart. Lamination usually begins at the head (the covered and generally dry part of the slate) rather than at the exposed tail. The layers flake at the edges, the nails break out of their holes and the slates slip down the roof. The British Standard for roofing slates therefore discriminates between slates capable of withstanding severe atmospheric pollution and those less durable, by means of an immersion test in sulphuric acid. Other tests are applied to check that the slates will withstand wetting and drying without splitting, and also to measure their water absorption.

Slates are available in a considerable range of sizes, and not only in different graded thicknesses but in three separate categories: those uniform in length and width, those uniform in length but of random width, and those of random sizes. Production of slates in the quarry is inevitably accompanied by considerable waste; this could be reduced to some extent and deliveries improved if the practice of specifying slates of uniform size—particularly in the popular sizes such as Countess (20 in. × 10 in.)—were relaxed in favour of accepting slates of uniform length but random width. These require only a little additional care in arrangement on the roof so that the butt joints between adjacent slates occur as nearly as possible centrally over the slate below. Random sized slates require additional care in setting out so that the margins of the slates diminish regularly from eaves to ridge and the specified lap is obtained in all cases.

The lap of a slate is the amount by which it overlaps the slates in the course *next but one* below. Side lap, which is the distance by which the side of a slate overlaps a slate in the course below, is also important, as it provides lateral protection against water creeping sideways between the slates and penetrating the roof. For this reason slates with a minimum width greater than half their length may be used on roofs of rather flat pitch. The lap (end lap) should be increased as the pitch of the roof is reduced. Generally a pitch of 35° is suitable for slates laid to a 3-in. lap.

Nailing is best done approximately at the centre-line of the slates, except with the very smallest sizes, as the slates then have greater security and do not tend to lift and rattle in high winds.

Tiles. Tiles are manufactured either from clay or concrete in a wide variety of patterns. The simplest forms are the 'plain' tiles, about 10½ in. × 6½ in. in size and provided with nail holes and projecting nibs for fixing to battens. Like slates they rely on a double overlap to shed water from the roof. More complicated designs are available, incorporating interlocking edges and sometimes wind stops and protected nail holes. These are laid with only a single overlap and are weathertight at pitches flatter than could be adopted for plain tiles.

Clay tile manufacture varies from hand making, by simple, primitive methods, to mechanized factory production. As tiles are less robust in form than bricks, and more severely exposed, the requirements for the clay are more strictly defined for tile-making than for brick-making. It must be substantially free from inclusions of limestone or chalk which on firing would form nodules of unslaked lime, and from soluble sulphates which might damage the tile by crystallization.

In the simplest process of forming, the clay is pressed by hand into a mould. The clay may also be moulded under a power press, or extruded into a continuous strip by an auger and cut off into tile widths. Interlocking tiles are normally made on a press. In these mechanical processes the tile body acquires a laminar structure; if this structure persists, damage may result later if water lodges and freezes between the laminae. The firing process, when controlled with sufficient precision, may correct any weakness due to lamination by heating the tile to incipient fusion, but this is not always achieved. There have been many failures of machine-made tiles by frost action, and some by crystallization of salts in planes of weakness caused by lamination. Lamination remains the principal weakness to be guarded against. The British Standard for the strength of clay tiles is a criterion for the general adequacy of manufacture and firing, but gives no absolute security as to frost resistance; it is still necessary for the architect and builder to satisfy themselves by enquiry that any particular tile is suitable for their purpose.

Concrete tiles are a precast concrete product, usually formed in a press and stacked on pallets to cure. Tests for transverse strength and permeability are laid down in the British Standards. Concrete tiles are unlikely to fail by lamination and those which conform to the Standard can be expected to be immune from frost failure.

Plain tiles should be laid to a pitch not flatter than 40°; at this pitch a lap of 2½ in. is generally sufficient, although on severely exposed sites it should be increased to 3 in. They are supported by the nibs bearing on battens, but added security is given by nailing. At least every fourth course should be nailed, and on more exposed sites and at steeper pitches it may be necessary to nail more frequently, up to the maximum of nailing every course.

For interlocking (single-lap) tiles, the B.S. Code of Practice CP 142 recommends a minimum pitch of 35°, but the considerable variations in design of interlocking tiles and in their durability make it difficult to make precise recommendations. Attack by frost is more severe on low-pitched roofs because the tiles remain wet for longer periods. Good quality clay and concrete tiles that can be demonstrated to be resistant to frost attack might be used at flatter pitches than recommended in the Code, and the ability of the design features of the tile to exclude water then becomes a deciding factor. The lap may be dictated by the design of the tiles and cannot be varied if the design incorporates interlocking heads; in other cases a lap of at least 3 in. is desirable. Every tile should be nailed, the number of nails being determined by the nail holes provided in the tile.

Asbestos-cement slates. Although commonly described as 'slates,' these are manufactured from asbestos fibre and Portland cement, and resemble natural roofing slates only in size, shape and method of laying. A British Standard governs quality and size, and it will usually be sufficient for the user to obtain an undertaking that the materials supplied comply with the Standard and are free from cracks or other visible defects.

The method of laying follows closely that for natural roofing slates, but the sizes commonly available are supplied with nail holes spaced only to suit 3-in. or 4-in. laps. The former is suitable for a pitch of 30°; on severely exposed sites a lap of 4 in. would give added protection, or a flatter pitch may be permitted with the greater lap in sites not abnormally exposed.

Because of the light weight of these slates there is a tendency for the tails to lift in a high wind, and the material is also liable to curl as it ages on the roof. A copper rivet should therefore be used to hold down the tails. The head of the rivet is held under adjacent edges of the slates, in the course below, and the pin passes through a hole formed centrally in the tail and is turned over.

Diamond pattern asbestos-cement slates are now very little used; the production even of rectangular slating is only a very small part of the output of the asbestos-cement industry in this country, and it could be argued that the sheet form of roof covering is a more logical and economical use of the material.

Shingles. The use of oak shingles as a roof covering dates back to the Romans and Saxons, evidence of which may be found in the name 'Saxon shakes' which still persists in this trade. Shortage in the supply of oak brought the craft almost to obsolescence, but it was taken by settlers to America where cedar was found to have some advantages over the oak formerly used (and the name 'cedar shakes' is still current there).

Western red cedar shingles are more durable than oak and more stable. Even so, their life of about sixty years cannot compare with that of good-quality tiles and slates. Oak shingles may have a life of about fifty years, but only if laid to a pitch of not less than 45°. A flatter pitch, say 30°, may be adopted for cedar shingles.

Shingles 16 in. long (other lengths are supplied) are commonly laid to a gauge of 5 in. at pitches of 30° and upwards. This provides a cover of not less than three thicknesses in any part of the roof. Between 20° and 30° pitch they should be laid to $3\frac{3}{4}$ in. gauge, which provides not less than four thicknesses in any part of the roof.

Copper nails should be used, as they are sufficiently durable to last for the life of the shingles. Galvanized or steel nails are unsuitable, as ferrous metals are attacked by corrosive agents in the timber.

Shingles should not be butted tightly against each other when laying; a gap of $\frac{3}{8}$–$\frac{1}{4}$ in. should be left to allow for moisture movement. Nailing is commonly done approximately along the centre-line of the shingles with two nails in each. It has been suggested that nailing with only one nail placed near the side edge of each shingle would allow unrestrained moisture movement without risk of splitting the shingles, but the more common practice seems to work satisfactorily.

An underlay of boarding or felt is not necessary as the shingles fit closely; such an underlay might indeed prove harmful by preventing the circulation of air to the underside of the shingles and so producing conditions favourable to rot.

Rigid sheets

Rigid sheets, corrugated or troughed in section, so as to be self-supporting over wide spans, are commonly available in lengths up to 10 ft or more, and with an effective covering width ranging upwards from 2 ft. The sheets are themselves impermeable and the effectiveness of the end lap determines the pitch that can be used. With longer lengths of sheeting fewer end laps will be needed, and on short spans may be eliminated completely; in such cases, a pitch as low as 10° might be adopted. More commonly, a pitch from 15° to 25° can be regarded as suitable. If the sheets are to be laid to flatter pitches than 15°, the usual 6-in. end lap should be increased to 9 in., and for added security the end laps should be sealed with a non-hardening mastic.

The sheets are light in weight and require supporting only by purlins spaced 3–6 ft apart, depending on the gauge of metal, section profile and loading. As the units are rather large, they are more suitable for covering large, plain areas of roof than for small intricate roofs intersected by hips, valleys and dormers. An underlay is not required to assist in excluding water, but may be provided as thermal insulation, as sound absorption, or to form a level surface at the underside of the sheeting to receive decoration.

Sheets are usually secured by means of hook bolts or drive screws, passed through the crowns of the corrugations or the troughs and fixed to purlins below. The holes through the sheeting should be waterproofed by means of bitumen or plastic washers.

The sheets may be curved (after corrugating) for the whole or a part of their length, and sheets so formed may be used to avoid the need for separate ridge coverings; alternatively, whole roofs may be covered with curved sheets, as in the Dutch barn.

Steel sheets. The durability of corrugated steel sheets depends on their effective and continuing protection. Most commonly they are supplied galvanized, and this may either be accepted as affording the necessary protection or, in heavily polluted industrial atmospheres, where the corrosion of the zinc coating is likely to be rapid, it may be regarded only as a good base for regular painting.

Some forms of sheet consist of a steel core, plain or galvanized, to both sides of which is bonded (under pressure) a coating of asbestos-based bitumen, asphalt-saturated felt, or asbestos-cement. Cutting or drilling the sheets exposes unprotected edges, which should be treated carefully according to the manufacturer's recommendations.

Aluminium sheets. Aluminium sheets are commonly supplied in lengths up to 16 ft or (from some manufacturers) 20 ft, so that roofs of considerable span can be laid without end laps. The thermal movement of sheets of this length may be considerable, but in practice the clearance of the fixing holes, coupled perhaps with slight deflection of the sheets, accommodates this movement without the sheets buckling.

The elimination of end laps makes possible pitches as flat as 10°; at such a pitch, any condensation that forms on the underside is likely to drip off the sheets rather than run down to the eaves, but even the more usual pitch of 15° may not be steep enough to prevent this.

Louvred ventilation openings can be formed in the sheets.

Some proprietary systems have been developed in which all fastenings are covered, so that the exposed surface is unbroken. Fixing is to clips, brackets or strips fastened to the roof structure. One pattern is obtainable in lengths up to 30 ft so that end laps are normally unnecessary; another pattern is supplied in rolls which are laid *along* the slope of the roof and have end laps, but side laps only at very wide intervals.

Asbestos-cement sheets. Several patterns of sheets are detailed in the B.S.690, and additional profiles are produced by some manufacturers. This variety has resulted from the search for stronger sheets that can be laid on wider-spaced purlins than the earlier standard or 6-in. corrugated sheets, for improved weather resistance at side laps, and for a less austere appearance.

One pattern incorporates upturned and downturned ends which form a drip similar to that in flat sheet metal roofing. This enables the sheeting to be laid to very low pitches, and it may in fact be regarded as a flat roof covering rather than a pitched roof covering.

A comprehensive range of flashing and weathering accessories is available, so that hips, valleys and other junctions can be made weathertight with the same material.

On exposure to the atmosphere, asbestos-cement carbonates slowly from the surface inwards. This is accompanied by some shrinkage and embrittlement. Shrinkage does not normally lead to failure, but if the sheets are too tightly bolted through holes with inadequate clearance, cracks may develop. Damage may also result from painting the sheets on one face only: carbonation is arrested by painting, and will then take place only from the unprotected face; shrinkage of one face only may produce bowing or distortion which (particularly if the sheets are tightly fixed) may ultimately produce cracks.

Embrittlement does not affect the weathertightness of the sheeting, but the reduced resistance to impact loads makes such roofs dangerous to walk on. The Building (Safety, Health and Welfare) Regulations, 1948, require ladders, duckboards or crawling boards to be provided for workmen who have to pass over, or work above, roofs covered with fragile materials, and also require prominent permanent notices to be displayed, drawing attention to the fragile nature of the coverings.

Translucent sheets. Translucent roofing sheets can be obtained to match the profile of most metal or asbestos-cement roof sheets. There is no British Standard for these sheets and their composition varies; the fire hazard they present also varies considerably.

Glass-fibre reinforced polyester resin sheets are probably the most common, but acrylic resin sheets and corrugated glass with wire reinforcement are also obtainable.

These sheets are commonly used singly at intervals in roofs of other materials, and have therefore to be laid to the same pitch as the main roof sheeting. They provide a convenient way of introducing some daylight through roofs, avoiding the need for flashings or special supports.

Polyester resin sheets vary considerably in the extent to which they retain their light-transmitting qualities. Some compare favourably in this respect with acrylic-resin sheets, but some—even among the more recently developed products—show a perceptible loss of light transmission after only a few months' exposure.

Fully-supported sheeting

Materials in this class include metal sheets (aluminium, copper, lead, zinc) and asphalt and bitumen, and are more commonly laid as coverings to flat roofs. When laid on sloping roofs, water exclusion does not normally present a problem; roof pitches are unrestricted.

However, some practical considerations require a slightly different technique to be employed from that used on flat roofs.

With metal sheeting, features such as drips, which are required on flat roofs to prevent the capillary flow of water through end laps, may be dispensed with on pitched roofs.

Bitumen felt roofing may be bonded to concrete with a bituminous adhesive, or may be nailed to boarded backgrounds in the manner adopted on flat roofs. The sheets should be laid up the slopes from eaves to ridge in multi-layer work, but across the roof slopes in single-layer work.

Asphalt will not adhere satisfactorily to steeply sloping surfaces unless a good mechanical key is provided. This can be done by stapling a layer of metal reinforcement to boarded backgrounds, or by forming grooves and hacking concrete surfaces. These, or similar, precautions are necessary on slopes steeper than 10°.

MAINTENANCE

Pitched roofs in general require very little maintenance, if properly designed and laid in the first instance, and if in selecting the covering proper consideration was given to the factors influencing durability, such as exposure to corrosive atmospheres and the degree of exposure of the roof.

A faulty selection of roof covering and design may lead to failure which cannot be remedied by any process that might fairly be described as maintenance.

Even a correctly designed roof, however, may spring a leak at some time during its life. Slates and tiles break away from their fixings, flashings become defective, valley gutters get choked. Any of these defects might result in water penetrating the structure and should be attended to promptly. Slates or tiles that come adrift can only be renewed or refixed when the fault occurs. Flashings, however, can be examined periodically and renewed when any sign of failure appears, before serious harm can come to the structure. An annual clearance of leaves and debris from valley gutters and eaves gutters will prevent them from becoming choked.

Slating and tiling are normally done by specialist firms whose operatives gain considerable skill and experience, but the repair of roofs is often left to a small jobbing builder. It is emphasized that repairs should be carried out by workmen no less skilled in their craft than those who laid the roof in the first instance.

Algae, lichens and mosses are commonly seen on roofs, particularly in rural districts, and the resulting appearance is often regarded as mellow, pleasing and generally desirable. These growths are rarely destructive, except that mosses may impede the shedding of water from roofs and may lead to blockage of gutters and downpipes. Requests received at the Building Research Station for advice on vegetation on roofs come about equally from those who wish to encourage and those who wish to destroy vegetable growths. For the former purpose, a wash of cow dung and water is the traditional treatment; human urine and skimmed milk are also said to be effective. For the removal of vegetation, a toxic wash can be used; several types are available.

Attempts to produce artificially the green patina generally admired on copper roofs, or to accelerate its formation, cannot be guaranteed to be permanent and may also interfere with its natural formation.

Chapter 9

SHELL ROOFS AND OTHER SPECIAL TYPES

PRINCIPLES OF DESIGN

THIN membranes, curved in one or more directions, may be used as a means of roofing, usually over single-storey buildings of relatively large area. Timber has been used in this way, and so have steel sheets, ceramics (including glass), plastics and even hardboard, but the great majority of these 'shell' roofs have been constructed in reinforced concrete.

There are many possible shapes and arrangements of the shell, or shells, and the necessary supporting elements. Shells can be classified according to their geometry into the following types:

(i) Rotation shells, whose surface is formed by rotating a curve about a straight line in its own plane. Thus, a spherical dome may be traced out by rotating part of a circle about a vertical axis (Fig. 9.1*a*).

(ii) Translation shells, whose surface is formed by moving a curve of one shape over an orthogonal curve of the same or different shape, thus producing domes or anticlastic shells depending on the sense of the curvature of one curve relative to that of the other (Fig. 9.1*b*). (Note that the hyperbolic paraboloid can be generated by a straight line moving over two other skewed straight lines.)

(iii) Conoidal shells, in which a straight line which generates the surface moves at one end over a curve and at the other end along a straight line, whilst remaining in parallel planes (Fig. 9.1*c*).

(iv) Conical shells, which are a special case of (i), where the curve is a straight line intersecting the axis (Fig. 9.1*d*).

(v) Cylindrical shells, which are a special case of (ii), where the generator is a straight line parallel to the axis (Fig. 9.1*e*).

When a load is applied to such a roof, one or more of three load-carrying actions may be brought into play in transferring the load to the ground or to the supporting structure: direct forces (thrusts and pulls tangential to the shell), shear forces in the same plane as the direct forces, and bending moments and twisting moments in two planes normal to the surface of the shell and at right-angles to each other (Fig. 9.2).

It is the ability of the shell membrane to carry load simultaneously by all these three mechanisms, and at the same time to provide a weather-excluding covering, that makes shell roofing such an efficient method of covering large areas unobstructed by intermediate columns.

169

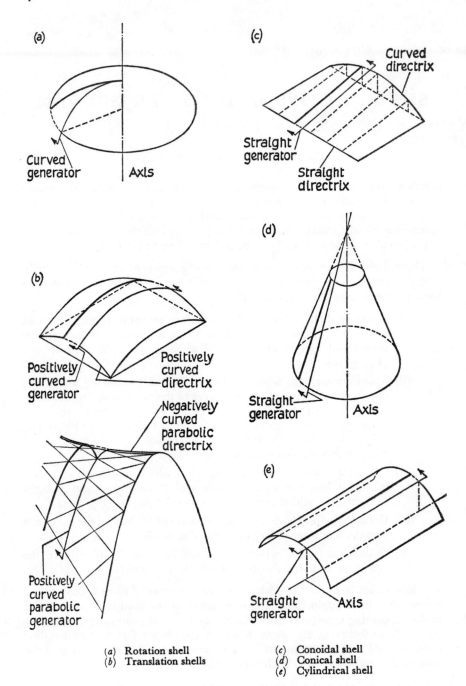

(a)   Rotation shell
(b)   Translation shells

(c)   Conoidal shell
(d)   Conical shell
(e)   Cylindrical shell

FIG. 9.1

Types of shell

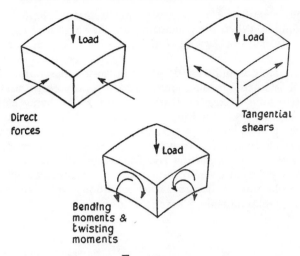

FIG. 9.2

Internal forces in shells

Good shell design, from the structural point of view, consists in arranging the shape of the shell, and the disposition and stiffness of its supports, so that the shear forces and direct forces will predominate, the latter in the form of thrusts so far as is possible, and so that the bending and twisting moments will be as small as possible, whatever the type of loading the shell may be expected to carry. The thin membrane is ill-adapted to carry large bending moments; indeed it is probably the combination of curvature, thrust, and shear that typifies 'shell action' in the mind of the structural engineer. Fortunately, nearly all the loads on roofs are fairly uniformly distributed, and large local bending moments such as are produced by concentrated loads do not usually have to be catered for. Small bending moments can be resisted, by a shell of the thickness that is in any case required to provide cover to the reinforcement; if, locally, the stresses somewhat exceed the capacity of the shell, its thickness can be slightly increased in those regions.

Each type of shell has its own peculiar combination of load-carrying actions. Dome-like shells of rotation (Plate 9.1a) carry their loads mainly by meridional compression and hoop tension; dome-like translation shells (Plate 9.1b) carry their loads mainly by shear to the gable frames at their edges, as do anticlastic shells such as the hyperbolic paraboloid (Plate 9.2a); conoidal shells (Plate 9.2b), usually employed to obtain a kind of northlight roof, have an action that is mainly circumferential arching with some slab-action; conical shells, suitably supported along their longer arc, carry their dead load mainly by compression in both the meridional and circumferential directions.

Although all of the types of shell listed above have been used for roofing, many of them have limited application, either because their plan form is inconvenient, or because they need special supporting arrangements at the edges which it may not be practicable to provide.

The cylindrical shell, on the other hand, lends itself to a number of arrangements, with edge conditions which may fairly easily be realized in

practice and, except where a precasting technique is adopted, has proved
the most popular. When the generating line has a greater length than the
chord width (usually at least $1\frac{1}{2}$ times) the shell is known as a 'long' shell
(Plate 9.3a), and if supported at the corners may be imagined to be acting
very approximately as an inverted bath or horse-trough spanning lengthwise.
Such a shell is in compression longitudinally at the crown and in tension
along the two long edges, the truss or beam action being completed by
tangential shear forces in the intermediate parts of the shell. Arch action in
the circumferential direction is virtually non-existent, such arch thrusts as
one intuitively expects being converted into tangential shear forces which
get larger towards the supporting end frames or stiffening beams, to which
the accumulated would-be arch thrusts are thus transferred (Fig. 9.3).

Unfortunately this ideal membrane condition, with extensional forces
only, cannot be maintained because it is not usually possible to provide the

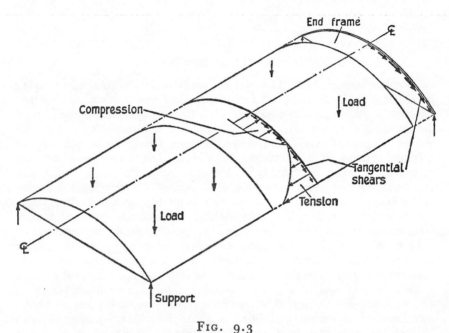

FIG. 9.3

Extensional forces in a cylindrical shell

requisite conditions at the edges of the shell; bending moments arise, particularly in the circumferential direction, and the extensional forces are modified.
Consequently, the 'hollow-beam theory' cannot generally be used to
calculate the stresses.

Very often edge beams are provided along the long edges of the shell.
These serve to increase the effective height and therefore reduce the longitudinal forces in the shell beam, to reduce the circumferential moments,
and to contain the main tensile reinforcement, which for large spans becomes
too bulky to be adequately incorporated within the thickness of the shell.

When spans become very large the bulk and weight of steel can be reduced by using longitudinal steel of higher tensile strength. As the cracking of the concrete would become excessive owing to the higher stresses present in such steel, it is post-tensioned, so that the concrete in the tensile zones is actually in compression before the dead load of the roof is taken up on striking the shuttering. Hence part of the load can be applied before this concrete goes over into tension and the width of the ensuing cracks is controlled by only the last part of the increment in steel stress which the load produces. The net vertical deflections of the shell are also reduced by this prestressing.

Post-tensioning of stiffening beams and trusses is even more often used, for the latter tend to be heavy and sometimes carry more than one bay width of shell. Also, in the most common form of stiffening beam the concrete tends to be in tension along the upper perimeter, as a result of transfer of shear from the shell, and along the lower perimeter as a result of the beam's own weight, i.e. the beam behaves in fact as a horizontal tie.

Another arrangement of the cylindrical shell is the 'short' shell, with the length much less than the chord width (Plate 9.3b). Longitudinal forces are then reduced, circumferential forces increase, and the load is mostly carried by shear to the supporting ribs or portal frames, which therefore become very massive when the chord width is large. Here again, failure to provide ideal membrane edge conditions results in bending moments, this time principally in the direction of the generating line.

Northlight shells consist, to all intents and purposes, of ordinary long shells tilted about one edge (Plate 9.4a). The effective depth from crown to chord line of such a shell tends to be rather small if the proportions of ordinary northlight roofs are adopted; it may be increased by using a rather wider barrel. The tensile forces in the gutter beams of northlight shells tend in any case to be large, and prestressing is very advantageous in this case. Alternatively, a truss in the plane of the northlight can be used.

An arrangement of two 'northlight' shells back-to-back forms a 'butterfly' shell (Plate 9.4b). Here the chord is somewhat small, and the stresses or the thickness will be rather large for the span involved.

Whatever the type of shell to be used, the architect, the structural designer and the contractor need to co-operate very closely, from the inception of the job if possible. The major dimensions and geometry of the shell will need to be decided upon. The necessary unobstructed area or span, the necessary clear height, the loads which the user may apply to the roof structure, and the quality of daylighting will probably be the main factors to be considered initially. Where a choice of shell type or arrangement is possible, questions of economy of materials may rule, and so may the practicalities of construction.

For reasons given above, shell roofs use the material contained in them in a very efficient way. Consumption of both steel and concrete per square foot of covered area is very low and this further reduces thicknesses, and foundation costs also. This economy in materials may be expected to become particularly noticeable when large areas unobstructed by columns have to be covered. Furthermore, shells tend to have a large reserve strength in certain circumstances because, if one of the load-carrying mechanisms fails, another may be brought into play.

The possibility of using curved surfaces of large area gives great scope to the architect in relation to the internal as well as the external appearance of the building. The resulting roof can have a clean, tidy appearance; it is also free from dust-retaining ledges and is easily cleaned, thus having special appeal for certain occupancies where cleanliness is essential. It must be said, however, that precisely because the roof possesses large unbroken areas, blemishes are particularly noticeable, and severe cracking, damp stains, honeycombed concrete or shuttering marks can ruin the appearance. Most of these faults can be avoided by obvious means; shuttering marks can, by suitable formwork design, be made regular and used to give a texture to the surface of the concrete.

Besides the cost of materials there are also construction and maintenance costs to be taken into account when assessing the relative merits of concrete shell and other types of roofing. If properly constructed in the first instance, shells should require little maintenance. Construction costs, however, tend to be high at times because of the high cost of the necessary formwork. They can be reduced if the formwork can be used several times, either by dismantling and re-erecting or by the use of movable sections of shuttering.

If this is to be done it must not be forgotten that the designer of the roof will have arranged that the loads are supported by structural actions that depend on the presence of a certain minimum portion of the structure, usually one shell bay complete with the ribs, beams or frames at its edges. Hence the shuttering for at least one bay must remain in position whilst that bay is being cast and cured. Economy by the re-use of formwork on a given job is therefore possible only if the structure has several bays which can be cast successively. Usually at least two sets of formwork will be required if reinforcement placing is not to cause delay.

In some countries, the cost of formwork and the period required for construction have been very greatly reduced by precasting shell units of a number of types, of medium dimensions, erecting them with cranes to form the major structure and fastening them together with *in situ* concrete, sometimes using a post-tensioning technique. In such cases the shell action for dead load is usually confined to the individual units and only the live loads are taken by shell action of the major structures.

DESIGN METHODS

Of the two general methods of design referred to in Chapter 2, that using the theory of elasticity is by far the most commonly used for the structural analysis of shells. The behaviour of shells at high loads has not yet been sufficiently investigated for load-factor methods of design to be practicable at present.

In computing the stresses by the theory of elasticity, it is assumed that the material of the shell is elastic (has always the same strain for a given stress); obeys Hooke's law (has a linear relationship between strain and stress, here assumed to be the same in tension and compression), and is homogeneous and isotropic (having the same properties in all directions).

Clearly, none of these assumptions is valid, even for a plain, uncracked, concrete shell. Moreover, a shell does not remain uncracked. It is subject to differential shrinkage and to other restraints to its free shrinkage which cause tensile stresses to be set up in addition to those due to the load. Because of its low tensile strength, the concrete cracks, and it is necessary to use reinforcement to distribute the cracking as well as to supply the tensile forces at the cracked sections. Such reinforcement alters the shell stiffness locally. It could hardly be said, therefore, that the shell fulfils the assumptions of the theory of elasticity.

Nevertheless, as with other structures where reinforced concrete is used, there is enough experimental evidence to show that behaviour at loads up to and just beyond those that cause initial cracking is quite well represented by the theory of elasticity. Local departures from the assumed mean values of the various physical properties concerned produce only local effects, which do not greatly upset the general distribution of stiffness which in turn controls the general distribution of stress. (As the loads increase, more and more cracking will occur, up to a certain limit, and the behaviour of the shell will depart more and more from the predictions of elasticity theory.)

The designer therefore uses the theory of elasticity (or some modification of it that makes the analysis tractable) to calculate the forces in the shell and in the members that act in combination with it. Where these forces are tensile, he adds steel reinforcement in appropriate quantity and checks that the permissible tensile stress in the steel and the permissible compressive stress in the concrete are nowhere exceeded. The steel thus added should be well distributed throughout the area of the concrete which it replaces in the structural interaction in the shell, otherwise the stresses may differ considerably from those derived from the theory.

The actual calculation of the forces is not difficult, but it is very complex and lengthy. A number of working aids may be invoked, such as the use of tables of functions based on certain parameters of the shell shape, and possibly, in the near future, the use of electronic computers.

DIMENSIONAL STABILITY

There are many reasons why a shell roof may change in its dimensions or in its position. Moisture movement, thermal movement, deflection due to load, lack of structural stability against overturning or against buckling—these all have to be taken into account in shell roof construction.

Moisture movement

Drying shrinkage of the shell concrete would cause little trouble if it took place uniformly throughout the structure and were not restrained in any way. In practice, shrinkage is restrained, and the concrete cracks at places where the sum of the stress due to this restraint and the stress due to load exceeds the tensile strength of the concrete. The factors tending to cause restraint are external restraint, differential shrinkage, and the presence of reinforcement.

Though external restraints are not usually met with in shell roof construction, they may occur if a new building is tied in some way to an existing one or to other buildings in the same suite. Restraint can also occur from strong panel infillings between columns if they are built before the shell is cast or too soon afterwards. All these restraints can be prevented by movement joints, such as may in any event be necessary to allow for thermal movements. Another type of external restraint is the 'nipping' of formwork, due to shrinkage of the concrete by evaporation from an unshuttered face, or to expansion of the timber by absorption of water. This can be avoided by proper curing methods at the exposed face and by easing the shuttering laterally (i.e. across the grain of the timber) as soon as the final set has taken place.

The fine surface cracks caused by differential shrinkage as the surface layers of concrete dry more quickly than the core are not usually objectionable. More serious is the differential shrinkage that may occur if one part of the structure is cast later than an adjacent part, or if it is thinner and dries out more quickly, thus tending to shear off at the junction; this tends to produce tension in the thinner member parallel to the junction.

When reinforcement is present the concrete bonds on to the bars and is thereby prevented from shrinking; the steel is put into compression and the concrete into tension. If a crack is formed it will open wider with slight slip of the concrete on the bars but the bond stresses will continue to provide an interaction between steel and concrete.

In shells the reinforcement is usually widely distributed, and will restrain shrinkage; the resulting shrinkage cracks will be smaller but more numerous if the reinforcing bars are smaller and more numerous. These bars also serve to distribute any cracking due to differential shrinkage or to unavoidable external restraint. Occasionally, the reinforcement is concentrated, for instance in solid end frames or deep edge beams; in such areas it may be necessary to provide additional bars to control the shrinkage cracking in the otherwise unreinforced part of the member, which is made worse by the concentration of steel.

Thermal movement

Temperature changes result in thermal movement, both of the shell proper, and also of ribs, beams, frames and other ancillary parts of the structure. The latter suffer mainly extensional movements, whereas the shell membrane undergoes movement both in its own plane (extensional movements) and also considerable bending movements, because it is thin and so less well able to restrain the deflections caused by changes in the length of its surface layers. The extensional movements of the membrane and its ancillary elements may cause trouble because they tend to be restrained by the supporting columns, by panel walls or by adjacent structures, thus introducing bending moments in the columns, shears or bending moments in the panels, loads on the building itself and unexpected ones on any nearby building. The problem becomes a serious one in multi-bay construction.

It is therefore necessary to provide movement joints to permit thermal movement, which for a temperature range of 70°F amounts to about $\frac{1}{2}$ in. in every 100 ft. Such joints must not interfere with the structural action of the shells and they will therefore usually be located between shell bays or groups of bays but in some circumstances they may be located within a shell if the structural design takes account of their presence. Figure 9.4 shows various ways of providing for thermal movement. These may be summarized as (a) doubling of columns and beams with the joint between them, (b) joint within the shell, with cantilevered portions on both sides, (c) widening the joint to several feet to form an expansion bay with a separate roof, or fenestration, and (d) use of roller and rocker bearings for large spans with extreme ranges of temperature.

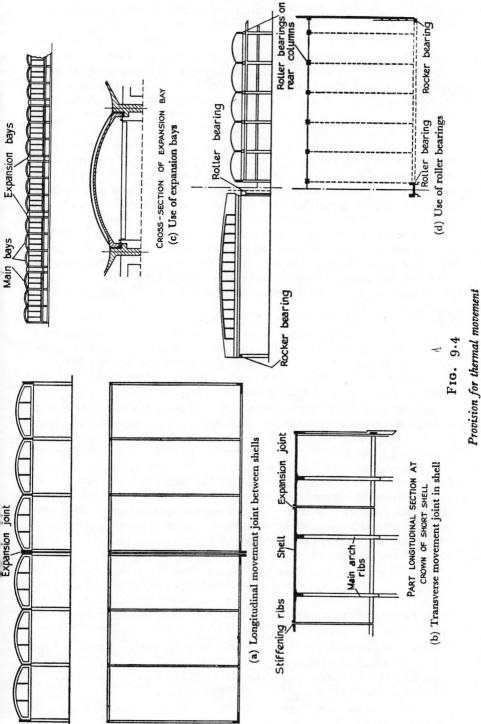

FIG. 9.4

Provision for thermal movement

Where long runs of glazing are present it will be necessary to provide a suitable joint to prevent damage by relative thermal, and other, movement.

Within the portions of the structure isolated by movement joints, the columns must be sufficiently flexible for the movement to occur without their experiencing excessive bending moments; at the same time the wind loads have to be resisted and it may be necessary to make at least two of the columns stronger for this purpose. It is also necessary to provide suitable clearances to ensure that walls and panels are not damaged by movement of the abutting structure.

The bending movements of the shell due to a temperature gradient through its thickness are unrestricted over the greater part of the area of the membrane, which is free to take up a position corresponding to its new temperature condition without being greatly stressed. However, shearing and bending stresses may arise at the junction of the membrane with any edge beams, end frames or arch ribs, because the latter are more massive and will undergo less thermal movement. If excessive stresses from this cause are likely, special reinforcement may be provided, but this is troublesome and it may be better to reduce the heat gain by providing external insulation and a reflective treatment (pp. 110, 134); this may be necessary in any case, to provide adequate conditions inside the building.

Deflections due to load

It is desirable for deflections under working loads to be limited, partly for the sake of appearance, partly to prevent damage to partitions, external walls, roof linings and coverings, fittings and services, and partly to ensure that the form of the structure when loaded does not differ so greatly from the designed conformations that the structural analysis is no longer valid.

With concrete shells the greater part of the deflection is due to dead load and will occur when the formwork is struck, before walls, fittings etc. have been erected. However, the possibility of increased deflections due to creep of the concrete should be looked into, for, although the compressive stresses in the concrete may be rather less than the permitted stresses, because the thickness of the shell is often controlled by the need to provide cover to the bars, the distance between supports tends to be rather larger than is usual in reinforced concrete constructions and the accumulated creep strain over this large span may produce appreciable deflection. The effect of creep on the curvature of the shell must not be overlooked, particularly if the curvature is small initially.

In the case of long edge beams, or trusses of wide span carrying the ends of shells, there is sometimes an apparent sag of the long horizontal soffit due to optical illusion. This, and some of the other effects of deflection, may be counteracted by cambering the undersides of beams and trusses or by prestressing.

Some settlement of foundations nearly always occurs—usually a little and fairly quickly in granular materials, but more and rather slowly in semi-permeable materials such as clay, in which the final settlement may be two to four times that at completion of construction.

A fairly general settlement may reduce clearances above a ground-bearing floor slab; it may thus damage services, or nip walls or partitions and possibly thereby affect the stresses in the shell. Differential settlement may, in addition, give rise to bending moments in supporting columns and other undesirable effects, especially in multi-bay buildings. There are two general methods of dealing with differential settlement. One is to design the building so that movement is permissible, but this is not easy to do in the case of shells. A preferable method is to provide for the points of support to be jacked back to a suitable level when necessary. A combination of both methods may be used.

Structural stability

There are two aspects of stability to be considered: one is stability against horizontal movement, and overturning, of the structure as a whole, or of a particular large part of it; the other is the stability of individual elements against buckling due to compressive stresses.

Horizontal movement of a shell-roofed building may tend to occur as a result of the horizontal component of wind forces, earthquake, or loads from the acceleration and braking of travelling cranes. Clearly, one point of the building must have its position fixed and another restrained in such a way as to prevent rotation. Such fixing is usually done through the contact of columns or other footings with the ground. The columns must be sufficiently strong to carry the resisting forces up to the necessary level. When the shell is mounted on roller and rocker bearings, care must be taken that the necessary restraints are also present.

Overturning tends to occur from the effect of the horizontal forces and the vertically upward (suction) component of any wind forces. It is guarded against by ensuring that the moment of the overturning forces about the axis of potential rotation does not exceed two-thirds of the moment of the restoring forces.

The second aspect of stability, that of buckling, is characterized by a large increase in deflection for a small increase in stress in the member concerned, the stresses being in any case less than those which would cause failure of the material itself. It occurs because in the new deflected position the member is much less stiff than in its original conformation. The buckling of columns is its most familiar form, and it is also seen in the buckling of the webs of plate girders and of thin reinforced concrete beams of long span. It inherently involves compressive stresses.

In the case of shell roofs, large parts of the shell membrane are subject to compression and therefore to the possibility of buckling. Generally, the thinner the shell and the larger its radius of curvature, the lower the stress at which buckling may occur. If creep under load takes place the radius of curvature may increase, and this will increase the chance of buckling. It is therefore necessary to keep the design stresses fairly low, both to reduce creep and to avoid exceeding the critical buckling stress.

In the case of shells of small span the design stresses in compression will be low, and it is usually only in the case of large spans that the critical buckling stresses may be approached. The most dangerous stresses are the longitudinal ones in the case of long shells of very large span and the circumferential ones in the case of short shells.

The type of buckling so far considered tends to produce wave-like corrugations of fairly large dimensions. Buckling of this type can be avoided by introducing stiffening ribs which prevent the formation of the corrugations and preserve the original shape of the shell. These ribs should be circumferential in the case of short shells, but long shells require ribs both circumferentially and longitudinally because the high longitudinal stresses tend to produce corrugations simultaneously in both directions. Other types of shell need treatment according to the shape into which they would buckle.

Experiments on metal shells have shown that buckling can occur at a lower load than conventional buckling theory would indicate, partly because of the introduction of bending moments at the junction between the shell proper and its supporting structure, and partly because any irregular curvature or thickness, or variations in the elastic properties of local areas of the shell, may cause a local 'snap-through' buckling of the shell, similar to the 'dimpling' of a table-tennis ball. Similar factors may operate in the case of reinforced concrete shell roofs. The ordinary form of stiffening rib would probably be unavailing against this type of behaviour, and it may be that double shell construction or thicker shells of perhaps lighter material will be necessary.

It should be emphasized that buckling is only likely to be a problem when spans are very large, or shells very thin.

DAYLIGHTING

There are a few cases, e.g. concert halls, planetaria, bulk storage buildings, where the daylighting of buildings covered by shell roofs is not of great importance, but for most occupancies daylighting is probably the second most important functional requirement. The provision of an adequate level, uniformity and type of illumination controls the type and arrangement of the roof structure only little less than do the demands of strength and stability.

An isolated shell of medium dimensions, of the dome, long shell or short shell type, will sometimes receive sufficient light from vertical glazing round its perimeter; but when covered areas are large, when multi-bay construction is used, or the sky is masked by adjacent shells, it becomes necessary to admit light at other, interior, points of the roofed area.

This may be done by raising the middle or alternate shells above the general level of the others, thus producing very large monitors. A second method is to tilt all the shells about one of their longer edges, thus converting a long barrel into a northlight shell (Plate 9.5a) or a short barrel (with other slight changes) into a conoid shell (Plate 9.2b). Anticlastic shells are naturally tilted upwards towards the corners and can be advantageously arranged so that they do not mask each other (Fig. 9.5). Many of the less orthodox shell roof arrangements are likewise well adapted for admitting daylight, because of their asymmetry. The third and commonly adopted method is to provide roof lights in the surface of the shell. These may be small individual lights; alternatively certain major areas of the roof may be given over to the admission of daylight.

One of the problems here is to prevent undue interference with the structural actions within the shell. For instance, it is not usually permissible to locate openings in regions of high shear such as the valley slopes of long shells, but many things can be done, even the latter, provided that they are taken into account in the structural design. Plates 9.1*b*, 9.3, 9.5*b* and 9.6 show typical arrangements.

A second problem is that of glare, particularly from high sun. This may

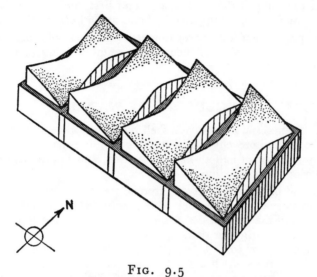

FIG. 9.5

Array of anticlastic shells

be reduced by suitable siting of the roof lights in the building, by dormer or monitor construction which convert a near-horizontal light into a vertical one, by the use of low-transmission glass or by light-coloured painting of the shell near the roof soffit and of the roof-light reveals.

A general feature of shell roofs is that the curved underside is free from obstruction from trusses, purlins and the like, and can with suitable treatment act as a good reflector of light, provided that adequate light can fall on it in the first place. This last condition, however, is not easy to arrange, particularly with the shallower types of shell.

CARRYING OF SERVICES

The services required in a building with a shell roof are best considered at an early stage of the design. Large point loads are not readily carried by the shell proper unless additional circumferential ribs are provided, and the pleasant appearance of the underside of the shell, which is one of its main features, is soon marred by excrescences. So far as possible, additions to the main structure are best made along edge or valley beams or round main arch ribs. Cables, piping, and runs of fluorescent lighting may be unobtrusive but accessible in such positions. Heating and ventilation ducts may be contained within the beams themselves, and unit heaters placed at the junctions of beams and columns.

Artificial lighting is the most troublesome service to arrange. A background lighting of the shell soffit from concealed fluorescent tubes along the sides of edge beams is pleasant and convenient, and takes advantage of the reflection from the shell, which may be increased by suitable decorative treatment. Additional direct lighting will often be necessary, located, if possible, on the edge beams, king posts or mullions, suspended from or flush with the soffit of the shell as a second best, and preferably not ever spoiling the appearance of the shell by being slung between the edge beams.

If it is expected that future attachments to the shell soffit may have to be provided for, it is as well to incorporate suitable fixing points from the beginning.

EXCLUSION OF WATER

It is normally necessary to provide shell roofs with some sort of waterproof membrane, both to prevent corrosion of the reinforcement whilst permitting the minimum cover of half-an-inch to be used, and to prevent penetration to the interior of the building.

Asphalt and brushed or sprayed bitumen treatments are possible but are not very satisfactory, because they tend to soften through solar heating. At the other end of the scale of permanence (and expense) is copper sheeting, the traditional covering for domes. A commonly used compromise is bituminous felt in two or three layers (the extra layer doubling the life of the covering). The layers of felt are lapped and stuck down to each other and to the roof, and bitumen-painted and gritted. Even with felt there is some tendency to soften and to pull away, especially when insulation external to the shell prevents loss of solar heat into the structure, and it is an advantage, for this and other reasons, to provide a coating of white stone chippings to reflect much of the incident sunlight. A lime and tallow wash is a cheaper but less permanent alternative.

Rain and melted snow rapidly find their way into the valley or eaves gutters; so does loose grit. Water impounded by snow and grit, or trapped by the deflection of the roof under load, may fail to drain away; it may add to the load on the roof, but its major disadvantage is usually that it rots the fibres in the roofing felt. Gutters must therefore be kept clear of grit by regular cleaning out, snow boards provided to keep a clear channel and to carry any traffic, and the gutters given a fall to carry the water away. This fall may sometimes be provided by tilting the whole roof, but usually a lightweight screed is placed above the structural concrete. Down-pipes may conveniently be formed within the columns.

OTHER SPECIAL TYPES OF ROOF

Folded-plate roofs

The curved surface of a cylindrical shell may be replaced by a series of flat slabs which intersect in pairs along certain generators of the original shell. These folded-plate roofs, or prismatic shells, depend rather more on transverse bending action than the shells which they replace and are conse-

(Sunderland & S. Shields Water Company)

(*a*) *Spherical dome of rotation*

(Cement and Concrete Association)

(*b*) *Translation dome*

PLATE 9.1

(a) *Hyperbolic paraboloid shells*

(b) *Conoid shells*

PLATE 9.2

(a) *Long cylindrical shells*

(Photos : Cement and Concrete Association)

(b) *Short cylindrical shells*

PLATE 9.3

(a) *Northlight shells*

(b) *Butterfly shell*

PLATE 9.4

(Cement and Concrete Association)

(a) *Daylighting of northlight shell*

(b) *Daylighting by longitudinal lights*

PLATE 9.5

(a) *Daylighting by circular lights*

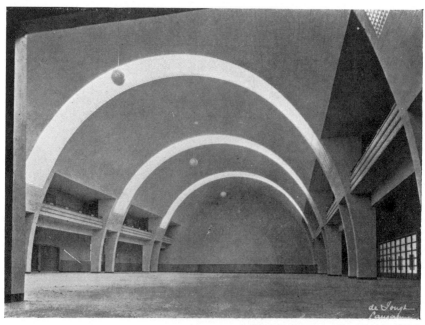

(Photos : Cement and Concrete Association)

(b)   *Daylighting by transverse lights*

PLATE 9.6

(*a*) *Folded plate roof*

(*b*) *Clad lattice roof*

PLATE 9.7

Beton- u. Monierbau A.G.

Saddle shaped hanging roof

PLATE 9.8

quently rather thicker, or more heavily reinforced. On the other hand they are better adapted to the carrying of concentrated loads (at the intersections), shuttering is simplified, and precasting can readily be used. Computation of the stresses is also easier; indeed an equivalent shell proper can be analysed by this means. These roofs also have a use as 'saw-tooth' roofs, of which a simple example is shown in Plate 9.7a.

Clad-lattice roofs

In a true shell the structural or load-carrying elements are combined with the cladding or weather-excluding elements in a single covering medium, but it is also possible for the two functions to be fulfilled by separate parts of the covering without losing the spatial, three-dimensional character of the construction. Whilst in some ways this might be considered a retrograde step, it is justified if shuttering or centering can be reduced, or if a material can then be used in an economical thickness that might otherwise lead to a risk of buckling.

Thus, metal sheeting alone cannot readily be used for large shells because, unless it is ribbed or corrugated, or an uneconomically thick section is used, the stresses due to load would exceed the buckling stress; but it is quite possible to carry the main forces by a lattice of tubes, bars, angles or built-up lattice struts, leaving the sheeting to carry only the smaller, local forces required to transmit the load to the lattice members. Similarly, in the case of concrete shells and folded-plate roofs, a tubular framework can be made up in the general shape of the shell and used as a main load-bearing framework to carry slabs or *in situ* concrete (Plate 9.7b). There is, of course, little shell action in the concrete in such cases, but the cost of the tubes can be set against the saving of time, centering and possibly shuttering.

Hanging roofs

Ideally, a shell made of a material naturally strong in compression but weak in tension would be in compression everywhere. On the other hand, there are now materials such as steel wire and man-made fibres which can be fairly readily produced in a form that is strong in tension though likely to buckle under compression. Such materials can form the structural basis of a roof, used in networks that are everywhere in tension. Whilst it is possible to suspend some kind of roof covering from such a network, the problems of protection against corrosion are easier to solve if the network is within the building or incorporated into the roof covering; moreover, use can then be made of prestressing.

Just as there are tensions at the perimeter of most shells, either in the shell itself or in the supporting structure, so there are necessary compression elements at the perimeter of most networks. A simple arrangement, for instance, is to have, supported on columns, a horizontal circular compression ring, to which are attached the radial wires of the network; the network carries slabs or some form of cladding with, of course, due attention to thermal movement, thermal insulation, exclusion of water and maintenance (Fig. 9.6).

Whilst in a plane (or slightly sagging) network of this kind, there is no buckling problem such as would arise with the corresponding membrane in compression, there is a different stability problem—that of aerodynamic stability. Suction effects of wind can cause oscillations of the roof, and the lighter the roof the worse these will be. One way of reducing the oscillations is to prestress the network; another is to tie the roof down with some form of inclined bracing. A third method is to break away from the plane network

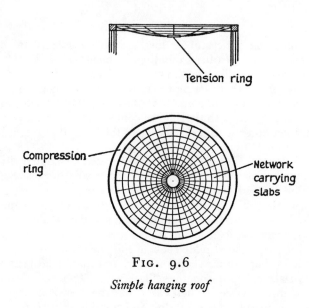

FIG. 9.6

Simple hanging roof

and use a saddle-shaped mesh in which one set of wires is concave upwards whilst an orthogonal set of wires, concave downwards, ties or prestresses the main load-bearing wires. Such an arrangement demands appropriate changes in the shape of the compression ring (Plate 9.8).

Such hanging roofs are the newest, in principle, of all forms of roof construction. Doubtless their use will throw up many problems of detailed design, of which there is as yet no experience in this country. Doubtless, too, the consideration of functional requirements will continue to be the main guiding principle in this as in other fields of building.

INDEX

Dd505852 K26 11/72   SBN 11 670297 4